APPLICATIONS FOR ENROLLMENT OF CHICKASAW NEWBORN ACT OF 1905 VOLUME III

TRANSCRIBED BY
JEFF BOWEN

NATIVE STUDY
Gallipolis, Ohio
USA

Copyright © 2013
by Jeff Bowen

ALL RIGHTS RESERVED
No part of this publication may be reproduced
or used in any form or manner whatsoever
without previous written permission from the
copyright holder or publisher.

Originally published:
Baltimore, Maryland
2013

Reprinted by:

Native Study LLC
Gallipolis, OH
www.nativestudy.com
2020

Library of Congress Control Number: 2020917160

ISBN: 978-1-64968-065-5

Made in the United States of America.

This series is dedicated to the descendants of the Chickasaw newborn listed in these applications.

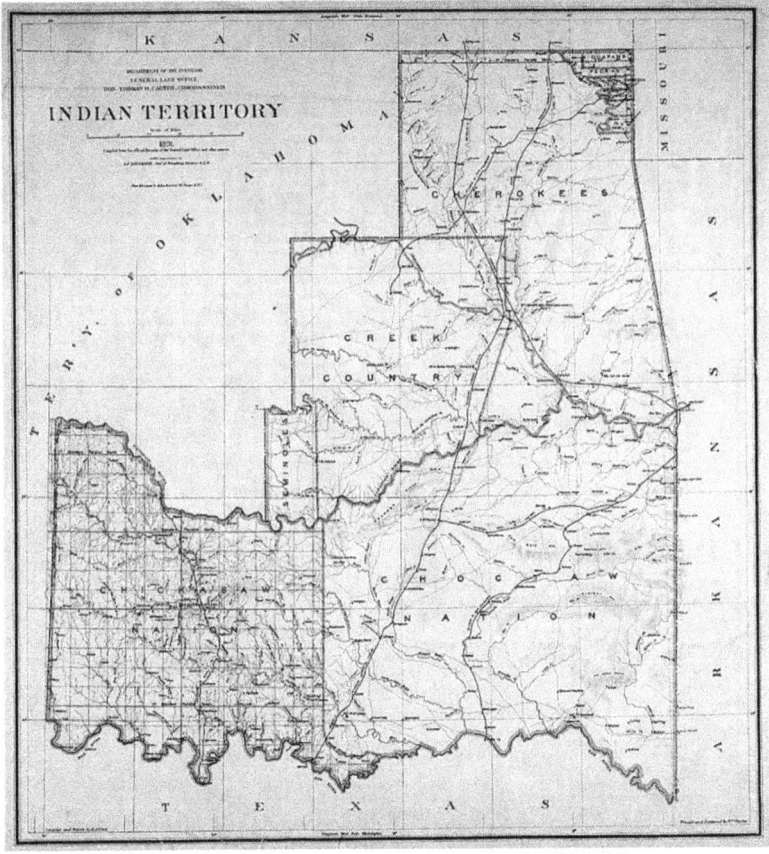

This map of Indian Territory shows how large the Choctaw and Chickasaw Nations' land base was that contained huge deposits of asphalt and coal. Just the size and territory involved was flooded with the "Grafters".

DEPARTMENT OF THE INTERIOR,
Commission to the Five Civilized Tribes.

Rules and Regulations Governing the Selection of Allotments and the Designation of Homesteads in the Choctaw and Chickasaw Nations.

1. Selections of allotments and designations of homesteads for adult citizens and selections of allotments for adult freedmen must be made in person except as herein otherwise provided.
2. Applications to have land set apart and homesteads designated for duly identified Mississippi Choctaws must be made personally before the Commission to the Five Civilized Tribes. Fathers may apply for their minor children and if the father be dead the mother may apply. Husbands may apply for wives. Applications for orphans, insane persons and persons of unsound mind may be made by duly appointed guardian or curator, and for aged and infirm persons and prisoners by agents duly authorized thereunto by power of attorney, in the discretion of said Commission.
3. At the time of the selection of allotment each citizen and duly identified Mississippi Choctaw shall designate as a homestead out of said selection land equal in value to one hundred and sixty acres of the average allottable land of the Choctaw and Chickasaw Nations, as nearly as may be.
4. Each Choctaw and Chickasaw freedman, at the time of selection shall designate as his or her allotment of the lands of the Choctaw and Chickasaw Nations, land equal in value to forty acres of the average allottable land of the Choctaw and Chickasaw Nations.
5. Citizens, freedmen and identified Mississippi Choctaws who are married, whether they have attained their majority or not, will be regarded as of age for the purpose of making selections.
6. Selections may be made by citizen and freedmen parents for unmarried male children under twenty-one years of age and for unmarried female children under eighteen years of age, and a male citizen or freedman may make selection for his wife, if she is entitled to make selection, unless she shall, at the time or previously thereto, protest in writing.
7. Where the father of an unmarried minor citizen, freedman or identified Mississippi Choctaw is a non-citizen, the citizen, freedman or identified Mississippi Choctaw mother of such children must make selection in person in behalf of said children.
8. Selections of allotments and designations of homesteads for minor citizens and selections of allotments for minor freedmen may be made by the citizen father or mother or freedman father or mother, as the case may be, or by a guardian, curator, or an administrator having charge of their estate, in the order named.
9. Selections of allotments and designations of homesteads for citizen, and selections of allotment for freedmen, prisoners, convicts, aged and infirm persons and soldiers and sailors of the United States on duty outside of Indian Territory, may be made by duly appointed agents under power of attorney, and for incompetents by guardians, curators, or other suitable person akin to them.
10. Selections may be made and homesteads designated by duly identified Mississippi Choctaws, who have, within one year after the date of their identification as such, made satisfactory proof of bona fide settlement within the Choctaw-Chickasaw country, at any time within six months after the date of their said identification.
11. Persons authorized to make selections by power of attorney, as provided in rules 2 and 9 hereof, must be the husband or wife, or a relative not further removed than a cousin of the first degree of the person for whom such selection is made.
12. It shall be the duty of the Commission to the Five Civilized Tribes to see that selections of allotments and designations of homesteads for the classes of persons mentioned in rules 2, 6, 7, 8 and 9 hereof, are made for the best interests of such persons.
13. Selections of allotments for citizens, freedmen and identified Mississippi Choctaws who have died subsequent to September 25, 1902, and before making a selection of allotment, shall be made by a duly appointed administrator or executor. If, however, such administrator or executor be not duly and expeditiously appointed, or fails to act promptly when appointed, or for any other cause such selections be not so made within a reasonable and practicable time, the Commission to the Five Civilized Tribes shall designate the lands thus to be allotted.
14. In determining the value of a selection the appraised value of the land selected shall be increased by the appraised value of such pine timber on such land as has heretofore been estimated by the Commission to the Five Civilized Tribes.
15. Selections of allotments may be made only by citizens and freedmen whose enrollment has been approved by the Secretary of the Interior, and by persons duly identified by the Commission to the Five Civilized Tribes as Mississippi Choctaws, and by none others.
16. When a selection of land has been made by a citizen, freedman or identified Mississippi Choctaw, and the land so selected is claimed by a person whose rights as a citizen or freedman have not been finally determined, contest for the land so selected may be instituted by the person claiming the land, formal application for the land being first made as is required by the Rules of Practice in Choctaw and Chickasaw allotment contest cases.

THE COMMISSION TO THE FIVE CIVILIZED TRIBES.
TAMS BIXBY, Chairman.

Muskogee, Indian Territory, March 24, 1903.

The above statement published prior to 1905, was established for what was supposed to be a set of guidelines when it came to allotments. But with supplemental agreements and Congressional legislation, time frames as well as rules and regulations often changed and were not the same for every tribe.

INTRODUCTION

The *Applications for Enrollment of Chickasaw Newborn Act of 1905*, National Archive film M-1301, Rolls 455-458, are found under the heading of Applications for Enrollment of the Commission to the Five Civilized Tribes. For this series, I have transcribed the application forms filled out by individuals applying for enrollment in the Five Civilized Tribes under the Dawes Commission. These applications contain considerably more information than stated on the census cards found in series M-1186. M-1301 possesses its own numerical sequence, separate from M-1186. To find each party's roll number you would have to reference M-1186.

The Chickasaw as well as the Choctaw allotments were likely some of the most sought after properties in Indian Territory. There was supposed to be a 25-year restriction on the sale or lease of any Indian lands so as to insure that the owners wouldn't be swindled, but that isn't what happened. This fact is borne out in the Dawes Commission General Allotment Act, of February 8, 1887, Section 5, which "Provides that after an Indian person is allotted land, the United States will hold the land 'in trust [1] for the sole use and benefit of the Indian' (or his heirs if the Indian landowner dies) for a period of 25 years. (Land held in trust by the United States government cannot be sold or in anyway alienated by the Indian landowner, since the United States government considers the underlying ownership of the land held by itself and not the tribe. After the period of trust ends, the Indian landowner is free to sell the land and is free from any encumbrance from the United States.)"[1] Instead, Native Americans were exploited by the devious. The Chickasaw and Choctaw Districts both had huge asphalt and coal deposits, so there was pressure from outsiders to acquire them from the minute they were discovered. After repeated attacks throughout the years and many legislative changes, President "Roosevelt finally signed the Five Tribes Bill at noon on April 26, 1906, the forces seeking to end all restrictions were disappointed. Section 19 removed restrictions from the sale of all inherited land but directed that no full-bloods could sell their land for twenty-five years. The Act also prohibited leases for more than one year without the approval of the Secretary of the Interior."[2]

Angie Debo described the opportunists that wanted these Native American allotments as, "Grafters". The parents of the newborns enumerated within this series would no sooner receive the approval for their child's allotment than there would be someone there with cash in hand holding a new deed or lease for the parents to sign their child's birthright away. Angie Debo said it best, "As the business incapacity of the allottees became apparent, a horde of despoilers fastened themselves upon their property." According to Debo, "The term 'grafter' was applied as a matter of course to dealers in Indian land, and was frankly accepted by them. The speculative fever also affected Government employees so that it was almost impossible to prevent them from making personal investments."[3]

---

[1] General Allotment Act, Act of Feb. 8, 1887 (24 Stat. 388, ch. 119, 25 USCA 331)
[2] The Dawes Commission and the Allotment of the Five Civilized Tribes, 1893-1914 by Kent Carter, pg. 173
[3] And Still the Waters Run, Angie Debo, p. 92.

INTRODUCTION

According to the Department of Interior in 1905, "It is estimated that there will be added to the final rolls of the citizens and freedmen of the Choctaw and Chickasaw nations the names of 2,000 persons, including 1,500 new-born children to be enrolled under the provisions of the act of Congress approved March 3, 1905."[4]

The quote below explains, in detail, the requirements for qualifying as a newborn Chickasaw, "By the act of Congress approved March 3, 1905 (H.R. 17474), entitled 'An act making appropriations for the current and contingent expenses of the Indian Department and for fulfilling treaty stipulations with various Indian tribes for the fiscal year ending June 30, 1906, and for other purposes,' it was provided as follows:

'That the Commission to the Five Civilized Tribes is hereby authorized for sixty days after the date of the approval of this act to receive and consider applications for enrollment of infant children born prior to September twenty-fifth, nineteen hundred and two, and who were living on said date, to citizens by blood of the Choctaw and Chickasaw tribes of Indians whose enrollment has been approved by the Secretary of the Interior prior to the date of the approval of this act; and to enroll and make allotments to such children.'

'That the Commission to the Five Civilized Tribes is authorized for sixty days after the date of the approval of this act to receive and consider applications for enrollment of children born subsequent to September twenty-fifth, nineteen hundred and two, and prior to March fourth, nineteen hundred and five, and who were living on said latter date, to citizens by blood of the Choctaw and Chickasaw tribes of Indians whose enrollment has been approved by the Secretary of the Interior prior to the date of the approval of this act; and to enroll and make allotments to such children.'

"Notice is hereby given that the Commission to the Five Civilized Tribes will, up to and inclusive of midnight, May 2, 1905, receive applications for the enrollment of infant children born prior to September 25, 1902, and who were living on said date, to citizens by blood of the Choctaw and Chickasaw tribes of Indians whose enrollment has been approved by the Secretary of the Interior prior to March 3, 1905."[5]

Following is the scope of these transcriptions: Besides the applications themselves, researchers will find the identities of other individuals within these applications -- doctors, lawyers, mid-wives, and other relatives -- that may help with your genealogical research.

Jeff Bowen
Gallipolis, Ohio
NativeStudy.com

---

[4] Annual Reports of the Department of the Interior For the Fiscal Year Ended June 30, 1905, p. 609.
[5] Annual Reports of the Department of the Interior For the Fiscal Year Ended June 30, 1905, p. 593.

Applications for Enrollment of Chickasaw Newborn
Act of 1905   Volume III

Chic. N.B - 160
    (Herman Hardwick
    Born November 11, 1902)
    (Waneta Hardwick
    Born August 17, 1904)

BIRTH AFFIDAVIT.

DEPARTMENT OF THE INTERIOR.
COMMISSION TO THE FIVE CIVILIZED TRIBES.

IN RE APPLICATION FOR ENROLLMENT, as a citizen of the   Chickasaw   Nation, of   Herman Hardwick   , born on the 11 day of Nov , 1902

Name of Father: Joe. B. Hardwick   a citizen of the   Chickasaw   Nation.
Name of Mother: Alma Bell Hardwick   a citizen of the   Chickasaw   Nation.
by marriage

                       Postoffice   Powell I.T.

AFFIDAVIT OF MOTHER.

UNITED STATES OF AMERICA, Indian Territory, ⎫
    Southern   DISTRICT. ⎭

    I,   Alma Bell Hardwick   , on oath state that I am Twenty two years of age and a citizen by   marriage   , of the   Chickasaw   Nation; that I am the lawful wife of   Joe B. Hardwick   , who is a citizen, by Blood   of the   Chickasaw   Nation; that a   male   child was born to me on 11 day of Nov. , 1902; that said child has been named   Herman Hardwick   , and was living March 4, 1905.

                       Alma Bell Hardwick

Witnesses To Mark:
  ⎧ Bettie Drennan
  ⎩ S.S. Lindsay

    Subscribed and sworn to before me this 24 day of   Mar   , 1905

                       P.F. Robinson
                          Notary Public.

Applications for Enrollment of Chickasaw Newborn
Act of 1905   Volume III

AFFIDAVIT OF ATTENDING PHYSICIAN OR MID-WIFE.

UNITED STATES OF AMERICA, Indian Territory,
Southern   DISTRICT.

I, Sarah S. Lindsay , a midwife , on oath state that I attended on Mrs. Alma Bell Hardwick , wife of Joe B Hardwick on the 11 day of Nov. , 1902; that there was born to her on said date a male child; that said child was living March 4, 1905, and is said to have been named Herman Hardwick

Sarah S. Lindsay

Witnesses To Mark:
 Bettie Drennan
 S. S. Lindsay

Subscribed and sworn to before me this 24 day of Mar , 1905

P.F. Robinson
Notary Public.

BIRTH AFFIDAVIT.

DEPARTMENT OF THE INTERIOR.
COMMISSION TO THE FIVE CIVILIZED TRIBES.

IN RE APPLICATION FOR ENROLLMENT, as a citizen of the Chickasaw Nation, of Waneta Hardwick , born on the 17 day of Aug , 1904

Name of Father: Joe. B. Hardwick a citizen of the Chickasaw Nation.
Name of Mother: Alma Bell Hardwick a citizen of the Chickasaw Nation.
by marriage

Postoffice Powell I.T.

AFFIDAVIT OF MOTHER.

UNITED STATES OF AMERICA, Indian Territory,
Southern   DISTRICT.

I, Alma Bell Hardwick , on oath state that I am Twenty two years of age and a citizen by marriage , of the Chickasaw Nation; that I am the lawful wife of Joe B. Hardwick , who is a citizen, by Blood of the Chickasaw Nation; that a Female child was born to me on 17 day of Aug. , 1904; that said child has been named Waneta Hardwick , and was living March 4, 1905.

Alma Bell Hardwick

Applications for Enrollment of Chickasaw Newborn
Act of 1905   Volume III

Witnesses To Mark:
- Allie Lindsay
- Effie Covington

Subscribed and sworn to before me this 24 day of   Mar   , 1905

P.F. Robinson
Notary Public.

AFFIDAVIT OF ATTENDING PHYSICIAN OR MID-WIFE.

UNITED STATES OF AMERICA, Indian Territory,
Southern   DISTRICT.

I,   Sarah S. Lindsay   , a   Midwife   , on oath state that I attended on Mrs.   Alma Bell Hardwick   , wife of   Joe B Hardwick   on the 17 day of Aug.   , 1904; that there was born to her on said date a   Female   child; that said child was living March 4, 1905, and is said to have been named Waneta Hardwick

Sarah S. Lindsay

Witnesses To Mark:
- Allie Lindsay
- Effie Covington

Subscribed and sworn to before me this 24 day of   Mar   , 1905

P.F. Robinson
Notary Public.

Chickasaw 1012.

Muskogee, Indian Territory, April 4, 1905.

Joe B. Hardwick,
　　Howell, Indian Territory.

Dear Sir:

Receipt is hereby acknowledged of the affidavits of Alma Belle[sic] Hardwick and Sarah S. Lindsay to the birth of Herman Hardwick and Waneta Hardwick, children of Joe B. and Alma Belle Hardwick, November 11, 1902 and August 17, 1904, respectively, and the same have been filed with our records as an application for the enrollment of said child.

Respectfully,

Commissioner in Charge.

Applications for Enrollment of Chickasaw Newborn
Act of 1905   Volume III

Chic. N.B - 161
   (Edna Crecia Mutz
   Born August 10, 1903)

BIRTH AFFIDAVIT.

DEPARTMENT OF THE INTERIOR.
COMMISSION TO THE FIVE CIVILIZED TRIBES.

   IN RE APPLICATION FOR ENROLLMENT, as a citizen of the   Chickasaw   Nation, of   Edna Crecia Mutz   , born on the 10th day of   Aug[sic]   , 1903

Name of Father: George Mutz   a citizen of the   Chickasaw   Nation.
Name of Mother: Ida Mutz   a citizen of the   Chickasaw   Nation.

            Postoffice   Kingston, I.T.

AFFIDAVIT OF MOTHER.

UNITED STATES OF AMERICA, Indian Territory,
   Southern   DISTRICT.

   I,   Ida Mutz   , on oath state that I am   26   years of age and a citizen by blood   , of the   Chickasaw   Nation; that I am the lawful wife of   George Mutz , who is a citizen, by intermarriage   of the   Chickasaw   Nation; that a   female child was born to me on 10th day of   August   , 1903; that said child has been named   Edna Crecia Mutz   , and was living March 4, 1905.

                        Ida Mutz
Witnesses To Mark:

   Subscribed and sworn to before me this 15th day of   Mar   , 1905

                  DP Johnston
                     Notary Public.

Applications for Enrollment of Chickasaw Newborn
Act of 1905 Volume III

AFFIDAVIT OF ATTENDING PHYSICIAN OR MID-WIFE.

UNITED STATES OF AMERICA, Indian Territory,
Southern DISTRICT.

    I, E.F. Lewis, a physician, on oath state that I attended on Mrs. Ida Mutz, wife of George Mutz on the 10th day of August, 1903; that there was born to her on said date a female child; that said child was living March 4, 1905, and is said to have been named Edna Crecia Mutz

                                      E.F. Lewis MD

Witnesses To Mark:
{

    Subscribed and sworn to before me this 15th day of Mar, 1905

                                       DP Johnston
                                          Notary Public.

(The Affidavits below typed as given.)

AFFIDAVIT OF ATTENDING PHYSICIAN OR MIDWIFE.

United States of America,
Indian Territory, Southern District.

    I, a Dr. E F Lewis a Physician on oath state that I attended on Mrs. Mutz, wife [sic] George Mutz of Kingston, on the 13th day of May 1903. that there was born to her on same date a female child, that said child is now living and is said to have been named Edna Crecia Mutz

                                      E. F. Lewis   M.D.

Witnesseth:--
    Brit Hardwick
    Eastman Hardwick

    Subscribed and sworn to before me this the 13th day of March 190 5.

                                      DP Johnston
                                        Notary Public.

Applications for Enrollment of Chickasaw Newborn
Act of 1905   Volume III

We hereby certify that we are well acquainted with   Dr. E.F. Lewis   and know him to be reputable and of good standing in the community.

                F. B. Massy
                W.R. Hume

New Born Affidavit:

    No. _____.

        Chickasaw
        ~~CHOCTAW~~ ENROLLING COMMISSION.

In the matter of the application for enrollment as a citizen of the   Chickasaw   Nation, of   Edna Crecia   born on the   10th   day of   May   190 3
Name of Father   Geo Mutz   a citizen of   Chickasaw   Nation, final enrollment *No.*   49 ?(?)
Name of mother   Ida Mutz   a citizen of   Chickasaw   Nation, final enrollment No.   366 (?)

              Post Office   Kingston, I. T.

Affidavit of Mother.

    United States of America,
Indian Territory,
    Southern District.

    I,   Ida Mutz   , on oath state that I am   26   years of age and a citizen by blood of the   Chickasaw   Nation, and as such have been placed upon the final roll of the   Chickasaw   nation, by the Hon. Secretary of the Interior my final enrollment No. being   49   and that a   female   child was born to me on the   10th   day of   May   190 3; that said child has been named   Edna Crecia   and is now living.

                Ida Mutz

Witnesseth:--
    Eastman Hardwick
    Brit Hardwick

    Subscribed and sworn to before me this the   13th   day of   March   190 5.

                DP Johnston
                    Notary Public.
My commission expires   19th   day of   Mar   190 7.

Applications for Enrollment of Chickasaw Newborn
Act of 1905 Volume III

9-1032

Muskogee, Indian Territory, March 20, 1905.

D. P. Johnson[sic],
    Kingston, Indian Territory.

Dear Sir:

    Receipt is hereby acknowledged of your letter of March 14, 1905, enclosed the affidavits of Ida Mutz and E. F. Lewis to the birth of Edna Crecia Mutz, child of George and Ida Mutz, May 10, 1903, and the same have been filed with our records as an application for the enrollment of said child.

        Respectfully,

                Chairman.

9 N B 161

Muskogee, Indian Territory, April 14, 1905.

George Mutz,
    Kingston, Indian Territory.

Dear Sir:

    There is inclosed you herewith for execution application for the enrollment of your infant child, Edna Crecia Mutz, born May 10, 1903.

    In the affidavit of the physician heretofore filed with the Commission, the date of the birth of said child is given as May 13, 1903. It is, therefore, necessary to have the application re-executed giving correct date of her birth.

    In having these affidavits executed care should be exercised to see that all names are written in full, as they appear in the body of the affidavit, and in the event that either of the persons signing the affidavit are unable to write, signatures by mark must be attested by two witnesses. Each affidavit must be executed before a Notary Public and the notarial seal and signature of the officer must be attached to each separate affidavit.

        Respectfully,

LM 14-135.   Commissioner in Charge.

Applications for Enrollment of Chickasaw Newborn
Act of 1905   Volume III

9 NB 161

Muskogee, Indian Territory, April 28, 1905.

George Mutz,
    Kingston, Indian Territory.

Dear Sir:

    Receipt is hereby acknowledged of your letter of April 24, 1905, asking is Edna Crecia Mutz has been enrolled or not.

    In reply to your letter you are informed that the affidavits heretofore forwarded to the birth of Edna Crecia Mutz have been filed with our records as an application for the enrollment of said child.

                  Respectfully,

                                Chairman.

9-NB-161.

Muskogee, Indian Territory, May 12, 1905.

George Mutz,
    Kingston, Indian Territory.

Dear Sir:

    There is enclosed you herewith for execution application for the enrollment of your infant child, Edna Crecia Mutz, born _ _ _ _ _ _ _ _ _ .

    In the affidavits of March 13, 1905, heretofore filed with the Commission, the mother gives the date of the applicant's birth as May 10, 1902[sic]; the physician gives it as May 13, 1903, while in the affidavits of April 15, 1905, the date of birth if given as August 10, 1903.

        Before this matter can be finally disposed of it will be necessary for you to file with the Commission the enclosed application properly executed, in which you will supply the correct date of the applicant's birth.

    In having these affidavits executed care should be exercised to see that all names are written in full, as they appear in the body of the affidavit, and in the event that either of the persons signing the affidavit are unable to write, signatures by mark must be attested by two witnesses. Each affidavit must be executed before a Notary Public and the notarial seal and signature of the officer must be attached to each separate affidavit.

Applications for Enrollment of Chickasaw Newborn
Act of 1905 Volume III

Respectfully,

Chairman.

V. 12/5.

Chickasaw NB 161

Muskogee, Indian Territory, May 19, 1905.

George Mutz,
    Kingston, Indian Territory.

Dear Sir:

    Receipt is hereby acknowledged of the affidavits of Ida Mutz and E F. Lewis to the birth of Edna Crecia Mutz, child of George and Ida Mutz, August 10, 1903, and the same have been filed with our records in the matter of the enrollment of said child.

Respectfully,

Chairman.

Chic. N.B - 162
    (Ernest Leon Massey
    Born May 13, 1903)

BIRTH AFFIDAVIT.

Department of the Interior,
COMMISSION TO THE FIVE CIVILIZED TRIBES.

IN RE APPLICATION FOR ENROLLMENT, as a citizen of the Chickasaw Nation, of Ernest Leon Massey , born on the 13th day of May , 190 3

Name of Father: Enoch L Massey   a ~~citizen of~~ the U S ~~Nation~~.
Name of Mother: Marietta Massey nee Huff   a citizen of the Chickasaw Nation.

Post-Office: Willis Ind. Ter.

Applications for Enrollment of Chickasaw Newborn
Act of 1905   Volume III

AFFIDAVIT OF MOTHER.

UNITED STATES OF AMERICA,
   INDIAN TERRITORY,
Southern   District.

I, Marietta Massey nee Huff , on oath state that I am 27 years of age and a citizen by blood , of the Chickasaw Nation; that I am the lawful wife of Enoch L Massey , who is a citizen, ~~by~~ _____ of the United States ~~Nation~~; that a male child was born to me on 13th day of May , 190 3, that said child has been named Ernest Leon Massey , and is now living.

Marietta Massey

WITNESSES TO MARK:

{

Subscribed and sworn to before me this 24th day of March , 190 5

C.H. Thomes
Notary Public.

AFFIDAVIT OF ATTENDING PHYSICIAN OR MID-WIFE.

UNITED STATES OF AMERICA,
   INDIAN TERRITORY,
Southern   District.

I, J. P. Collins , a physician , on oath state that I attended on Mrs. Marietta Massey , wife of Enoch L Massey on the 13th day of May , 190 3; that there was born to her on said date a male child; that said child is now living and is said to have been named Ernest Leon Massey

J.P. Collins

WITNESSES TO MARK:

{

Subscribed and sworn to before me this 25th day of March , 190 .

C.H. Thomes
Notary Public.

Applications for Enrollment of Chickasaw Newborn
Act of 1905   Volume III

Chickasaw 1023.

Muskogee, Indian Territory, April 3, 1905.

Enoch L. Massey,
    Willis, Indian Territory.

Dear Sir:

    Receipt is hereby acknowledged of the affidavits of Marietta Massey and J. P. Collins to the birth of Ernest Leon Massey, son of Enoch L. and Marietta Massey, May 13, 1903, and the same have been filed with our records as an application for the enrollment of said child.

                  Respectfully,

                                  Chairman.

Chic. N.B - 163
    (Charley Archerd
    Born August 14, 1903)

INDIAN TERRITORY,
SOUTHERN DISTRICT.

    I, C. M. Campbell, Clerk of the United States Court, Southern District, Indian Territory, do hereby certify that the above and foregoing is a true and correct copy of the Marriage License and Certificate of Marriage filed for record in my office at Ardmore on the 27th day of October, 1903, as the same appears duly recorded in volume F, page 553, Marriage Records

    IN TESTIMONY WHEREOF, I have hereunto set my hand and affixed the seal of said Court at my office in Ardmore, Indian Territory this 26th day of May, A.D. 1905.

                          C. M. Campbell, Clerk

                    By   N.H. McCoy   Chief Deputy.

Applications for Enrollment of Chickasaw Newborn
Act of 1905 Volume III

CERTIFICATE OF
RECORD OF MARRIAGE

UNITED STATES OF AMERICA,
INDIAN TERRITORY, } sct.
SOUTHERN DISTRICT.

I, C. M. CAMPBELL, Clerk of the United States Court, in the Territory and District aforesaid Do HEREBY CERTIFY, that the License for and Certificate of Marriage of

Mr   Henry Archerd   and

M   Mary Gayle

were filed in my office in said Territory and District the   27th   day of October   A.D., 190 2   and duly recorded in Book F   of Marriage Record, Page   553

WITNESS my hand and Seal of said Court, at Ardmore, this   27th   day of   October   A.D. 190 2

C. M. Campbell
CLERK.

Return this license to the United States Clerk at Ardmore, that it may be recorded, when it will be mailed to the proper address.

Texas Printing Company, Fort Worth.

DEPARTMENT OF THE INTERIOR,
COMMISSION TO THE FIVE CIVILIZED TRIBES.

FILED

JUN - 1905   Tams Bixby CHAIRMAN.

No person is authorized to perform the Marriage Ceremony in the Indian Territory unless the proper credentials have first been recorded in the Clerk's office.

MARRIAGE LICENSE.

No. 1457

UNITED STATES OF AMERICA,
INDIAN TERRITORY, } SS.   To Any Person Authorized by Law to Solemnize
SOUTHERN DISTRICT.   Marriage, Greeting:

YOU ARE HEREBY COMMANDED to solemnize the Rite and publish the Banns of Matrimony between Mr.   Henry Archerd
of   Madill   in the Indian Territory, aged   twenty-five   years, and
M   Mary Gayle   of   Madill   in the Indian Territory,

Applications for Enrollment of Chickasaw Newborn
Act of 1905 Volume III

aged twenty *years, according to law; and do you officially sign and return this license to the parties therein named.*

WITNESS my hand and official Seal, this 16th day of October A. D. 190 2

C. M. Campbell
Clerk of the United States Court.

Certificate of Marriage.

UNITED STATES OF AMERICA,
INDIAN TERRITORY, } SS.
SOUTHERN DISTRICT.

I, D. J. McDonald, Local Elder of M. E. Church South *do hereby certify that on the* 22nd *day of* October A. D. 190 2 *, I did duly and according to law, as commanded in the foregoing License, solemnize the Rite and publish the Banns of Matrimony between the parties therein named.*

WITNESS my hand this 25th day of October A. D. 190 2

My credentials are recorded in the office of the Clerk of the United States Court, Indian Territory, Southern District, at Ardmore, Book C *, Page* 46

D. J. McDonald
L.E. Methodist E.C.S.

NOTE. (a)- This License and Certificate of Marriages must be returned to the office of the Clerk of the United States Court in the Indian Territory, at Ardmore, within sixty days from the date thereof, or the party to whom the License was issued will be liable in the amount of ONE HUNDRED DOLLARS ($100).

BIRTH AFFIDAVIT.

DEPARTMENT OF THE INTERIOR.
COMMISSION TO THE FIVE CIVILIZED TRIBES.

IN RE APPLICATION FOR ENROLLMENT, as a citizen of the Chickasaw Nation, of Charley Archerd , born on the 14th day of Aug , 1903

Name of Father: Henry Adolphus Archerd a citizen of the Chickasaw Nation.
Name of Mother: Mary Buckner Archerd a citizen of the United States Nation.

Postoffice Madill, Indian Territory

Applications for Enrollment of Chickasaw Newborn
Act of 1905   Volume III

AFFIDAVIT OF MOTHER.

UNITED STATES OF AMERICA, Indian Territory, }
  Southern   DISTRICT.

I, Mary Buckner Archerd , on oath state that I am Twenty Three years of age and a citizen by ...., of the United States Nation; that I am the lawful wife of Henry Adolphus , who is a citizen, by blood of the Chickasaw Nation; that a male child was born to me on 14th day of August , 1905[sic]; that said child has been named Charley Archerd , and was living March 4, 1905.

                                  Mary B. Archerd
Witnesses To Mark:
 {

Subscribed and sworn to before me this Twenty Seventh day of March , 1905

                                  Summers Hardy
                                  Notary Public.

AFFIDAVIT OF ATTENDING PHYSICIAN OR MID-WIFE.

UNITED STATES OF AMERICA, Indian Territory, }
  Southern   DISTRICT.

I, Martha L Trail , a Midwife , on oath state that I attended on Mrs. Mary Buckner Archerd , wife of Henry Adolphus Archerd on the 14th day of August , 1905[sic]; that there was born to her on said date a male child; that said child was living March 4, 1905, and is said to have been named Charley Archerd

                                  Martha L Trail
Witnesses To Mark:
 {

Subscribed and sworn to before me this 27" day of March , 1905

                                  Summers Hardy
                                  Notary Public.

Applications for Enrollment of Chickasaw Newborn
Act of 1905 Volume III

BIRTH AFFIDAVIT.

DEPARTMENT OF THE INTERIOR.
COMMISSION TO THE FIVE CIVILIZED TRIBES.

IN RE APPLICATION FOR ENROLLMENT, as a citizen of the   Chickasaw   Nation, of   Charley Archerd   , born on the   14th day of August   , 1903

Name of Father: Henry Adolphus Archerd   a citizen of the   Chickasaw   Nation.
Name of Mother: Mary Buckner Archerd   a citizen of the United States   Nation.

Postoffice   Madill, I T

AFFIDAVIT OF MOTHER.

UNITED STATES OF AMERICA, Indian Territory, }
    Southern   DISTRICT.

     I,   Mary Buckner Archerd   , on oath state that I am   23   years of age and a citizen by   ——————   , of the   United States   Nation; that I am the lawful wife of Henry Adolphus Archerd   , who is a citizen, by   blood   of the   Chickasaw Nation; that a   male   child was born to me on   14th day of   August   , 1903; that said child has been named   Charley Archerd   , and was living March 4, 1905.

                                         Mary Buckner Archerd
Witnesses To Mark:
{

     Subscribed and sworn to before me this   19" day of   April   , 1905

                                         Summers Hardy
                                               Notary Public.

AFFIDAVIT OF ATTENDING PHYSICIAN OR MID-WIFE.

UNITED STATES OF AMERICA, Indian Territory, }
    Southern   DISTRICT.

     I,   Martha L Trail   , a   midwife   , on oath state that I attended on Mrs.   Mary Buckner Archerd   , wife of Henry Adolphus Archerd   on the   14th day of   August   , 1903; that there was born to her on said date a   male   child; that said child was living March 4, 1905, and is said to have been named   Charley Archerd

                                         Martha L Trail
Witnesses To Mark:
{

Applications for Enrollment of Chickasaw Newborn
Act of 1905   Volume III

Subscribed and sworn to before me this 19" day of April , 1905

Summers Hardy
Notary Public.

---

9 N B 163

Muskogee, Indian Territory, April 14, 1905.

Henry Adolphus Archerd,
    Madill, Indian Territory.

Dear Sir:

    There is inclosed you herewith for execution application for the enrollment of your infant child, Charley Archerd, born August 14, 1903.

    The affidavits heretofore filed with the Commission, give the date of the birth of said child as August 14, 1905. It will, therefore, be necessary to have the application re-executed, showing the correct date of his birth.

    In having these affidavits executed care should be exercised to see that all names are written in full, as they appear in the body of the affidavit, and in the event that either of the persons signing the affidavit are unable to write, signatures by mark must be attested by two witnesses. Each affidavit must be executed before a Notary Public and the notarial seal and signature of the officer must be attached to each separate affidavit.

Respectfully,

LM 14-170   Commissioner in Charge.

Chickasaw N. B. 163.

Muskogee, Indian Territory, April 22, 1905.

Henry Adolphus Archerd,
    Madill, Indian Territory.

Dear Sir:

    Receipt is hereby acknowledged of the affidavits of Mary Buckner Archerd and Martha L. Trail to the birth of Charley Archerd, son of Henry Adolphus and Mary Buckner Archerd, August 14, 1903, and the same have been filed with our records in the matter of the enrollment of said child.

Applications for Enrollment of Chickasaw Newborn
Act of 1905   Volume III

Respectfully,

Chairman.

———————

9-NB-163.

Muskogee, Indian Territory, May 13, 1905.

Henry Adolphus Archerd,
    Madill, Indian Territory.

Dear Sir:

    Referring to the application for the enrollment of your infant child, Charley Archerd, born August 14, 1905, it is noted that the applicant claims through you.

    In this event it will be necessary that you file with the Commission either the original or a certified copy of the license and certificate of your marriage to Mary Buckner Archerd.

    Please give this matter your immediate attention.

Respectfully,

Chairman.

———————

9 N.B. 163.

Muskogee, Indian Territory, June 5, 1905.

Henry A. Archerd,
    Ardmore, Indian Territory.

Dear Sir:

    Receipt is hereby acknowledged of your letter of May 26, transmitting certified copy of the marriage license and certificate between Henry Archerd and Mary Gayle, which you offer in support of the application for the enrollment of your child, Charlie[sic] Archerd, and the same has been filed with the record in this case.

Respectfully,

Commissioner in Charge.

Applications for Enrollment of Chickasaw Newborn
Act of 1905   Volume III

9-NB-163

Muskogee, Indian Territory, July 21, 1905.

Henry A. Archard,
    Madill, Indian Territory.

Dear Sir:

    Receipt is hereby acknowledged of your letter of July 17, 1905, in which you state that you forwarded your marriage license and certificate in the matter of the enrollment of your child Charley Archard[sic] and you ask if the same was received.

    In reply to your letter you are advised that the marriage license and certificate between Henry Archard and Mary Gale[sic] were received at this office and receipt thereof was acknowledged to you at Ardmore, Indian Territory on June 5, 1905.

    You are further advised that the name of your child Charley Archard has been placed upon a schedule of citizens by blood of the Chickasaw Nation which has been forwarded the Secretary of the Interior and you will be notified when his enrollment is approved by the Department.

                              Respectfully,

                                              Commissioner.

Chic. N.B. - 164
    (Either Sealy
    Born December 12, 1903)

BIRTH AFFIDAVIT.

DEPARTMENT OF THE INTERIOR.
COMMISSION TO THE FIVE CIVILIZED TRIBES.

    IN RE APPLICATION FOR ENROLLMENT, as a citizen of the   Chickasaw   Nation, of   Either Sealy   , born on the   12th day of Dec   , 1903

Name of Father: Will Sealy   a citizen of the   Chickasaw Nation.
Name of Mother: Sussie Sealy   a citizen of the   ———   Nation.

                            Postoffice   Kingston I.T.

Applications for Enrollment of Chickasaw Newborn
Act of 1905 Volume III

AFFIDAVIT OF MOTHER.

UNITED STATES OF AMERICA, Indian Territory,
Southern DISTRICT.

I, Sussie Sealy, on oath state that I am 20 years of age and a citizen by ———, of the ——— Nation; that I am the lawful wife of Will Sealy, who is a citizen, by blood of the Chickasaw Nation; that a female child was born to me on 12th day of Dec, 1903; that said child has been named Either Sealy, and was living March 4, 1905.

Sussie Seely[sic]

Witnesses To Mark:
{

Subscribed and sworn to before me this 18th day of March, 1905

DP Johnston
Notary Public.

AFFIDAVIT OF ATTENDING PHYSICIAN OR MID-WIFE.

UNITED STATES OF AMERICA, Indian Territory,
Southern DISTRICT.

I, E F Lewis, a Physician, on oath state that I attended on Mrs. Will Sealy, wife of Will Sealy on the 12th day of Dec, 1903; that there was born to her on said date a female child; that said child was living March 4, 1905, and is said to have been named Either Sealy

E.F. Lewis

Witnesses To Mark:
{

Subscribed and sworn to before me this 18th day of March, 1905

DP Johnston
Notary Public.

Chic. N.B. - 165
(Zella Bernice Gardner
Born January 18, 1903)

Applications for Enrollment of Chickasaw Newborn
Act of 1905   Volume III

BIRTH AFFIDAVIT.

DEPARTMENT OF THE INTERIOR.
COMMISSION TO THE FIVE CIVILIZED TRIBES.

IN RE APPLICATION FOR ENROLLMENT, as a citizen of the   Chickasaw   Nation, of   Zella Bernice Gardner   , born on the   18   day of   January   , 1903

Name of Father: Benjamin Shannon Gardner   a citizen of the   Chickasaw Nation.
Name of Mother: Annie Gardner   a citizen of the   Chickasaw Nation.

Postoffice   McMillan Ind Ter

AFFIDAVIT OF MOTHER.

UNITED STATES OF AMERICA, Indian Territory,
Southern   DISTRICT.

I,   Annie Gardner   , on oath state that I am   35   years of age and a citizen by   blood   , of the   Chickasaw   Nation; that I am the lawful wife of   Benjamin Shannon Gardner   , who is a citizen, by Intermarriage   of the   Chickasaw Nation; that a   girl   child was born to me on   18   day of   January   , 1903; that said child has been named   Zella Bernice Gardner   , and was living March 4, 1905.

Annie Gardner

Witnesses To Mark:
{

Subscribed and sworn to before me this   20   day of   March   , 1905

W C Campbell
Notary Public.

AFFIDAVIT OF ATTENDING PHYSICIAN OR MID-WIFE.

UNITED STATES OF AMERICA, Indian Territory,
Southern   DISTRICT.

I,   J *(Illegible)*   , a   Physician   , on oath state that I attended on Mrs.   Annie Gardner   , wife of   Benjamin Shannon Gardner   on the   18   day of   Jan   , 1903; that there was born to her on said date a   female   child; that said child was living March 4, 1905, and is said to have been named   Zella Bernice Gardner

Jay *(Illegible)* M.D.

Witnesses To Mark:
{

Applications for Enrollment of Chickasaw Newborn
Act of 1905   Volume III

Subscribed and sworn to before me this 20   day of   March   , 1905

> W C Campbell
> Notary Public.

Chickasaw N B 165

Muskogee, Indian Territory, May 16, 1905.

B. S. Gardner,   6/27/05 McMillan I.T.
   Ardmore, Indian Territory.

Dear Sir:

   Receipt is hereby acknowledged of your letter of May 12, asking if the birth certificate of Zella Gardner was received, and in reply you are advised that the affidavits heretofore forwarded to the birth of Zella Bernice Gardner have been filed with our records as an application for the enrollment of said child.

> Respectfully,
>
> Chairman.

Chic. N.B. - 166
   (James Anderson Harrison
   Born February 10, 1905)

BIRTH AFFIDAVIT.

DEPARTMENT OF THE INTERIOR.
COMMISSION TO THE FIVE CIVILIZED TRIBES.

IN RE APPLICATION FOR ENROLLMENT, as a citizen of the   Chickasaw   Nation, of   James Anderson Harrison   , born on the   10   day of Feb , 1905
Name of Father: George W Harrison   a citizen of the   Chickasaw   Nation.
Name of Mother: Betty Maud[sic] Harrison   a citizen of the   Chickasaw   Nation.

> Postoffice   Oswalt I. Ter.

Applications for Enrollment of Chickasaw Newborn
Act of 1905   Volume III

AFFIDAVIT OF MOTHER.

UNITED STATES OF AMERICA, Indian Territory, }
Southern   DISTRICT.

I,   Bettie Maud Harrison   , on oath state that I am 24   years of age and a citizen by   Birth , of the   Chickasaw   Nation; that I am the lawful wife of Geo W Harrison   , who is a citizen, by Marriage   of the   Chickasaw Nation; that a   male   child was born to me on   10 day of   Feb , 1905; that said child has been named   Jas. Anderson Harrison   , and was living March 4, 1905.

                                       Mrs Bettie Maude Harrison

Witnesses To Mark:
  { Geo W Coffman
  { John C Howell

Subscribed and sworn to before me this 25 day of   March   , 1905

                                       E.S. Hammond
                                       Notary Public.

AFFIDAVIT OF ATTENDING PHYSICIAN OR MID-WIFE.

UNITED STATES OF AMERICA, Indian Territory, }
Southern   DISTRICT.

I,   W. M. Kearney   , a   Physician   , on oath state that I attended on Mrs. Bettie Maud Harrison   , wife of   Geo. W. Harrison   on the 10 day of Feb , 1905; that there was born to her on said date a   male   child; that said child was living March 4, 1905, and is said to have been named Jas. Anderson Harrison

                                         WM Kearney

Witnesses To Mark:
  { Geo W Coffman
  { John C Howell

Subscribed and sworn to before me this 25 day of   March   , 1905

                                       E.S. Hammond
                                       Notary Public.

Applications for Enrollment of Chickasaw Newborn
Act of 1905   Volume III

Chic. N.B. - 167
    (Byrd Love Draughon
    Born November 16, 1903)

BIRTH AFFIDAVIT.

DEPARTMENT OF THE INTERIOR.
COMMISSION TO THE FIVE CIVILIZED TRIBES.

IN RE APPLICATION FOR ENROLLMENT, as a citizen of the   Chickasaw   Nation, of   Byrd Love Draughon   , born on the 16th day of   November   , 1903

Name of Father: H E Draughon   a citizen of the   Chickasaw   Nation.
Name of Mother: Ruby Belle Draughon   a citizen of the   Chickasaw   Nation.
                      (nee Love)
                      Postoffice   Marietta Ind Ter

AFFIDAVIT OF MOTHER.

UNITED STATES OF AMERICA, Indian Territory, }
   Southern   DISTRICT.

    I, Ruby Bell Draughon   , on oath state that I am   24   years of age and a citizen by   blood   , of the   Chickasaw   Nation; that I am the lawful wife of   H E Draughon   , who is a citizen, by   Intermarriage   of the   Chickasaw Nation; that a   Female   child was born to me on   16th day of   November   , 1903; that said child has been named   Byrd Love Draughon   , and was living March 4, 1905.

                          Ruby Belle (Love) Draughon

Witnesses To Mark:
{

    Subscribed and sworn to before me this   14 day of   Mar   , 1905

                         D G Bartlett
                         Notary Public.

AFFIDAVIT OF ATTENDING PHYSICIAN OR MID-WIFE.

UNITED STATES OF AMERICA, Indian Territory, }
   Southern   DISTRICT.

    I,   J D Batson   , a Physician   , on oath state that I attended on Mrs. HE Draughon , wife of HE Draughon   on the 16th day of November ,

Applications for Enrollment of Chickasaw Newborn
Act of 1905   Volume III

1903; that there was born to her on said date a   Female   child; that said child was living March 4, 1905, and is said to have been named Byrd Love Draughon

J D Batson M.D.

Witnesses To Mark:

{

Subscribed and sworn to before me this   14 day of   Mar   , 1905

D G Bartlett
Notary Public.

7-198
9-1033

Muskogee, Indian Territory, March 20, 1905.

D. G. Bartlett,
  Marietta, Indian Territory.

Dear Sir:

  Receipt is hereby acknowledged of your letter of March 14, 1905, enclosing the affidavits of Minnie Holden Askew and D. Autrey to the birth of Dorthey Hazell Askew, daughter of Thomas D. and Minnie Holder Askew, August 28, 1904, also the affidavits of Ruby Belle Draughon (Love) and J. D. Batson to the birth of Byrd Love Draughon, daughter of H. E. and Ruby Belle Draughon, November 16, 1903, and the same have been filed with our records as an application for the enrollment of said child.

Respectfully,

Chairman.

Chic. N.B. - 168
  (John Noletubby
  Born August 22, 1903)

Applications for Enrollment of Chickasaw Newborn
Act of 1905 Volume III

BIRTH AFFIDAVIT.

DEPARTMENT OF THE INTERIOR.
COMMISSION TO THE FIVE CIVILIZED TRIBES.

IN RE APPLICATION FOR ENROLLMENT, as a citizen of the Chickasaw Nation, of John Noletubby, born on the 22nd day of Aug, 1903

Name of Father: John Anderson Noletubby   a citizen of the Chickasaw Nation.
Name of Mother: Land Noletubby   a citizen of the Chickasaw Nation.

Postoffice   Stringtown, I.T.

AFFIDAVIT OF MOTHER.

UNITED STATES OF AMERICA, Indian Territory,
Central Judicial   DISTRICT.

I, Land Noletubby, on oath state that I am 28 years of age and a citizen by marriage, of the Chickasaw Nation; that I am the lawful wife of John Anderson Noletubby, who is a citizen, by blood of the Chickasaw Nation; that a male child was born to me on 22nd day of Aug, 1903; that said child has been named John Noletubby, and was living March 4, 1905.

Land Noletubby

Witnesses To Mark:

{

Subscribed and sworn to before me this 22nd day of Mch, 1905

D.S. Kennedy
Notary Public.

AFFIDAVIT OF ATTENDING PHYSICIAN OR MID-WIFE.

UNITED STATES OF AMERICA, Indian Territory,
Central Judicial   DISTRICT.

I, J.A. Dabney, a Physician, on oath state that I attended on Mrs. Land Noletubby, wife of John Anderson Noletubby on the 22nd day of Aug, 1903; that there was born to her on said date a male child; that said child was living March 4, 1905, and is said to have been named John Noletubby

JA Dabney M.D.

Witnesses To Mark:

{

Applications for Enrollment of Chickasaw Newborn
Act of 1905 Volume III

Subscribed and sworn to before me this 22nd day of   Mch   , 1905

                                  D.S. Kennedy
                                  Notary Public.

DEPARTMENT OF THE INTERIOR,
COMMISSION TO THE FIVE CIVILIZED TRIBES.

In the matter of the application for the enrollment of the infant child,   Johnnie Noletubby   , born on the   22   day of   August   , as a citizen of the   Chickasaw Nation.

Name of Father: Johnson A Noletubby   of   Stringtown   , I.T.
Name of Mother: Land Noletubby   of   Stringtown   , I.T.

UNITED STATES OF AMERICA,::
    INDIAN TERRITORY,   :: SS
    CENTRAL DISTRICT.   ::

    I, Land Noletubby , being duly sworn, state that I am   29   years of age, and a citizen of the   Chickasaw   Nation by   Intermarriage   ; that there was born to me on the   22nd   day of   August   , 190 3 , a   male   child; that aid child is now living, and has been named   Johnnie Noletubby   .

                                  Land Noletubby

Witnesses to mark:

_____

Subscribed and sworn to before me this   12th   day of December   , 190 4 .

                                  EA Newman
                                Notary Public.

UNITED STATES OF AMERICA,::
    INDIAN TERRITORY,   :: SS
    CENTRAL DISTRICT.   ::

    I,   Martha Watson   , a   Midwife   , being duly sworn, on oath state that I am   54   years of age, and that my post office us[sic]   Stringtown   , I. T., that I attended on Mrs.   Land Noletubby   on the   22   day of   August   , 1903 and that there was born to her on said date a   male   child; that said child is still living, and is said to have been named   Johnnie Noletubby   .

                                  Martha Watson

Witnesses to mark:

_____

_____

Applications for Enrollment of Chickasaw Newborn
Act of 1905   Volume III

Subscribed and sworn to before me this 12th day of December , 190 4 .

EA Newman
Notary Public.

9-1057

Muskogee, Indian Territory, March 28, 1905.

John Anderson Noletubby,
    Stringtown, Indian Territory.

Dear Sir:

    Receipt is hereby acknowledged of the affidavits of Land Noletubby and J. A. Dabney to the birth of John Noletubby son of John Anderson and Land Noletubby, August 22, 1903, and the same have been filed with our records as an application for the enrollment of said child.

Respectfully,

Chairman.

Chic. N.B. - 169
    (Joseph Peter
    Born November 2, 1904)

BIRTH AFFIDAVIT.

DEPARTMENT OF THE INTERIOR.
COMMISSION TO THE FIVE CIVILIZED TRIBES.

    IN RE APPLICATION FOR ENROLLMENT, as a citizen of the Chickasaw Nation, of Joseph Peter , born on the 2nd day of November , 1904

Name of Father: Harvey Peter   a citizen of the Chickasaw Nation.
Name of Mother: Jane Peter   a citizen of the Chickasaw Nation.

Postoffice   Filmore[sic] I.T.

Applications for Enrollment of Chickasaw Newborn
Act of 1905   Volume III

AFFIDAVIT OF MOTHER.

UNITED STATES OF AMERICA, Indian Territory, }
   Southern   DISTRICT.

I, Jane Peter , on oath state that I am 28 years of age and a citizen by blood , of the Chickasaw Nation; that I am the lawful wife of Harvey Peter , who is a citizen, by blood of the Chickasaw Nation; that a male child was born to me on the 2nd day of November , 1904; that said child has been named Joseph Peter , and was living March 4, 1905.

Jane Peter

Witnesses To Mark:
{

Subscribed and sworn to before me this 20 day of April , 1905

JE Williams
Notary Public.

AFFIDAVIT OF ATTENDING PHYSICIAN OR MID-WIFE.

UNITED STATES OF AMERICA, Indian Territory, }
   Southern   DISTRICT.

I, Susan Carney , a mid-wife , on oath state that I attended on Mrs. Jane Peter , wife of Harvey Peter on the 2nd day of November , 1904; that there was born to her on said date a male child; that said child was living March 4, 1905, and is said to have been named Joseph Peter

her
Susan x Carney
mark

Witnesses To Mark:
{ JE Williams
  Harvey Peter

Subscribed and sworn to before me this 20 day of April , 1905

JE Williams
Notary Public.

Applications for Enrollment of Chickasaw Newborn
Act of 1905   Volume III

BIRTH AFFIDAVIT.

DEPARTMENT OF THE INTERIOR.

Commission to the Five Civilized Tribes.

IN RE APPLICATION FOR ENROLLMENT as a citizen of the Chickasaw Nation of JOSEPH PETER   , born on the 2nd   day of   November   , 1904.

    Name of Father:-   Harvey Peter   , a citizen by blood of the   Chickasaw Nation.
    Name of Mother:-   Jane Peter   , a citizen by   blood   of the Chickasaw Nation.
                      Post-office:-   Fillmore   , Ind. Ter.

UNITED STATES OF AMERICA,)
Southern District,   )ss.
Indian Territory .   )
)

AFFIDAVIT OF MOTHER.

                I, Jane Peter, formerly Jane Conover, on oath state that I am twenty-eight years old and a citizen by blood of the Chickasaw Nation; that I am the lawful wife of Harvey Peter, who is a citizen by blood of the Chickasaw Nation; that a male child was born to me on the second day of November, 1904; that said child has been named Joseph Peter, and is now living.
                                          Jane Peter

    Subscribed and sworn to before me on this the 20th day of February, 1905.

                                J.B. O'Bryan
                                    Notary Public. -----

UNITED STATES OF AMERICA,)
Southern District,   )ss.
Indian Territory .   )
)

AFFIDAVIT OF MID-WIFE.

          I, Peggy Colbert, on oath state that I attended on Mrs. Jane Peter, the affiant above named, acting as mid-wife, she being the wife of Harvey Peter, on the second day of November, 1904; that there was born to her on said date a male child; that said child is now living and is said to have been named Joseph Peter.
                                            her
                                  Peggie x Colbert
                                      mark

Applications for Enrollment of Chickasaw Newborn
Act of 1905   Volume III

Witness to mark
(Name Illegible) (Illegible) ?.T.
SW Maples   " "

Subscribed and sworn to before me on this the 28 day of February, 1905.

JG Gardner
Notary Public. -------------

9-1064

Muskogee, Indian Territory, March 4, 1905.

Jane Peter,
    Filmore[sic], Indian Territory,

Dear Madam:

    Receipt is hereby acknowledged of your affidavit and the affidavit of Peggy Colbert relative to the birth of Joseph Peter, infant son of Harvey and Jane Peter, November 2, 1904, and the same have been filed with the records of the Commission.

Respectfully,

Commissioner in Charge.

9 N.B. 169

Muskogee, Indian Territory, April 13, 1905.

Harvey Peter,
    Fillmore, Indian Territory.

Dear Sir:

    There is herewith inclosed you for execution application for the enrollment of your infant child, Joseph Peter, born November 2, 1904.

    The affidavits heretofore filed with the Commission show the child was living on February 28, 1905. It is necessary, for the child to be enrolled, that he was living on March 4, 1905. Please insert the age of the mother in space provided for the purpose.

    In having these affidavits executed care should be exercised to see that all names are written in full, as they appear in the body of the affidavit, and in the event that either

Applications for Enrollment of Chickasaw Newborn
Act of 1905 Volume III

of the persons signing the affidavit are unable to write, signatures by mark must be attested by two witnesses. Each affidavit must be executed before a Notary Public and the notarial seal and signature of the officer must be attached to each separate affidavit.

Respectfully,

LM 13-26   Commissioner in Charge.

Chic. N.B. - 170
   *(Otis Kemp
   Born January 19, 1905)*

BIRTH AFFIDAVIT.   No 14

DEPARTMENT OF THE INTERIOR.
COMMISSION TO THE FIVE CIVILIZED TRIBES.

IN RE APPLICATION FOR ENROLLMENT, as a citizen of the   Chickasaw   Nation, of ...., born on the 19 day of January , 1905

Name of Father: Wellington Martin Kemp   a citizen of the Chickasaw Nation.
Name of Mother: Susan A Kemp   a citizen of the Chickasaw Nation.

Postoffice   Paucaunly[sic]

AFFIDAVIT OF MOTHER.

UNITED STATES OF AMERICA, Indian Territory,
   Central   DISTRICT.

I, Susan A Kemp   , on oath state that I am 35 years of age and a citizen by   intermarriage   , of the   Chickasaw   Nation; that I am the lawful wife of Wellington Martin Kemp   , who is a citizen, by   blood   of the   Chickasaw Nation; that a   male   child was born to me on 19 day of January , 1905, that said child has been named   Otis   , and is now living.

Susan A Kemp

Witnesses To Mark:
   { Artie Vantrees
   { W.M. Kemp

31

Applications for Enrollment of Chickasaw Newborn
Act of 1905   Volume III

Subscribed and sworn to before me this 23 day of January , 1905.

S M Mead
Notary Public.

AFFIDAVIT OF ATTENDING PHYSICIAN OR MID-WIFE.

UNITED STATES OF AMERICA, Indian Territory, }
Central   DISTRICT. }

I,   C A Kerby   , a   Midwife   , on oath state that I attended on Mrs. Susan A Kemp , wife of Wellington M Kemp on the 19 day of January , 1905; that there was born to her on said date a male child; that said child is now living and is said to have been named Otis

C A Kerby

Witnesses To Mark:
{ Artie Vantrees
{ W.M. Kemp

Subscribed and sworn to before me this 23 day of January , 1905.

S M Mead
Notary Public.

9-1069

Muskogee, Indian Territory, March 31, 1905.

Wellington Martin Kemp,
    Paucaunla, Indian Territory.

Dear Sir:

Receipt is hereby acknowledged of the affidavits of Susan A. Kemp and C. A. Kirby[sic] to the birth of Otis Kemp son of Wellington Martin and Susan A. Kemp, January 19, 1905, and the same have been filed with our records as an application for the enrollment of said child.

Respectfully,

Chairman.

Applications for Enrollment of Chickasaw Newborn
Act of 1905 Volume III

Chic. N.B. - 171
    (Nicolos or Nickless Phelps
    Born January 17, 1903)
    (Douglas Phelps
    Born February 7, 1905)

BIRTH AFFIDAVIT.

DEPARTMENT OF THE INTERIOR,
COMMISSION TO THE FIVE CIVILIZED TRIBES.

In Re Application for Enrollment, as a citizen of the Chicosaw[sic] Nation, of   Nicolos Phelps   , born on the   17   day of   Jan   , 1903

Name of Father: Andrew Phelps   a citizen of the (By Marriage) Nation.
Name of Mother: Emma Phelps   a citizen of the   Chicosaw   Nation.

        Post-office   Antlers, I.T.

AFFIDAVIT OF MOTHER.

UNITED STATES OF AMERICA, ⎫
   ~~INDIAN TERRITORY,~~   ⎬
   Central   District. ⎭

    I,   Emma Phelps   , on oath state that I am   25   years of age and a citizen by   Blood   , of the   Chicosaw   Nation; that I am the lawful wife of   Andrew Phelps   , who is a citizen, by   marriage of the   Chicosaw   Nation; that a   Boy   child was born to me on   17   day of   Jan   , 1903 , that said child has been named   Nicolos Phelps   , and is now living.

                          her
                      Emma x Phelps
WITNESSES TO MARK: mark
   { T.B. Draper
     J.C. McGinnis

    Subscribed and sworn to before me this   24 day of   Mch , 1905.

                         C.E. Walker
                            NOTARY PUBLIC.

Applications for Enrollment of Chickasaw Newborn
Act of 1905 Volume III

AFFIDAVIT OF ATTENDING PHYSICIAN OR MID-WIFE.

UNITED STATES OF AMERICA, ⎫
~~INDIAN TERRITORY,~~
Central   District. ⎭

I, Bessie Brown   , a Midwife   , on oath state that I attended on Mrs. Emma Phelps , wife of Andrew Phelps   on the 17   day of Jan , 1903; that there was born to her on said date a   male   child; that said child is now living and is said to have been named Nicolos Phelps

                                    Bessie Brown

WITNESSES TO MARK:

Subscribed and sworn to before me this 24 day of   Mch , 1905.

                        C.E. Walker
                        NOTARY PUBLIC.

BIRTH AFFIDAVIT.   No 10

DEPARTMENT OF THE INTERIOR.
COMMISSION TO THE FIVE CIVILIZED TRIBES.

IN RE APPLICATION FOR ENROLLMENT, as a citizen of the   Chickasaw   Nation, of Nickless Phelps   , born on the 17th   day of January , 1903

Name of Father: Andrew Phelps   a citizen of the   U.S.   Nation.
Name of Mother: Emma Phelps   a citizen of the Chickasaw Nation.

                Postoffice   Robbers Roost I.T.

AFFIDAVIT OF MOTHER.

UNITED STATES OF AMERICA, Indian Territory, ⎫
Central   DISTRICT. ⎭

I, Emma Phelps   , on oath state that I am   24 years of age and a citizen by blood , of the   Chickasaw   Nation; that I am the lawful wife of   Andrew Phelps   , who is a citizen, by ....of the   U.S. Nation; that a   male   child was born to me on   17th   day of   January   , 1903, that said child has been named Nickless Phelps   , and is now living.   her
                        Emma x Phelps
                             mark

34

Applications for Enrollment of Chickasaw Newborn
Act of 1905   Volume III

Witnesses To Mark:
{ *(Name Illegible)*
{ *(Name Illegible)*

    Subscribed and sworn to before me this   25th   day of   January , 1905.

                       C. T. Luttrell
                            Notary Public.

AFFIDAVIT OF ATTENDING PHYSICIAN OR MID-WIFE.

UNITED STATES OF AMERICA, Indian Territory, }
....DISTRICT. }

    I,   Elvira Kieffer   , a   midwife   , on oath state that I attended on Mrs. Emma Phelps , wife of   Andrew Phelps   on the   17th   day of January, 1903; that there was born to her on said date a   male   child; that said child is now living and is said to have been named Nickless Phelps

                       Elvira Keiffer

Witnesses To Mark:
{ George Seeley
{ Ollie Curtis

    Subscribed and sworn to before me this   25th   day of   January , 1905.

                       C. T. Luttrell
                            Notary Public.
              Commission expires March 22nd 1908

BIRTH AFFIDAVIT.
DEPARTMENT OF THE INTERIOR.
COMMISSION TO THE FIVE CIVILIZED TRIBES.

    IN RE APPLICATION FOR ENROLLMENT, as a citizen of the   Chickasaw   Nation, of Douglas Phelps   , born on the   7th   day of   Feb , 1..........

Name of Father: Andrew Phelps   a citizen of the   U.S.   Nation.
Name of Mother: Emma Phelps   a citizen of the   Chickasaw Nation.

                Postoffice   Robbers I.T.

Applications for Enrollment of Chickasaw Newborn
Act of 1905   Volume III

\AFFIDAVIT OF MOTHER.

UNITED STATES OF AMERICA, Indian Territory, }
    Central   DISTRICT.

    I, Emma Phelps , on oath state that I am 24 years of age and a citizen by blood , of the Chickasaw Nation; that I am the lawful wife of Andrew Phelps , who is a citizen, ~~by~~ of U.S. of the ——— Nation; that a male child was born to me on 7th day of February , 1905, that said child has been named Douglas Phelps , and is now living.

                              her
                        Emma x Phelps
                              mark

Witnesses To Mark:
  { *(Name Illegible)*
    W H Maupin

    Subscribed and sworn to before me this 14th day of Feb , 1905.

                        C. T. Luttrell
                            Notary Public.

AFFIDAVIT OF ATTENDING PHYSICIAN OR MID-WIFE.

UNITED STATES OF AMERICA, Indian Territory, }
    Central   DISTRICT.

    I, G.W. Green , a Physician , on oath state that I attended on Mrs. Emma Phelps , wife of Andrew Phelps on the 7th day of Feb , 1905; that there was born to her on said date a male child; that said child is now living and is said to have been named Douglas Phelps

                        G.W. Green M.D.

Witnesses To Mark:
  { *(Name Illegible)*
    W H Maupin

    Subscribed and sworn to before me this 14th day of Feb , 1905.

                        C. T. Luttrell
My office expires Mar 22nd 1908

Applications for Enrollment of Chickasaw Newborn
Act of 1905   Volume III

BIRTH AFFIDAVIT.

DEPARTMENT OF THE INTERIOR.
COMMISSION TO THE FIVE CIVILIZED TRIBES.

IN RE APPLICATION FOR ENROLLMENT, as a citizen of the   Chickasaw   Nation, of   Nickless Phelps   , born on the   17th day of   Jan   , 1903

Name of Father: Andrew Phelps   a citizen of the   U.S.   Nation.
Name of Mother: Emma Phelps   a citizen of the   Chickasaw   Nation.

Postoffice   Robbers Roost I.T.

AFFIDAVIT OF MOTHER.

UNITED STATES OF AMERICA, Indian Territory, }
Central   DISTRICT.   }

I,   Emma Phelps   , on oath state that I am   24   years of age and a citizen by blood   , of the   Chickasaw   Nation; that I am the lawful wife of   Andrew Phelps   , who is a citizen, by ....of the   U.S. Nation; that a   male   child was born to me on   17th day of   Jan.   1903   , 1....... that said child has been named   Nickless Phelps   , and is now living.

            her
          Emma x Phelps
            mark

Witnesses To Mark:
{ D.H. Hanna
{ Roberson Kemp

Subscribed and sworn to before me this   1st day of   April   , 1905.

          C. T. Luttrell
            Notary Public.

AFFIDAVIT OF ATTENDING PHYSICIAN OR MID-WIFE.

UNITED STATES OF AMERICA, Indian Territory, }
Central   DISTRICT.   }

I,   Elvira Keffer[sic]   , a mid-wife   , on oath state that I attended on Mrs.   Emma Phelps   , wife of   Andrew Phelps   on the   17th day of   Jan , 1903; that there was born to her on said date a   male   child; that said child is now living and is said to have been named Nickless Phelps

            her
          Elvira x Keffer
            mark

Applications for Enrollment of Chickasaw Newborn
Act of 1905 Volume III

Witnesses To Mark:
{ D.H. Hanna
{ Roberson Kemp

    Subscribed and sworn to before me this 1st day of April , 1905.

                                   C. T. Luttrell
                                         Notary Public.
                      Commission expires March 22nd 1908

BIRTH AFFIDAVIT.

DEPARTMENT OF THE INTERIOR.
COMMISSION TO THE FIVE CIVILIZED TRIBES.

    IN RE APPLICATION FOR ENROLLMENT, as a citizen of the   Chickasaw   Nation, of   Douglas Phelps   , born on the 7 day of February , 1905

Name of Father: Andrew Phelps   a citizen of the   U.S.   Nation.
Name of Mother: Emma Phelps   a citizen of the   Chickasaw   Nation.

                          Postoffice   Robbers, Ind. Ter,

AFFIDAVIT OF MOTHER.

UNITED STATES OF AMERICA, Indian Territory, }
   Central   DISTRICT. }

    I, Emma Phelps   , on oath state that I am 24 years of age and a citizen by blood , of the   Chickasaw   Nation; that I am the lawful wife of Andrew Phelps   , who is a citizen, ~~by~~——— of the   United States Nation; that a   male   child was born to me on   7th   day of   February , 1905; that said child has been named Douglas Phelps   , and was living March 4, 1905.

                                             her
                                   Emma x Phelps
Witnesses To Mark: mark
{ Fannie Luttrell
{ D.H. Hanna

    Subscribed and sworn to before me this 18th day of May   , 1905

                                   C.T. Luttrell
                                     Notary Public.

Applications for Enrollment of Chickasaw Newborn
Act of 1905   Volume III

AFFIDAVIT OF ATTENDING PHYSICIAN OR MID-WIFE.

UNITED STATES OF AMERICA, Indian Territory,
Central   DISTRICT.

I,   G.W. Greene   , a   Physician   , on oath state that I attended on Mrs.   Emma Phelps   , wife of   Andrew Phelps   on the 7th day of   February, 1905; that there was born to her on said date a   male   child; that said child was living March 4, 1905, and is said to have been named   Douglas Phelps

G.W. Greene M.D.

Witnesses To Mark:

{

Subscribed and sworn to before me this 18th day of   May   , 1905

C.T. Luttrell
Notary Public.

9-1078.

Muskogee, Indian Territory, March 30, 1903.

Andrew Phelps,
Antlers, Indian Territory.

Dear Sir:

Referring to the application for enrollment as a citizen of the Chickasaw Nation of Nicolos Phelps, infant son of Andrew and Emma Phelps, born January 17, 1903, recently submitted by you; your attention is invited to Section twenty-eight of the act of Congress approved July 1, 1902, which was ratified by the citizens of the Choctaw and Chickasaw Nations September 25, 1902, as follows:

"The names of all persons living on the date of the final ratification of this agreement entitled to be enrolled as provided in section 27 hereof shall be placed upon the rolls made by said Commission; and no child born thereafter to a citizen or freedman and no person intermarried thereafter to a citizen shall be entitled to enrollment or to participate in the distribution of the tribal property of the Choctaws and Chickasaws."

Under the above legislation, the Commission is without authority to enroll this child.

Respectfully,

Chairman.

Applications for Enrollment of Chickasaw Newborn
Act of 1905 Volume III

9-1078

Muskogee, Indian Territory, May 7, 1904.

Emma Phelps,
    Robbersroost, Indian Territory.

Dear Madam:

    Receipt is hereby acknowledged of your letter of the 1st inst., stating that you have noticed a clause in the Indian Appropriation Bill authorizing the enrollment of children born since September 22, 1902, and you request to be advised whether it will be necessary for you to furnish any further evidence relative to the birth of your infant son, Nicholas Phelps, born January 17, 1903.

    You are advised that under existing legislation, the Commission is now without authority to enroll infant children born subsequent to September 25, 1902.

Respectfully,

Commissioner in Charge.

9-1078

Muskogee, Indian Territory, February 18, 1905.

Emma Phelps,
    Robbersroost, Indian Territory.

Dear Madam:

    Receipt is hereby acknowledged of your affidavit and the affidavit of G. W. Green to the birth of Douglas Phelps, infant son of Andrew and Emma Phelps, February 7, 1905, which it is presumed have been forwarded as an application for the enrollment of said child.

    You are advised that under the provisions of the act of Congress approved July 1, 1902, no children born to citizens of the Choctaw and Chickasaw Nations subsequent to September 25, 1902, the date of the ratification of said act, are entitled to enrollment and allotment in the Choctaw and Chickasaw Nations.

Respectfully,

Chairman.

Applications for Enrollment of Chickasaw Newborn
Act of 1905 Volume III

9-1078

Muskogee, Indian Territory, February 27, 1905.

Emma Phelps,
    Robbersroost, Indian Territory.

Dear Madam:

    Receipt is hereby acknowledged of your letter of February 18, 1905, in which you ask if a record was made of the application for the enrollment of your child Douglas Phelps and request that the affidavits be returned you in order that they may be submitted to the Chickasaw Enrolling Commission.

    In reply to your letter you are informed that the affidavits relative to the birth of your child Douglas Phelps have been placed with the other records in the matter of the enrollment of yourself and your family and it is not deemed advisable to return them.

    The communication of the Commission of February 18, enclosed with your letter is herewith returned.

    Respectfully,

Commissioner in Charge.

9-1078

Muskogee, Indian Territory, March 20, 1905.

Emma Phelps,
    Robbersroost, Indian Territory.

Dear Madam:

    Receipt is hereby acknowledged of your letter of March 14, 1905, stating that you have two children born since September 25, 1902, and asking if the application you have already submitted will be sufficient.

    In reply to your letter you are informed that the affidavits heretofore filed by you to the birth of your son Douglas Cooper[sic], February 7, 1905, have been filed with our records as an application for the enrollment of said child. It does not appear, however, that application has been made to this Commission for the enrollment of another child born to you since September 25, 1902.

    Respectfully,

Chairman.

Applications for Enrollment of Chickasaw Newborn
Act of 1905   Volume III

9-1078

Muskogee, Indian Territory, March 30, 1905.

Emma Phelps,
 Robbersroost, Indian Territory.

Dear Madam:

Receipt is hereby acknowledged of your letter of March 23, 1905, in which you state that the correct name of the child for whom you have already made application is Douglas Phelps and that you have another child whom you desire to have enrolled, and request a blank for that purpose.

In reply to your letter you are informed that the affidavits heretofore forwarded to the birth of your child show that his name is Douglas Phelps as it so appears upon our records.

In compliance with your request there is inclosed herewith blank for the enrollment of an infant child.

Respectfully,

Chairman.

EB 1-30

Chickasaw 1078.

Muskogee, Indian Territory, April 11, 1905.

Andrew Phelps,
 Robbers Roost, Indian Territory.

Dear Sir:

Receipt is hereby acknowledged of the affidavits of Emma Phelps and Elvira Keffer to the birth of Nickless Phelps, son of Andrew and Emma Phelps, January 17, 1903, and the same have been filed with our records as an application for the enrollment of said child.

Respectfully,

Commissioner in Charge.

Applications for Enrollment of Chickasaw Newborn
Act of 1905   Volume III

9-1078

Muskogee, Indian Territory, April 14, 1905.

Emma Phelps,
    Robbersroost, Indian Territory.

Dear Madam:

    Receipt is hereby acknowledged of your letter of April 3, 1905, in which you ask if the name of Douglas Phelps has ever come to the land office as you desire to file on his allotment.

    In reply to your letter you are informed that the affidavits heretofore forwarded to the birth of your children, Douglas and Nickless Phelps have been filed with our records as applications for the enrollment of these children, but no selection of allotment can be permitted for children for whom application was made under the act of Congress approved March 3, 1905, until their enrollment has been approved by the Secretary of the Interior.

    In compliance with your request there is inclosed herewith plat showing unallotted lands in the section named in your letter.

Respectfully,

Commissioner in Charge.

EB 1-14

Chickasaw N B 171

Muskogee, Indian Territory, May 20, 1905.

Andrew Phelps,
    Robbers Roost, Indian Territory.

Dear Sir:

    Receipt is hereby acknowledged of the affidavits of Emma Phelps and G. W. Greene to the birth of Douglas Phelps, son of Andrew and Emma Phelps, February 7, 1905, and the same have been filed with our records in the matter of the enrollment of said child.

Respectfully,

Chairman.

Applications for Enrollment of Chickasaw Newborn
Act of 1905 Volume III

9-NB-171.

Muskogee, Indian Territory, May 15, 1905.

Andrew Phelps,
    Robbers, Indian Territory.

Dear Sir:

    There is enclosed you herewith for execution application for the enrollment of your infant child, Douglas Phelps, born February 7, 1905.

    The affidavits heretofore filed with the Commission show the child was living on February 14, 1905. It is necessary, for the child to be enrolled, that he was living on March 4, 1905.

    In having these affidavits executed care should be exercised to see that all names are written in full, as they appear in the body of the affidavit, and in the event that either of the persons signing the affidavit are unable to write, signatures by mark must be attested by two witnesses. Each affidavit must be executed before a Notary Public and the notarial seal and signature of the officer must be attached to each separate affidavit.

Respectfully,

Chairman.

Chic. N.B. - 172
*(George Martin Rowler or Roller
Born February 17, 1904)*

BIRTH AFFIDAVIT.   *No 72*

DEPARTMENT OF THE INTERIOR.
COMMISSION TO THE FIVE CIVILIZED TRIBES.

IN RE APPLICATION FOR ENROLLMENT, as a citizen of the Chickasaw Nation, of George Martin Rowler, born on the 17 day of February, 1904

Name of Father: Jack E Rowler   a citizen of the Chickasaw Nation.
Name of Mother: Lucy Rowler   a citizen of the Chickasaw Nation.

Applications for Enrollment of Chickasaw Newborn
Act of 1905   Volume III

Postoffice   Mead

AFFIDAVIT OF MOTHER.

UNITED STATES OF AMERICA, Indian Territory, }
   Central   DISTRICT. }

I, Lucy Rowler , on oath state that I am   22   years of age and a citizen by blood , of the   Chickasaw   Nation; that I am the lawful wife of   Jack E Rowler , who is a citizen, by   intermarriage   of the   Chickasaw   Nation; that a   male   child was born to me on   17   day of   February , 1904, that said child has been named   George Martin   , and is now living.

Mrs J E Roller

Witnesses To Mark:
 { America Johnson
 { *(Name Illegible)*

Subscribed and sworn to before me this 31 day of   January , 1905.

S M Mead
Notary Public.

AFFIDAVIT OF ATTENDING PHYSICIAN OR MID-WIFE.

UNITED STATES OF AMERICA, Indian Territory, }
   Central   DISTRICT. }

I,   America Johnson   , a   Midwife   , on oath state that I attended on Mrs.   Lucy Rowler , wife of   J E Rowler   on the   17   day of   February , 1904; that there was born to her on said date a   male   child; that said child is now living and is said to have been named George Martin

America Johnson

Witnesses To Mark:
 { America Johnson
 { *(Name Illegible)*

Subscribed and sworn to before me this 31 day of   January , 1905.

S M Mead
Notary Public.

Applications for Enrollment of Chickasaw Newborn
Act of 1905 Volume III

BIRTH AFFIDAVIT.

DEPARTMENT OF THE INTERIOR.
COMMISSION TO THE FIVE CIVILIZED TRIBES.

IN RE APPLICATION FOR ENROLLMENT, as a citizen of the Chickasaw Nation, of George Martin Roller, born on the 17th day of February, 1904

Name of Father: Jack E Roller a citizen of the Chickasaw Nation.
Name of Mother: Lucy Krouse Roller a citizen of the Chickasaw Nation.

Postoffice   Mead Ind Terr

AFFIDAVIT OF MOTHER.

UNITED STATES OF AMERICA, Indian Territory, }
Central   DISTRICT.

I, Lucy Krouse Roller, on oath state that I am 22 yr years of age and a citizen by Blood, of the Chickasaw Nation; that I am the lawful wife of Jack E Roller, who is a citizen, by Marriage of the Chickasaw Nation; that a male child was born to me on 17th day of February, 1904; that said child has been named George Martin Roller, and was living March 4, 1905.

Lucy Krouse Roller

Witnesses To Mark:
{ L F Harvey
  John Malcolm

Subscribed and sworn to before me this 29th day of March, 1905

W.L. Seearce
Notary Public.

AFFIDAVIT OF ATTENDING PHYSICIAN OR MID-WIFE.

UNITED STATES OF AMERICA, Indian Territory, }
Central   DISTRICT.

I, America Johnson, a mid wife, on oath state that I attended on Mrs. Lucy Krouse Roller, wife of Jack E Roller on the 17th day of February, 1904; that there was born to her on said date a male child; that said child was living March 4, 1905, and is said to have been named George Martin Roller

her
America (x) Johnson
mark

Applications for Enrollment of Chickasaw Newborn
Act of 1905   Volume III

Witnesses To Mark:
{ L F Harvey
{ John Malcolm

    Subscribed and sworn to before me this   29th day of   March   , 1905

                              W.L. Seearce
                                Notary Public.

                                                9-1087

                  Muskogee, Indian Territory, April 4, 1905.

Jack E. Roller,
    Mead, Indian Territory.

Dear Sir:

    Receipt is hereby acknowledged of the affidavits of Lucy Krouse Roller and America Johnson to the birth of Geroge[sic] Martin Roller, son of Jack E. and Lucy Krouse Roller, February 17, 1904, and the same have been filed with our records as an application for the enrollment of said child.

                              Respectfully,

                                              Chairman.

<u>Chic. N.B. - 173</u>
        (Abrigale Webb
        Born January 17, 1905)
        (John Wesley Webb
        Born November 2, 1903)

Applications for Enrollment of Chickasaw Newborn
Act of 1905   Volume III

BIRTH AFFIDAVIT.

DEPARTMENT OF THE INTERIOR.
COMMISSION TO THE FIVE CIVILIZED TRIBES.

IN RE APPLICATION FOR ENROLLMENT, as a citizen of the Chickasaw Nation, of Abrigale Webb, born on the 17 day of January, 1905

Name of Father: George W Webb   a citizen of the Chickasaw Nation.
Name of Mother: Luna Webb   a citizen of the Chickasaw Nation.

Postoffice   Kemp I.T.

AFFIDAVIT OF MOTHER.

UNITED STATES OF AMERICA, Indian Territory,
Central   DISTRICT.

I, Luna Webb, on oath state that I am 22 years of age and a citizen by marriage, of the Chickasaw Nation; that I am the lawful wife of George W Webb, who is a citizen, by blood of the Chickasaw Nation; that a female child was born to me on 17 day of January, 1905; that said child has been named Abrigale Webb, and was living March 4, 1905.

Luna Webb

Witnesses To Mark:
{

Subscribed and sworn to before me this 27 day of March, 1905

O.R. Fowler
Notary Public.

AFFIDAVIT OF ATTENDING PHYSICIAN OR MID-WIFE.

UNITED STATES OF AMERICA, Indian Territory,
Central   DISTRICT.

I, G H Ellis, a Physician, on oath state that I attended on Mrs. Luna Webb, wife of George W Webb on the 17 day of January, 1905; that there was born to her on said date a female child; that said child was living March 4, 1905, and is said to have been named Abrigale Webb

G.H. Ellis M.D.

Witnesses To Mark:
{

Applications for Enrollment of Chickasaw Newborn
Act of 1905   Volume III

Subscribed and sworn to before me this 17 day of January[sic], 1905

O.R. Fowler
Notary Public.

BIRTH AFFIDAVIT.

DEPARTMENT OF THE INTERIOR.
COMMISSION TO THE FIVE CIVILIZED TRIBES.

IN RE APPLICATION FOR ENROLLMENT, as a citizen of the Chickasaw Nation, of John Wesley Webb, born on the 2 day of Nov., 1902[sic]

Name of Father: George W Webb   a citizen of the Chickasaw Nation.
Name of Mother: Luna Webb   a citizen of the Chickasaw Nation.

Postoffice   Kemp I.T.

AFFIDAVIT OF MOTHER.

UNITED STATES OF AMERICA, Indian Territory, }
  Central   DISTRICT.

I, Luna Webb, on oath state that I am 22 years of age and a citizen by Marriage, of the Chickasaw Nation; that I am the lawful wife of George W Webb, who is a citizen, by blood of the Chickasaw Nation; that a Male child was born to me on 2 day of Nov, 1902; that said child has been named John Wesley Webb, and was living March 4, 1905.

Luna Webb

Witnesses To Mark:
{

Subscribed and sworn to before me this 27 day of March, 1905

O.R. Fowler
Notary Public.

AFFIDAVIT OF ATTENDING PHYSICIAN OR MID-WIFE.

UNITED STATES OF AMERICA, Indian Territory, }
  Central   DISTRICT.

I, G H Ellis, a Physician, on oath state that I attended on Mrs. Luna Webb, wife of George W Webb on the 2 day of Nov,

Applications for Enrollment of Chickasaw Newborn
Act of 1905   Volume III

1902; that there was born to her on said date a   Male   child; that said child was living March 4, 1905, and is said to have been named   John Wesley Webb

G.H. Ellis M.D.

Witnesses To Mark:
{

Subscribed and sworn to before me this 27 day of   March   , 1905

O.R. Fowler
Notary Public.

BIRTH AFFIDAVIT.

DEPARTMENT OF THE INTERIOR.
COMMISSION TO THE FIVE CIVILIZED TRIBES.

IN RE APPLICATION FOR ENROLLMENT, as a citizen of the   Chickasaw   Nation, of   Abrigale Webb   , born on the   17th day of   January   , 1905

Name of Father: George W Webb   a citizen of the   Chickasaw   Nation.
Name of Mother: Luna Webb   a citizen of the   Chickasaw   Nation.

Postoffice   Kemp I.T.

AFFIDAVIT OF MOTHER.

UNITED STATES OF AMERICA, Indian Territory, }
    Central   DISTRICT.

I, Luna Webb   , on oath state that I am   21   years of age and a citizen by marriage   , of the   Chickasaw   Nation; that I am the lawful wife of   George W Webb   , who is a citizen, by blood   of the   Chickasaw   Nation; that a   female   child was born to me on 17th day of   January   , 1905; that said child has been named   Abrigale Webb   , and was living March 4, 1905.

Luna Webb

Witnesses To Mark:
{

Subscribed and sworn to before me this 17 day of   April   , 1905

O.R. Fowler
Notary Public.

Applications for Enrollment of Chickasaw Newborn
Act of 1905 Volume III

AFFIDAVIT OF ATTENDING PHYSICIAN OR MID-WIFE.

UNITED STATES OF AMERICA, Indian Territory,
Central DISTRICT.

I, G H Ellis, a Physician, on oath state that I attended on Mrs. Luna Webb, wife of George W Webb on the 17th day of January, 1905; that there was born to her on said date a female child; that said child was living March 4, 1905, and is said to have been named Abrigale Webb

G.H. Ellis M.D.

Witnesses To Mark:

{ Subscribed and sworn to before me this 17 day of April, 1905

O.R. Fowler
Notary Public.

BIRTH AFFIDAVIT.

DEPARTMENT OF THE INTERIOR.
COMMISSION TO THE FIVE CIVILIZED TRIBES.

IN RE APPLICATION FOR ENROLLMENT, as a citizen of the Chickasaw Nation, of John Wesley Webb, born on the 2 day of Nov., 1903

Name of Father: George W Webb   a citizen of the Chickasaw Nation.
Name of Mother: Luna Webb   a citizen of the Chickasaw Nation.

Postoffice   Kemp I.T.

AFFIDAVIT OF MOTHER.

UNITED STATES OF AMERICA, Indian Territory,
Central DISTRICT.

I, Luna Webb, on oath state that I am 21 years of age and a citizen by Marriage, of the Chickasaw Nation; that I am the lawful wife of George W Webb, who is a citizen, by blood of the Chickasaw Nation; that a Male child was born to me on 2 day of Nov, 1903; that said child has been named John Wesley Webb, and was living March 4, 1905.

Luna Webb

Witnesses To Mark:
{

Applications for Enrollment of Chickasaw Newborn
Act of 1905   Volume III

Subscribed and sworn to before me this   17   day of   April   , 1905

                              O.R. Fowler
                              Notary Public.

AFFIDAVIT OF ATTENDING PHYSICIAN OR MID-WIFE.

UNITED STATES OF AMERICA, Indian Territory,
   Central   DISTRICT.

    I,   G H Ellis   , a   Physician   , on oath state that I attended on Mrs. Luna Webb   , wife of   George W Webb   on the   2 day of   Nov , 1903; that there was born to her on said date a   Male   child; that said child was living March 4, 1905, and is said to have been named   John Wesley Webb

                              G.H. Ellis M.D.

Witnesses To Mark:

Subscribed and sworn to before me this   17   day of   April   , 1905

                              O.R. Fowler
                              Notary Public.

Applications for Enrollment of Chickasaw Newborn
Act of 1905   Volume III

No. 3118

Certificate of Record of Marriages.

DEPARTMENT OF THE INTERIOR,
Commission to the Five Civilized Tribes.
FILED
APR 20 1905
Tams Bixby CHAIRMAN.

UNITED STATES OF AMERICA, }
INDIAN TERRITORY,   } SCT:
Central   DISTRICT. }

I,   E.J. Fannin   , Clerk of the United States Court in the Indian Territory and District aforesaid, do hereby CERTIFY, that the License for and Certificate of the Marriage of

Mr.   G.W. Webb   and

Miss Luna Hollingsworth   was

filed in my office in said Territory and District the 14 day of   Dec   A.D., 190 2 and duly recorded in Book 10 of Marriage Record, Page 316

WITNESS my hand and seal of said Court, at   So McAlester   , this 14 day of   Dec   , A.D. 190 2

E.J. Fannin
Clerk.

By   Geo Grace   Deputy.

APR 19 1905

No. 3118

FORM NO. 598.

MARRIAGE LICENSE.

UNITES STATES OF AMERICA, }
THE INDIAN TERRITORY,   } ss:
Central   DISTRICT. }

To any Person Authorized by Law to Solemnize Marriage—Greeting:

You are hereby commanded to solemnize the Rite and publish the Banns of Matrimony *between* Mr.   G.W. Webb   *of*   Colbert   *in the Indian Territory, aged*   22   *years, and M*iss Luna Hollingsworth   .

Applications for Enrollment of Chickasaw Newborn
Act of 1905 Volume III

of (Illegible) *in the Indian Territory, aged* 19 *years, according to law, and do you officially sign and return this License to the parties therein named.*

WITNESS my hand and official seal, this 11 day of Nov A. D. 190 2

E J Fannin
Clerk of the United States Court.

Geo Grace   *Deputy*

CERTIFICATE OF MARRIAGE.

UNITES STATES OF AMERICA,
THE INDIAN TERRITORY, } ss: I,   A M Belcher
_____DISTRICT.   *a*   Minister

do hereby CERTIFY, that on the 16 day of Nov A, D. 190 2 ; I did duly and according to law, as commanded in the foregoing License, solemnize the Rite and publish the BANNS OF MATRIMONY between the parties therein named.

Witness my hand this 16 day of Nov , A. D. 190 2

My credentials are recorded in the office of the Clerk of the United States Court in the Indian Territory, Central District, Book A Page 11

A M Belcher
a

Chickasaw 1100.

Muskogee, Indian Territory, April 1, 1905.

George W. Webb,
    Kemp, Indian Territory.

Dear Sir:

Receipt is hereby acknowledged of the affidavits of Luna Webb and G. H. Ellis to the birth of John Wesley Webb and Abrigale Webb, children of George W. and Luna Webb, November 2, 1902[sic], and January 17, 1905, respectively, and the same have been filed with our records as an application for the enrollment of said children.

Applications for Enrollment of Chickasaw Newborn
Act of 1905 Volume III

Respectfully,

Chairman.

---

9 N B 173

Muskogee, Indian Territory, April 13, 1905.

George W. Webb,
    Kemp, Indian Territory.

Dear Sir:

    There is inclosed you herewith for execution application for the enrollment of your infant child, Abrigale Webb, born January 17, 1905.

    The affidavit of the physician heretofore filed with the Commission shows the child was living on January 17, 1905. It is necessary for the child to be enrolled, that all the affidavits show she was living on March 4, 1905.

    You are further advised that before the application can be finally disposed of, it will be necessary that you furnish the Commission either the original or a certified copy of the license and certificate of your marriage to her mother, Luna Webb, forwarding same with the return of the inclosed application.

    In having these affidavits executed care should be exercised to see that all names are written in full, as they appear in the body of the affidavit, and in the event that either of the persons signing the affidavit are unable to write, signatures by mark must be attested by two witnesses. Each affidavit must be executed before a Notary Public and the notarial seal and signature of the officer must be attached to each separate affidavit.

Respectfully,

LM 13-30.   Commissioner in Charge.

Applications for Enrollment of Chickasaw Newborn
Act of 1905   Volume III

Chickasaw N.B.
173.

Muskogee, Indian Territory, April 21, 1905.

George W. Webb,
    Kemp, Indian Territory.

Dear Sir:

    Receipt is hereby acknowledged of the affidavits of Lune Webb and G. H. Ellis to the birth of John Wesley Webb and Abrigale Webb, children of George W. and Luna Webb, November 2, 1903 and January 17, 1905, respectively, and the same have been filed with our records in the matter of the enrollment of said children.

    Receipt is also acknowledged of the marriage license and certificate between George W. Webb and Luna Hollingsworth and the same have been filed in support of the application for the enrollment of the above named children.

Respectfully,

Chairman.

Chic. N.B. - 174
    (John Otis or Johny Odus Duncan
    Born June 29, 1903)

BIRTH AFFIDAVIT. #91

DEPARTMENT OF THE INTERIOR.
COMMISSION TO THE FIVE CIVILIZED TRIBES.

IN RE APPLICATION FOR ENROLLMENT, as a citizen of the Chickasaw Nation, of John Otis Duncan, born on the 29 day of June, 1903

Name of Father: James Duncan   a citizen of the Chickasaw Nation.
Name of Mother: Samantha Duncan   a citizen of the Chickasaw Nation.

Postoffice   Kemp

Applications for Enrollment of Chickasaw Newborn
Act of 1905 Volume III

AFFIDAVIT OF MOTHER.

UNITED STATES OF AMERICA, Indian Territory,　}
　Central　　　　　　　　DISTRICT.

　　　I, Samantha Duncan　, on oath state that I am　22　years of age and a citizen by　intermarriage　, of the　Chickasaw　Nation; that I am the lawful wife of　James Duncan　, who is a citizen, by　blood　of the　Chickasaw Nation; that a　male　child was born to me on　29　day of　June　, 1903, that said child has been named　John Otis　, and is now living.

　　　　　　　　　　　　　　　　　Samantha Duncan

Witnesses To Mark:
　{ T.W. Short
　　Cleo Short

　　　Subscribed and sworn to before me this　14　day of　February　, 1905.

　　　　　　　　　　　　　　　　　S M Mead
　　　　　　　　　　　　　　　　　　Notary Public.

AFFIDAVIT OF ATTENDING PHYSICIAN OR MID-WIFE.

UNITED STATES OF AMERICA, Indian Territory,　}
　Central　　　　　　　　DISTRICT.

　　　I,　E L Mead　, a Physician　, on oath state that I attended on Mrs.　Samantha Duncan　, wife of　James Duncan　on the 29th day of June , 1903; that there was born to her on said date a　male　child; that said child is now living and is said to have been named　Johnie Otis

　　　　　　　　　　　　　　　　　E L Mead

Witnesses To Mark:
　{ T.W. Short
　　Cleo Short

　　　Subscribed and sworn to before me this　27　day of　January　, 1905.

　　　　　　　　　　　　　　　　　S M Mead
　　　　　　　　　　　　　　　　　　Notary Public.

Applications for Enrollment of Chickasaw Newborn
Act of 1905 Volume III

BIRTH AFFIDAVIT.

DEPARTMENT OF THE INTERIOR.
COMMISSION TO THE FIVE CIVILIZED TRIBES.

IN RE APPLICATION FOR ENROLLMENT, as a citizen of the Chickasaw Nation, of Johny Odus Duncan, born on the 29 day of June, 1903

Name of Father: James Duncan   a citizen of the Chickasaw Nation.
Name of Mother: Addie Duncan   a citizen of the Chickasaw Nation.

Postoffice   Kemp, Indian Terrietory[sic].

AFFIDAVIT OF MOTHER.

UNITED STATES OF AMERICA, Indian Territory,
Central   DISTRICT.

I, Addie Duncan, on oath state that I am 22 years of age and a citizen by Marriage, of the Chickasaw Nation; that I am the lawful wife of James Duncan, who is a citizen, by blood of the Chickasaw Nation; that a male child was born to me on 29 day of June, 1903; that said child has been named Johny Odus Duncan, and was living March 4, 1905.

Addie Duncan

Witnesses To Mark:
{

Subscribed and sworn to before me this 27 day of March, 1905

O.R. Fowler
Notary Public.

AFFIDAVIT OF ATTENDING PHYSICIAN OR MID-WIFE.

UNITED STATES OF AMERICA, Indian Territory,
Central   DISTRICT.

I, E.L. Mead, a physician, on oath state that I attended on Mrs. Addie Duncan, wife of James Duncan on the 19[sic] day of June, 1903; that there was born to her on said date a male child; that said child was living March 4, 1905, and is said to have been named Johny Odus Duncan

E L Mead

Witnesses To Mark:
{

Applications for Enrollment of Chickasaw Newborn
Act of 1905   Volume III

Subscribed and sworn to before me this 27 day of   March   , 1905

                                    O.R. Fowler
                                    Notary Public.

BIRTH AFFIDAVIT.

DEPARTMENT OF THE INTERIOR.
COMMISSION TO THE FIVE CIVILIZED TRIBES.

    IN RE APPLICATION FOR ENROLLMENT, as a citizen of the   Chickasaw   Nation, of   Johny Odus Duncan   , born on the 29th day of June   , 1903

Name of Father: James Duncan   a citizen of the   Chickasaw   Nation.
Name of Mother: Addie Duncan   a citizen of the   Chickasaw   Nation.

                        Postoffice   Kemp I.T.

AFFIDAVIT OF MOTHER.

UNITED STATES OF AMERICA, Indian Territory,
    Central District   DISTRICT.

    I,   Addie Duncan   , on oath state that I am   22   years of age and a citizen by ——— , of the   United States   Nation; that I am the lawful wife of   James Duncan   , who is a citizen, by blood   of the   Chickasaw   Nation; that a male   child was born to me on 29th day of   June   , 1903; that said child has been named   Johny Odus Duncan   , and was living March 4, 1905.

                                    Addie Duncan

Witnesses To Mark:

    Subscribed and sworn to before me this   25 day of   April   , 1905

                                    O.R. Fowler
                                    Notary Public.

AFFIDAVIT OF ATTENDING PHYSICIAN OR MID-WIFE.

UNITED STATES OF AMERICA, Indian Territory,
    Central   DISTRICT.

    I,   E.L. Mead   , a   physician   , on oath state that I attended on Mrs.   Addie Duncan   , wife of   James Duncan   on the 29th day of   June   , 1903;

Applications for Enrollment of Chickasaw Newborn
Act of 1905   Volume III

that there was born to her on said date a   male   child; that said child was living March 4, 1905, and is said to have been named Johny Odus Duncan

E L Mead

Witnesses To Mark:

{

Subscribed and sworn to before me this   25   day of   April   , 1905

O.R. Fowler
Notary Public.

(Marriage Certificate below the ink too light to read.)

Marriage Certificate.

State of Texas,
County of Grayson.   }   To Whom it may Concern:

Be it known that I hereby certify that in accordance with and by authority of the laws of the state of Texas on the   26   day of   Oct.   A.D., 190 1   I united Mr.   and M   in the holy bonds of wedlock. Witness my signature this   day of   A.D. 190

Officiating _____

P.O. _____

Chickasaw 1107.

James Duncan,
   Kemp, Indian Territory.

Dear Sir:

   Receipt is hereby acknowledged of the affidavits of Addie Duncan and E. L. Mead to the birth of Johny Odus Duncan, son of James and Addie Duncan, June 29, 1903, and the same have been filed with our records as an application for the enrollment of said child.

Respectfully,

Commissioner in Charge.

Applications for Enrollment of Chickasaw Newborn
Act of 1905   Volume III

9 N B 174

Muskogee, Indian Territory, April 14, 1905.

James Duncan,
    Kemp, Indian Territory.

Dear Sir:

    There is inclosed you herewith for execution application for the enrollment of your infant child, Johny Odus Duncan, born June 29, 1903.

    In the affidavit of the physician heretofore filed with the Commission, the date of the birth of said child is given as June 19, 1903. It will, therefore, be necessary to have application re-executed, giving the correct date of his birth.

    You are further advised, however, that before said application can be finally disposed of, it will be necessary for you to furnish the Commission either the original or a certified copy of the license and certificate of your marriage to his mother, Addie Duncan, forwarding same with the return of the inclosed application.

    In having these affidavits executed care should be exercised to see that all names are written in full, as they appear in the body of the affidavit, and in the event that either of the persons signing the affidavit are unable to write, signatures by mark must be attested by two witnesses. Each affidavit must be executed before a Notary Public and the notarial seal and signature of the officer must be attached to each separate affidavit.

    Respectfully,

LM 14-155   Commissioner in Charge.

9-N B 174.

Muskogee, Indian Territory, April 28, 1905.

James Duncan,
    Kemp, Indian Territory.

Dear Sir:

    Receipt is hereby acknowledged of the affidavits of Addie Duncan and E. L. Mead to the birth of Johny Odus Duncan, son of James and Addie Duncan, June 29, 1903, and the same have been filed with our records as an application for the enrollment of said child.

    Respectfully,

                                                   Chairman.

Applications for Enrollment of Chickasaw Newborn
Act of 1905   Volume III

Chic. N.B. - 175
   (Lyda Amanda Moore
   Born November 16, 1903)

BIRTH AFFIDAVIT.

DEPARTMENT OF THE INTERIOR.
COMMISSION TO THE FIVE CIVILIZED TRIBES.

IN RE APPLICATION FOR ENROLLMENT, as a citizen of the Chickasaw Nation, of Lyda Amanda Moore, born on the 16th day of November, 1903

Name of Father: Thomas Nowel Moore   a citizen of the Chickasaw Nation.
Name of Mother: Louisa J. Moore   a citizen of the U.S. Nation.

Postoffice   Ego Ind T.

AFFIDAVIT OF MOTHER.

UNITED STATES OF AMERICA, Indian Territory, }
   Central   DISTRICT.

   I, Louisa J. Moore, on oath state that I am 34 years of age and a citizen by Intermarriage, of the Chickasaw Nation; that I am the lawful wife of Thomas Nowel Moore, who is a citizen, by Blood of the Chickasaw Nation; that a Female child was born to me on 16th day of November, 1903; that said child has been named Lyda Amanda Moore, and was living March 4, 1905.

                                       her
                              Louisa J. x Moore
Witnesses To Mark: mark
   { Miss Melvia Ford
   { Mrs Deler Golden

   Subscribed and sworn to before me this 22nd day of March, 1905

                              J. T. Hoover
                                 Notary Public.

Applications for Enrollment of Chickasaw Newborn
Act of 1905   Volume III

AFFIDAVIT OF ATTENDING PHYSICIAN OR MID-WIFE.

UNITED STATES OF AMERICA, Indian Territory, }
.... DISTRICT.

    I, Thomas M. Morgan, a Physician, on oath state that I attended on Mrs. Louisa J. Moore, wife of Thomas Nowel Moore on the 16th day of November, 1903; that there was born to her on said date a Female child; that said child was living March 4, 1905, and is said to have been named Lydia[sic] Amanda Moore

                                          Thos M. Morgan M.D.

Witnesses To Mark:
{

    Subscribed and sworn to before me this 21st day of March, 1905

                                      J.T. Hoover
                                      Notary Public.

$W^m O.B.$

COMMISSIONERS:		
TAMS BIXBY,	**DEPARTMENT OF THE INTERIOR,**	REFER IN REPLY TO THE FOLLOWING:
THOMAS B. NEEDLES,	**COMMISSIONER TO THE FIVE CIVILIZED TRIBES.**	
C.R. BRECKINRIDGE.		9-1111
WM. O. BEALL		
Secretary		

        ADDRESS ONLY THE
  COMMISSION TO THE FIVE CIVILIZED TRIBES.

                        Muskogee, Indian Territory, March 28, 1905.

Thomas Nowel Moore,
    Eagle, Indian Territory.

Dear Sir:

    Receipt is hereby acknowledged of the affidavits of Louisa J. Moore and Thomas N[sic]. Morgan to the birth of Lyda Amanda Moore, daughter of Thomas Nowel and Louisa J. Moore, November 16, 1903, and the same have been filed with our records as an application for the enrollment of said child.

                                Respectfully,
                                Tams Bixby
                                  Chairman.

Applications for Enrollment of Chickasaw Newborn
Act of 1905 Volume III

9 NB 175

Muskogee, Indian Territory, April 27, 1905.

T. N. Moore,
    Ego, Indian Territory.

Dear Sir:

    Receipt is hereby acknowledged of your letter of April 19, 1905, asking if the application for the enrollment of Lyda Amanda Moore has been received.

    In reply to your letter you are informed that the affidavits heretofore forwarded to the birth of your child, Lyda Amanda Moore have been filed with our records as an application for the enrollment of said child.

                    Respectfully,

                                  Chairman.

Chic. N.B. - 176
    (Francis Albert Murray
    Born September 10, 1904)

BIRTH AFFIDAVIT.   #146

DEPARTMENT OF THE INTERIOR.
COMMISSION TO THE FIVE CIVILIZED TRIBES.

IN RE APPLICATION FOR ENROLLMENT, as a citizen of the Chickasaw Nation, of Francis Albert Murry[sic], born on the 10 day of September, 1904

Name of Father: Meigs Colbert Murry   a citizen of the Chickasaw Nation.
Name of Mother: May Murry   a citizen of the Chickasaw Nation.

                Postoffice   Colber[sic]

Applications for Enrollment of Chickasaw Newborn
Act of 1905   Volume III

AFFIDAVIT OF MOTHER.

UNITED STATES OF AMERICA, Indian Territory, }
    Central   DISTRICT. }

    I, May Murry, on oath state that I am 26 years of age and a citizen by Intermarriage, of the Chickasaw Nation; that I am the lawful wife of Meigs Colbert Murry, who is a citizen, by blood of the Chickasaw Nation; that a male child was born to me on 10 day of September, 1904, that said child has been named Francis Albert, and is now living.

                                  Maye Murray

Witnesses To Mark:
   { Henton Murray
     Mattie Murray

    Subscribed and sworn to before me this 20 day of February, 1905.

                                  S M Mead
                                        Notary Public.

AFFIDAVIT OF ATTENDING PHYSICIAN OR MID-WIFE.

UNITED STATES OF AMERICA, Indian Territory, }
    Central   DISTRICT. }

    I, C.C. Yeiser, a M.D., on oath state that I attended on Mrs. May Murry, wife of Meigs Colbert Murry on the 10 day of September, 1904; that there was born to her on said date a male child; that said child is now living and is said to have been named Francis Albert

                                  C.C. Yeiser M.D.

Witnesses To Mark:
   { Henton Murray
     Mattie Murray

    Subscribed and sworn to before me this 20 day of February, 1905.

                                  S M Mead
                                        Notary Public.

Applications for Enrollment of Chickasaw Newborn
Act of 1905 Volume III

BIRTH AFFIDAVIT.

DEPARTMENT OF THE INTERIOR.
COMMISSION TO THE FIVE CIVILIZED TRIBES.

IN RE APPLICATION FOR ENROLLMENT, as a citizen of the Chickasaw Nation, of Francis Albert Murray , born on the 10 day of Sept , 1904

Name of Father: Meigs Colbert Murray a citizen of the Chickasaw Nation.
Name of Mother: Maye Murray a citizen of the Chickasaw Nation.

Postoffice Colbert IT

AFFIDAVIT OF MOTHER.

UNITED STATES OF AMERICA, Indian Territory,
Central DISTRICT.

I, Maye Murray , on oath state that I am 26 years of age and a citizen by Marrige[sic] , of the Chickasaw Nation; that I am the lawful wife of Meigs Colbert Murray , who is a citizen, by Blood of the Chickasaw Nation; that a Male child was born to me on 10 day of Sepr , 1904; that said child has been named Francis Albert Murray , and was living March 4, 1905.

Maye Murray

Witnesses To Mark:
{

Subscribed and sworn to before me this 29 day of March , 1905

Chas E Bacon
Notary Public.

AFFIDAVIT OF ATTENDING PHYSICIAN OR MID-WIFE.

UNITED STATES OF AMERICA, Indian Territory,
Central DISTRICT.

I, C C Yeiser , a M.D. , on oath state that I attended on Mrs. Maye Murray , wife of Meigs Colbert Murray on the 10 day of Sept , 1905[sic]; that there was born to her on said date a male child; that said child was living March 4, 1905, and is said to have been named Francis Albert Murray

C.C. Yeiser M.D.

Witnesses To Mark:
{

Applications for Enrollment of Chickasaw Newborn
Act of 1905   Volume III

Subscribed and sworn to before me this 29 day of   March   , 1905

Chas E Bacon
Notary Public.

BIRTH AFFIDAVIT.

DEPARTMENT OF THE INTERIOR.
COMMISSION TO THE FIVE CIVILIZED TRIBES.

IN RE APPLICATION FOR ENROLLMENT, as a citizen of the   Chickasaw   Nation, of   Francis Albert Murray   , born on the 10th day of   September , 1904

Name of Father: Meigs Colbert Murray   a citizen of the   Chickasaw   Nation.
Name of Mother: Maye Murray   a citizen of the   Chickasaw   Nation.

Postoffice   Colbert Ind. Ter.

AFFIDAVIT OF MOTHER.

UNITED STATES OF AMERICA, Indian Territory, }
.... DISTRICT. }

I,   Maye Murray   , on oath state that I am   26   years of age and a citizen ~~by~~ ...., of the   United States   Nation; that I am the lawful wife of   Meigs Colbert Murray   , who is a citizen, by blood   of the   Chickasaw   Nation; that a .... child was born to me on 10th day of   September   , 1904; that said child has been named   Francis Albert Murray   , and was living March 4, 1905.

Maye Murray

Witnesses To Mark:
{

Subscribed and sworn to before me this   15   day of   April   , 1905

Chas E Bacon
Notary Public.

AFFIDAVIT OF ATTENDING PHYSICIAN OR MID-WIFE.

UNITED STATES OF AMERICA, Indian Territory, }
.... DISTRICT. }

I,   C C Yeiser   , a   M.D.   , on oath state that I attended on Mrs.   Maye Murray   , wife of   Meigs Colbert Murray   on the 10th day of

Applications for Enrollment of Chickasaw Newborn
Act of 1905 Volume III

September   , 1904; that there was born to her on said date a   male   child; that said child was living March 4, 1905, and is said to have been named Francis Albert Murray

C.C. Yeiser M.D.

Witnesses To Mark:
{

Subscribed and sworn to before me this 15 day of   April   , 1905

Chas E Bacon
Notary Public.

9-1112

Muskogee, Indian Territory April 3, 1905.

Meigs Colbert Murray,
    Colbert, Indian Territory.

Dear Sir:

    Receipt is hereby acknowledged of the affidavits of Maye Murray and C. C. Yeiser to the birth of Francis Albert Murray, son of Meigs Colbert and Maye Murray, September 10, 1904, and the same have been filed with our records as an application for the enrollment of said child.

Respectfully,

Chairman.

---

9 N B 176

Muskogee, Indian Territory, April 14, 1905.

Meigs Colbert Murray,
    Colbert, Indian Territory.

Dear Sir:

    There is inclosed you herewith for execution application for the enrollment of your infant child, Francis Albert Murray, born September 10, 1904.

    In the affidavit of the physician, heretofore filed with the Commission, the date of the birth of said child is given as September 10, 1905. It will, therefore, be necessary for the application to be re-executed, giving the correct date of his birth.

Applications for Enrollment of Chickasaw Newborn
Act of 1905   Volume III

In having these affidavits executed care should be exercised to see that all names are written in full, as they appear in the body of the affidavit, and in the event that either of the persons signing the affidavit are unable to write, signatures by mark must be attested by two witnesses. Each affidavit must be executed before a Notary Public and the notarial seal and signature of the officer must be attached to each separate affidavit.

Respectfully,

LM 14-140.   Commissioner in Charge.

Chickasaw N.B. 176.

Muskogee, Indian Territory, April 19, 1905.

Meigs Colbert Murray,
    Colbert, Indian Territory.

Dear Sir:

Receipt is hereby acknowledged of the affidavits of Maye Murray and C. C. Yeiser to the birth of Francis Albert Murray, son of Meigs Colbert and Maye Murray, September 10, 1904, and the same have been filed with our records in the matter of the enrollment of said child.

Respectfully,

Chairman.

Chic. N.B. - 177
    (Sadie Bell Gooding
    Born August 22, 1904)

Applications for Enrollment of Chickasaw Newborn
Act of 1905   Volume III

BIRTH AFFIDAVIT.

DEPARTMENT OF THE INTERIOR.
COMMISSION TO THE FIVE CIVILIZED TRIBES.

IN RE APPLICATION FOR ENROLLMENT, as a citizen of the Chickasaw Nation, of   Sadie Bell Gooding   , born on the   22   day of   Aug   , 1904

Name of Father: Charles Lemuel Gooding   a citizen of the   Chickasaw Nation.
Name of Mother: Nellie[sic] May Gooding   a citizen of the   Chickasaw Nation.

Postoffice   Colbert I.T.

AFFIDAVIT OF MOTHER.

UNITED STATES OF AMERICA, Indian Territory, }
      Central   DISTRICT.   }

I,   Willie May Gooding   , on oath state that I am   24   years of age and a citizen by ...., of the .... Nation; that I am the lawful wife of Charles Lemuel Gooding   , who is a citizen, by Blood   of the   Chickasaw Nation; that a   Female   child was born to me on   22   day of   August   , 1904; that said child has been named   Sadie Bell Gooding   , and was living March 4, 1905.

Willie May Gooding

Witnesses To Mark:
{

Subscribed and sworn to before me this   29th   day of   March   , 1905

EK Smith
Notary Public.

AFFIDAVIT OF ATTENDING PHYSICIAN OR MID-WIFE.

UNITED STATES OF AMERICA, Indian Territory, }
      Central   DISTRICT.   }

I,   W H McCarley M.D.   , a   Physician   , on oath state that I attended on Mrs.   Willie May Gooding   , wife of   Charles Lemuel Gooding   on the   22 day of   August   , 1904; that there was born to her on said date a   Female   child; that said child was living March 4, 1905, and is said to have been named Sadie Bell Gooding

WH McCarley M.D.

Witnesses To Mark:
{

Applications for Enrollment of Chickasaw Newborn
Act of 1905   Volume III

Subscribed and sworn to before me this   29th   day of   March   , 1905

        EK Smith
         Notary Public.

              9-1113

    Muskogee, Indian Territory, April 4, 1905.

Charles Lenuel[sic] Gooding,
  Colbert, Indian Territory.

Dear Sir:

  Receipt is hereby acknowledged of your letter of March 29, 1905, enclosing affidavits of Willie May Gooding and W. H. McCarley to the birth of Sadie Bell Gooding, daughter of Charles Lenuel[sic] and Willie May Gooding, August 22, 1904, and the same have been filed with our records as an application for the enrollment of said child.

       Respectfully,

         Commissioner in Charge.

This is to certify I am a regular practicing physician, located at Colbert Ind Ty. On Aug 22nd 1904 I attended Mrs. Willie Gooding, wife of Lem Gooding, in confinement and there was borned[sic] a Female child and child is still living.

      Very Respt,
       WH McCarley M.D.

This Jan 17th 1904

  Colbert I.T. Feb Eleventh 1905
Sworn and subscribed to before me EK Smith a Notary Public in and for the Central district of the Indian Territory.

       EK Smith
        Notary Public

    #139

Applications for Enrollment of Chickasaw Newborn
Act of 1905 Volume III

Chic. N.B. - 178
(Walter Harlin Lemon or Lemons
Born December 15, 1902)

BIRTH AFFIDAVIT.   *#III*

DEPARTMENT OF THE INTERIOR.
COMMISSION TO THE FIVE CIVILIZED TRIBES.

IN RE APPLICATION FOR ENROLLMENT, as a citizen of the   Chickasaw   Nation, of   Walter Harlin Lemon   , born on the   15   day of   December   , 1902

Name of Father: R B Lemon   a citizen of the   Chickasaw   Nation.
Name of Mother: Maria C Lemon   a citizen of the   Chickasaw   Nation.

Postoffice   Sterrett

AFFIDAVIT OF MOTHER.

UNITED STATES OF AMERICA, Indian Territory,
    Central   DISTRICT.

I,   Maria C Lemon   , on oath state that I am   36   years of age and a citizen by   blood   , of the   Chickasaw   Nation; that I am the lawful wife of   R B Lemon   , who is a citizen, by   intermarage[sic]   of the   Chickasaw   Nation; that a   male   child was born to me on   15   day of   December   , 1902, that said child has been named   Walter Harlin   , and is now living.

                                    Maria C Lemon
Witnesses To Mark:
 { S.M. Mead Jr
 { G.E. Mead

Subscribed and sworn to before me this   22   day of   February   , 1905.

                                    S.M. Mead
                                         Notary Public.

Applications for Enrollment of Chickasaw Newborn
Act of 1905   Volume III

AFFIDAVIT OF ATTENDING PHYSICIAN OR MID-WIFE.

UNITED STATES OF AMERICA, Indian Territory, } DISTRICT.

I, C C Yeiser , a M D , on oath state that I attended on Mrs. Maria C , wife of R.B. Lemon on the 15 day of Dec , 1902; that there was born to her on said date a male child; that said child is now living and is said to have been named Walter Harlin

C.C. Yeiser M.D.

Witnesses To Mark:
{ S.M. Mead Jr
  G.E. Mead

Subscribed and sworn to before me this 22 day of February , 1905.

S.M. Mead
Notary Public.

BIRTH AFFIDAVIT.

DEPARTMENT OF THE INTERIOR.
COMMISSION TO THE FIVE CIVILIZED TRIBES.

IN RE APPLICATION FOR ENROLLMENT, as a citizen of the   Chickasaw   Nation, of Walter Harlin Lemons , born on the 15th day of December , 1902

Name of Father: Robert Breckinridge Lemon[sic] a citizen of the Chickasaw Nation.
Name of Mother: Maria C Lemons   a citizen of the Chickasaw Nation.

Postoffice   Sterrett Indian Territory

AFFIDAVIT OF MOTHER.

UNITED STATES OF AMERICA, Indian Territory, } Central Judicial   DISTRICT.

I, Maria C Lemons , on oath state that I am 36 years of age and a citizen by Blood , of the Chickasaw   Nation; that I am the lawful wife of Robert Breckinridge Lemons , who is a citizen, by Marriage of the   Chickasaw Nation; that a male   child was born to me on the 15th day of December , 1902; that said child has been named Walter Harlin Lemons , and was living March 4, 1905.

Maria C. Lemon[sic]

Applications for Enrollment of Chickasaw Newborn
Act of 1905 Volume III

Witnesses To Mark:
{

Subscribed and sworn to before me this 25th day of March , 1905

GW Goodwin
Notary Public.

AFFIDAVIT OF ATTENDING PHYSICIAN OR MID-WIFE.

UNITED STATES OF AMERICA, Indian Territory, }
Central Judicial   DISTRICT.

I, C.C. Yeiser , a Physician , on oath state that I attended on Mrs. Maria C Lemons , wife of Robert Breckinridge Lemons on the 15th day of December , 1902; that there was born to her on said date a male child; that said child was living March 4, 1905, and is said to have been named Walter Harlin Lemons

C.C. Yeiser M.D.

Witnesses To Mark:
{

Subscribed and sworn to before me this 25th day of March , 1905

G.W. Goodwin
Notary Public.

Chic. N.B. - 179
  (Ittis Marie Potts
  Born December 23, 1903)

Chickasaw 1131.

Muskogee, Indian Territory, April 4, 1905.

Joe B. Potts,
  Colbert, Indian Territory.

Dear Sir:

Receipt is hereby acknowledged of the affidavits of Nannie V. Potts and C. C. Yeiser to the birth of Ittis Marie Potts, daughter of Joe B. and Nannie V. Potts, December

Applications for Enrollment of Chickasaw Newborn
Act of 1905   Volume III

23, 1903, and the same have been filed with our records as an application for the enrollment of said child.

Respectfully,

Commissioner in Charge.

BIRTH AFFIDAVIT.   #110

DEPARTMENT OF THE INTERIOR.
COMMISSION TO THE FIVE CIVILIZED TRIBES.

    IN RE APPLICATION FOR ENROLLMENT, as a citizen of the   Chickasaw   Nation, of   Ittis Marie Potts   , born on the   23   day of   December , 1902[sic]

Name of Father: J B Potts   a citizen of the   Chickasaw   Nation.
Name of Mother: Nannie V. Potts   a citizen of the   Chickasaw   Nation.

Postoffice   Colbert

AFFIDAVIT OF MOTHER.

UNITED STATES OF AMERICA, Indian Territory, ⎫
    Central   **DISTRICT.** ⎭

    I,   Nannie V. Potts   , on oath state that I am   42   years of age and a citizen by   Intermarriage   , of the   Chickasaw   Nation; that I am the lawful wife of J B Potts   , who is a citizen, by   blood   of the   Chickasaw   Nation; that a female   child was born to me on   23   day of   December   , 1902, that said child has been named   Ittis Marie   , and is now living.

Nannie V. Potts

Witnesses To Mark:
  ⎧ CW Colbert
  ⎩ F.E. Mead

    Subscribed and sworn to before me this   20 day of   February   , 1905.

S.M. Mead
Notary Public.

Applications for Enrollment of Chickasaw Newborn
Act of 1905   Volume III

AFFIDAVIT OF ATTENDING PHYSICIAN OR MID-WIFE.

UNITED STATES OF AMERICA, Indian Territory, ⎫
   Central   DISTRICT. ⎭

   I, C C Yeiser   , a   M.D.   , on oath state that I attended on Mrs. N.V. Potts , wife of J B Potts on the 23 day of December , 1902; that there was born to her on said date a   female   child; that said child is now living and is said to have been named Ittis

                                          C.C. Yeiser M.D.

Witnesses To Mark:
   { CW Colbert
     F.E. Mead

   Subscribed and sworn to before me this 20 day of February , 1905.

                                      S.M. Mead
                                              Notary Public.

BIRTH AFFIDAVIT.
DEPARTMENT OF THE INTERIOR.
COMMISSION TO THE FIVE CIVILIZED TRIBES.

   IN RE APPLICATION FOR ENROLLMENT, as a citizen of the   Chickasaw   Nation, of Ittis Marie Potts   , born on the 23 day of Dec , 1903

Name of Father: Joe B Potts   a citizen of the   Chickasaw Nation.
Name of Mother: Nannie V Potts   a citizen of the   Chickasaw Nation.

                        Postoffice   Colbert IT

AFFIDAVIT OF MOTHER.

UNITED STATES OF AMERICA, Indian Territory, ⎫
   Central   DISTRICT. ⎭

   I, Nannie V. Potts   , on oath state that I am 44 years of age and a citizen by   Marrige[sic]   , of the   Chickasaw   Nation; that I am the lawful wife of Joe B Potts   , who is a citizen, by Blood   of the   Chickasaw   Nation; that a Female   child was born to me on 23 day of Dec , 1903; that said child has been named Ittis Marie Potts   , and was living March 4, 1905.

                                      Nannie V Potts

Witnesses To Mark:
   {

Applications for Enrollment of Chickasaw Newborn
Act of 1905   Volume III

Subscribed and sworn to before me this 29   day of   March   , 1905

Chas E Bacon
Notary Public.

AFFIDAVIT OF ATTENDING PHYSICIAN OR MID-WIFE.

UNITED STATES OF AMERICA, Indian Territory,
   Central   **DISTRICT.**

I,   C C Yeiser   , a   M.D.   , on oath state that I attended on Mrs.   Nannie V Potts   , wife of   Joe B Potts   on the   23 day of   Dec   , 1903; that there was born to her on said date a   Female   child; that said child was living March 4, 1905, and is said to have been named   Ittis Marie Potts

C.C. Yeiser M.D.

Witnesses To Mark:
{

Subscribed and sworn to before me this 29   day of   March   , 1905

Chas E Bacon
Notary Public.

Chic. N.B. - 180
   (Mildred Francile Colbert
   Born July 31, 1903)

BIRTH AFFIDAVIT.
DEPARTMENT OF THE INTERIOR.
COMMISSION TO THE FIVE CIVILIZED TRIBES.

IN RE APPLICATION FOR ENROLLMENT, as a citizen of the   Chickasaw   Nation, of   Mildred Francile Colbert   , born on the 31   day of   July , 1903

Name of Father: Harley E Colbert   a citizen of the   Chickasaw Nation.
Name of Mother: Pearl Colbert   a citizen of the   Chickasaw Nation.

Postoffice   Colbert I.T.

Applications for Enrollment of Chickasaw Newborn
Act of 1905 Volume III

AFFIDAVIT OF MOTHER.

UNITED STATES OF AMERICA, Indian Territory,
Central   DISTRICT.

I, Pearl Colbert , on oath state that I am 23 years of age and a citizen by Blood , of the Chickasaw Nation; that I am the lawful wife of Harley E Colbert , who is a citizen, by Blood of the Chickasaw Nation; that a Female child was born to me on 31 day of July , 1903; that said child has been named Mildred Francile , and was living March 4, 1905.

Pearl ₽ Colbert

Witnesses To Mark:
{

Subscribed and sworn to before me this 25th day of March , 1905

EK Smith
Notary Public.

AFFIDAVIT OF ATTENDING PHYSICIAN OR MID-WIFE.

UNITED STATES OF AMERICA, Indian Territory,
Central   DISTRICT.

I, W H McCarley MD , a Physician , on oath state that I attended on Mrs. Pearl Colbert , wife of Mr. Harley E Colbert on the 31 day of July , 1903; that there was born to her on said date a Female child; that said child was living March 4, 1905, and is said to have been named Mildred Francile Colbert

WH McCarley M.D.

Witnesses To Mark:
{

Subscribed and sworn to before me this 25th day of March , 1905

EK Smith
Notary Public.

Applications for Enrollment of Chickasaw Newborn
Act of 1905 Volume III

BIRTH AFFIDAVIT.   #84

DEPARTMENT OF THE INTERIOR.
COMMISSION TO THE FIVE CIVILIZED TRIBES.

IN RE APPLICATION FOR ENROLLMENT, as a citizen of the   Chickasaw   Nation, of   Francile Colbert   , born on the   31   day of   July   , 1903

Name of Father: H E Colbert   a citizen of the   Chickasaw   Nation.
Name of Mother: Pearl Colbert   a citizen of the   Chickasaw   Nation.

Postoffice   Colbert

AFFIDAVIT OF MOTHER.

UNITED STATES OF AMERICA, Indian Territory,
   Central   DISTRICT.

I, Pearl Colbert   , on oath state that I am   23   years of age and a citizen by blood   , of the   Chickasaw   Nation; that I am the lawful wife of   H E Colbert , who is a citizen, by   blood   of the   Chickasaw   Nation; that a   female   child was born to me on   31   day of   July   , 1903, that said child has been named Francile   , and is now living.

                                    Pearl Colbert
Witnesses To Mark:
 { Jewel Colbert
 { C.W. Colbert

Subscribed and sworn to before me this   13   day of   February   , 1905.

                                    S M Mead
                                    Notary Public.

This is to certify I am a regular practicing physician located at Colbert Ind Ty. On July 31st 1903 I attending Mrs Pearl Colbert wife of Mr. Harley Colbert in confinement and there was borned (sic) a female child and child is still living

                    Very Respt
Jan 17th 1905   *WHM Carley M.D.*

Sworn and subscribed to before me EK Smith a Notary Public in and for the Central district of the Indian Territory this Eleventh Day of Feb 1905

                    EK Smith
    #84   *Notary Public*

Applications for Enrollment of Chickasaw Newborn
Act of 1905   Volume III

9-1131

Muskogee, Indian Territory, March 31, 1905.

Harley E. Colbert,
    Colbert, Indian Territory.

Dear Sir:

    Receipt is hereby acknowledged of the affidavits of Pearl P. Colbert and W. H. McCarley, M. D., to the birth of Mildred Francis[sic] Colbert daughter of Harley E and Pearl P. Colbert, July 31, 1903, and the same have been filed with our records as an application for the enrollment of said child.

Respectfully,

Chairman.

Chic. N.B. - 181
    (Henriyetta or Henretta Grinslade
    Born July 8, 1904)

BIRTH AFFIDAVIT.
DEPARTMENT OF THE INTERIOR.
COMMISSION TO THE FIVE CIVILIZED TRIBES.

IN RE APPLICATION FOR ENROLLMENT, as a citizen of the Chickasaw Nation, of Henriyetta Grinslade , born on the 8 day of July , 1904

Name of Father: Henry Grinslade   a citizen of the Chickasaw Nation.
Name of Mother: Sallie Grinslade   a citizen of the Chickasaw Nation.

Postoffice   Paucaunla I.T.

Applications for Enrollment of Chickasaw Newborn
Act of 1905   Volume III

AFFIDAVIT OF MOTHER.

UNITED STATES OF AMERICA, Indian Territory,
Central   DISTRICT.

I,   Sallie Grinslade   , on oath state that I am   37   years of age and a citizen by   Blood   , of the   Chickasaw   Nation; that I am the lawful wife of   Henry Grinslade   , who is a citizen, by Marriage   of the   Chickasaw   Nation; that a   Female   child was born to me on   8   day of   July   , 1905[sic]; that said child has been named   Henriyetta   , and was living March 4, 1905.

          Sallie Grinslade

Witnesses To Mark:

{ Mrs Anna Kemp

  Subscribed and sworn to before me this   30th day of   March   , 1905

          B.C. Wigand
            Notary Public.

AFFIDAVIT OF ATTENDING PHYSICIAN OR MID-WIFE.

UNITED STATES OF AMERICA, Indian Territory,
Central   DISTRICT.

I,   H.W. Klostermann M.D. , a ...., on oath state that I attended on Mrs.   Sallie Grinslade   , wife of   Henry Grinslade   on the   8   day of   July   , 1904; that there was born to her on said date a   Female   child; that said child was living March 4, 1905, and is said to have been named   Henriyetta Grinslade

          H.W. Klostermann M.D.

Witnesses To Mark:

{

  Subscribed and sworn to before me this   30th day of   March   , 1905

          B.C. Wigand
            Notary Public.

Applications for Enrollment of Chickasaw Newborn
Act of 1905   Volume III

BIRTH AFFIDAVIT.   #90

DEPARTMENT OF THE INTERIOR.
COMMISSION TO THE FIVE CIVILIZED TRIBES.

IN RE APPLICATION FOR ENROLLMENT, as a citizen of the   Chickasaw   Nation, of   Henretta Grinslade   , born on the   8   day of   July   , 1904

Name of Father: Henry Grinslade   a citizen of the   Chickasaw   Nation.
Name of Mother: Sallie Grinslade   a citizen of the   Chickasaw   Nation.

Postoffice   Paucaunla

AFFIDAVIT OF MOTHER.

UNITED STATES OF AMERICA, Indian Territory, }
   Central   DISTRICT. }

I,   Sallie Grinslade   , on oath state that I am   32   years of age and a citizen by   blood   , of the   Chickasaw   Nation; that I am the lawful wife of   Henry Grinslade   , who is a citizen, by   intermarriage   of the   Chickasaw   Nation; that a   female   child was born to me on   8   day of   July   , 1904, that said child has been named   Henretta   , and is now living.

Sallie Grinslade

Witnesses To Mark:
 { Henry Grinslade
 { Annie King

Subscribed and sworn to before me this   9   day of   February   , 1905.

S.M. Mead
Notary Public.

AFFIDAVIT OF ATTENDING PHYSICIAN OR MID-WIFE.

UNITED STATES OF AMERICA, Indian Territory, }
.... DISTRICT. }

I,   Dr. H.W. Klostermann   , a   Physician   , on oath state that I attended on Mrs.   Sally Grinslade   , wife of   Henry Grinslade   on the   8   day of   July , 1904; that there was born to her on said date a   Female   child; that said child is now living and is said to have been named   Henriyetta

Dr HW Klostermann

Applications for Enrollment of Chickasaw Newborn
Act of 1905   Volume III

Witnesses To Mark:
{ Henry Grinslade
{ Annie King

Subscribed and sworn to before me this 9 day of February , 1905.

S.M. Mead
Notary Public.

BIRTH AFFIDAVIT.

DEPARTMENT OF THE INTERIOR.
COMMISSION TO THE FIVE CIVILIZED TRIBES.

IN RE APPLICATION FOR ENROLLMENT, as a citizen of the   Chickasaw   Nation, of   Henriyetta Grinslade   , born on the 8th day of July , 1904

Name of Father: Henry Grinslade   a citizen of the   Chickasaw   Nation.
Name of Mother: Sallie Grinslade   a citizen of the   Chickasaw   Nation.

Postoffice   Paucaunla, I.T.

AFFIDAVIT OF MOTHER.

UNITED STATES OF AMERICA, Indian Territory,}
Central   DISTRICT.}

I, Sallie Grinslade , on oath state that I am 37 years of age and a citizen by blood , of the Chickasaw Nation; that I am the lawful wife of Henry Grinslade , who is a citizen, by intermarriage of the Chickasaw Nation; that a female child was born to me on 8th day of July , 1904; that said child has been named Henriyetta Grinslade , and was living March 4, 1905.

Sallie Grinslade

Witnesses To Mark:
{ Wash Marshall

Subscribed and sworn to before me this 21 th[sic] day of   April   , 1905

B.C. Wigand
Notary Public.

Applications for Enrollment of Chickasaw Newborn
Act of 1905   Volume III

AFFIDAVIT OF ATTENDING PHYSICIAN OR MID-WIFE.

UNITED STATES OF AMERICA, Indian Territory, }
    Central   DISTRICT.

   I,   H.W. Klostermann , a   Phys.   , on oath state that I attended on Mrs. Sallie Grinslade   , wife of   Henry Grinslade   on the 8th day of July , 1904; that there was born to her on said date a   female   child; that said child was living March 4, 1905, and is said to have been named Henriyetta Grinslade

                                H.W. Klostermann M.D.
Witnesses To Mark:
   { Wash Marshall

   Subscribed and sworn to before me this   21$^{th[sic]}$ day of   April   , 1905

                                B.C. Wigand
                                    Notary Public.

                                        Chickasaw 1138.

                Muskogee, Indian Territory, April 4, 1905.

Henry Grinslade,
    Paucaunla, Indian Territory.

Dear Sir:

   Receipt is hereby acknowledged of the affidavits of Sallie Grinslade and H. W. Klostermann to the birth of Henrietta[sic] Grinslade, daughter of Henry and Sallie Grinslade, July 8, 1904, and the same have been filed with our records as an application for the enrollment of said child.

                    Respectfully,

                                Commissioner in Charge.

Applications for Enrollment of Chickasaw Newborn
Act of 1905   Volume III

9 N B 181

Muskogee, Indian Territory, April 14, 1905.

Henry Grinslade,
    Paucaunla, Indian Territory.

Dear Sir:

    There is inclosed you herewith for execution application for the enrollment of your infant child, Henriyetta Grinslade, born July 8, 1904.

    In the affidavit of the mother, heretofore filed with the Commission, the date of the birth of said child is given as July 8, 1905. It will, therefore be necessary to have the application re-executed.

    In having these affidavits executed care should be exercised to see that all names are written in full, as they appear in the body of the affidavit, and in the event that either of the persons signing the affidavit are unable to write, signatures by mark must be attested by two witnesses. Each affidavit must be executed before a Notary Public and the notarial seal and signature of the officer must be attached to each separate affidavit.

        Respectfully,

LM 14-120.   Commissioner in Charge.

---

9 NB 181

Muskogee, Indian Territory, April 26, 1905.

Henry Grinslade,
    Paucaunla, Indian Territory.

Dear Sir:

    Receipt is hereby acknowledged of the affidavits of Sallie Grinslade and H. W. Klostermann to the birth of Henriyetta Grinslade, daughter of Henry and Sallie Grinslade, July 8, 1904, and the same have been filed with our records in the matter of the enrollment of said child.

        Respectfully,

        Chairman.

Applications for Enrollment of Chickasaw Newborn
Act of 1905 Volume III

Chic. N.B. - 182
(Charlie Perkins
Born November 4, 1902)
(Walter William Perkins, Jr.
Born May 29, 1904)

BIRTH AFFIDAVIT. #97

DEPARTMENT OF THE INTERIOR.
COMMISSION TO THE FIVE CIVILIZED TRIBES.

IN RE APPLICATION FOR ENROLLMENT, as a citizen of the Chickasaw Nation, of Charlie Perkins, born on the 4 day of November, 1902

Name of Father: W W Perkins   a citizen of the Chickasaw Nation.
Name of Mother: Laura B Perkins   a citizen of the Chickasaw Nation.

Postoffice   Sterrett

AFFIDAVIT OF MOTHER.

UNITED STATES OF AMERICA, Indian Territory,
Central   DISTRICT.

    I, Laura B Perkins, on oath state that I am 25 years of age and a citizen by blood, of the Chickasaw Nation; that I am the lawful wife of W W Perkins, who is a citizen, by intermarriage of the Chickasaw Nation; that a female child was born to me on 4 day of November, 1902, that said child has been named Charlie, and is now living.

                                 Laura B Perkins

Witnesses To Mark:
   { L.L. Mead
   { Mrs F. E. Mead

    Subscribed and sworn to before me this 13 day of February, 1905.

                                 S.M. Mead
                                      Notary Public.

Applications for Enrollment of Chickasaw Newborn
Act of 1905   Volume III

AFFIDAVIT OF ATTENDING PHYSICIAN OR MID-WIFE.

UNITED STATES OF AMERICA, Indian Territory,
Central   DISTRICT.

I,   C C Yeiser   , a   M.D.   , on oath state that I attended on Mrs. Laura B Perkins   , wife of W W Perkins   on the   4   day of November , 1902; that there was born to her on said date a   female   child; that said child is now living and is said to have been named Charlie

C C Yeiser M.D.

Witnesses To Mark:
- L.L. Mead
- Mrs F. E. Mead

Subscribed and sworn to before me this 13   day of   February   , 1905.

S.M. Mead
Notary Public.

BIRTH AFFIDAVIT.

DEPARTMENT OF THE INTERIOR.
COMMISSION TO THE FIVE CIVILIZED TRIBES.

IN RE APPLICATION FOR ENROLLMENT, as a citizen of the   Chickasaw   Nation, of   Charlie Perkins   , born on the   4 day of   November   , 1902

Name of Father: Walter William Perkins   a citizen of the   Chickasaw   Nation.
Name of Mother: Laura Belle Perkins   a citizen of the   Chickasaw   Nation.

Postoffice   Sterrett Ind Ter

AFFIDAVIT OF MOTHER.

UNITED STATES OF AMERICA, Indian Territory,
Central   DISTRICT.

I,   Laura Belle Perkins   , on oath state that I am   26   years of age and a citizen by   blood   , of the   Chickasaw   Nation; that I am the lawful wife of Walter William Perkins   , who is a citizen, by marriage   of the   Chickasaw   Nation; that a   female   child was born to me on 4"   day of   November   , 1902; that said child has been named   Charlie Perkins   , and was living March 4, 1905.

Laura Belle Perkins

Applications for Enrollment of Chickasaw Newborn
Act of 1905   Volume III

Witnesses To Mark:

    Subscribed and sworn to before me this   25   day of   March   , 1905

                                 S.M. Mead
                                 Notary Public.

AFFIDAVIT OF ATTENDING PHYSICIAN OR MID-WIFE.

UNITED STATES OF AMERICA, Indian Territory,
      Central   DISTRICT.

    I,   C C Yeiser   , a   M.D.   , on oath state that I attended on Mrs. Laura Bell Perkins   , wife of   Walter William Perkins   on the 4   day of   Nov   , 1902; that there was born to her on said date a   Female   child; that said child was living March 4, 1905, and is said to have been named   Charlie Perkins

                                C.C. Yeiser M.D.

Witnesses To Mark:

    Subscribed and sworn to before me this   25   day of   March   , 1905

                                 S.M. Mead
                                 Notary Public.

BIRTH AFFIDAVIT.   #96

DEPARTMENT OF THE INTERIOR.
COMMISSION TO THE FIVE CIVILIZED TRIBES.

    IN RE APPLICATION FOR ENROLLMENT, as a citizen of the   Chickasaw   Nation, of   Walter W Perkins Jr   , born on the   29   day of   May   , 1904

Name of Father: W W Perkins Sr   a citizen of the   Chickasaw Nation.
Name of Mother: Laura B Perkins   a citizen of the   Chickasaw Nation.

                        Postoffice   Sterrett

Applications for Enrollment of Chickasaw Newborn
Act of 1905   Volume III

AFFIDAVIT OF MOTHER.

UNITED STATES OF AMERICA, Indian Territory,}
Central   DISTRICT.

I, Laura B Perkins, on oath state that I am 25 years of age and a citizen by blood, of the Chickasaw Nation; that I am the lawful wife of W W Perkins, who is a citizen, by intermarriage of the Chickasaw Nation; that a male child was born to me on 29 day of May, 1904, that said child has been named Walter William, and is now living.

Laura B Perkins

Witnesses To Mark:
{ L.L. Mead
{ Mrs F. E. Mead

Subscribed and sworn to before me this 13 day of February, 1905.

S.M. Mead
Notary Public.

AFFIDAVIT OF ATTENDING PHYSICIAN OR MID-WIFE.

UNITED STATES OF AMERICA, Indian Territory,}
Central   DISTRICT.

I, C C Yeiser, a M.D., on oath state that I attended on Mrs. Laura B Perkins, wife of W W Perkins on the 29 day of May, 1904; that there was born to her on said date a male child; that said child is now living and is said to have been named Walter William

C C Yeiser M.D.

Witnesses To Mark:
{ L.L. Mead
{ Mrs F. E. Mead

Subscribed and sworn to before me this 13 day of February, 1905.

S.M. Mead
Notary Public.

Applications for Enrollment of Chickasaw Newborn
Act of 1905   Volume III

BIRTH AFFIDAVIT.

DEPARTMENT OF THE INTERIOR.
COMMISSION TO THE FIVE CIVILIZED TRIBES.

IN RE APPLICATION FOR ENROLLMENT, as a citizen of the Chickasaw Nation, of Walter William Perkins Jr , born on the 29" day of May , 1904

Name of Father: Walter William Perkins   a citizen of the Chickasaw Nation.
Name of Mother: Laura Belle Perkins   a citizen of the Chickasaw Nation.

Postoffice   Sterrett Ind Ter

AFFIDAVIT OF MOTHER.

UNITED STATES OF AMERICA, Indian Territory,
Central   DISTRICT.

I, Laura Belle Perkins , on oath state that I am 26 years of age and a citizen by blood , of the Chickasaw Nation; that I am the lawful wife of Walter William Perkins , who is a citizen, by marriage of the Chickasaw Nation; that a male child was born to me on 29" day of May , 1904; that said child has been named Walter William Perkins Jr , and was living March 4, 1905.

Laura Belle Perkins

Witnesses To Mark:
{

Subscribed and sworn to before me this 25 day of March , 1905

S.M. Mead
Notary Public.

AFFIDAVIT OF ATTENDING PHYSICIAN OR MID-WIFE.

UNITED STATES OF AMERICA, Indian Territory,
Central   DISTRICT.

I, C C Yeiser , a M.D. , on oath state that I attended on Mrs. Laura Bell Perkins , wife of Walter William Perkins on the 29 day of May , 1904; that there was born to her on said date a Male child; that said child was living March 4, 1905, and is said to have been named Walter William Perkins

C.C. Yeiser M.D.

Applications for Enrollment of Chickasaw Newborn
Act of 1905   Volume III

Witnesses To Mark:

Subscribed and sworn to before me this   25   day of   March   , 1905

S.M. Mead
Notary Public.

Chic. N.B. - 183
   (Winona Gardner
   Born October 2, 1903)

AFFIDAVIT OF ATTENDING PHYSICIAN OR MIDWIFE

UNITED STATES OF AMERICA
INDIAN TERRITORY
_____ DISTRICT

I,   I. N. Carrell   a   Physician on oath state that I attended on Mrs.   Susie Gardner   wife of   Robert Gardner   on the   2nd day of   October , 190 3, that there was born to her on said date a   Female   child, that said child is now living, and is said to have been named   Winona Gardner

I.N. Carrell   M.D.

WITNESSETH:
Must be two witnesses who are citizens and know the child.

Subscribed and sworn to before me this, the   18th   day of   March   190 5

G.B. Slater   Notary Public. JC Ky
Notary Public, Jefferson Co, Ky,
My commission expires Jan. 5th, 1908

We hereby certify that we are well acquainted with _____ a _____ and know _____ to be reputable and of good standing in the community.

Applications for Enrollment of Chickasaw Newborn
Act of 1905   Volume III

NEW-BORN AFFIDAVIT.

Number..............

...Chickasaw Enrolling Commission...

IN THE MATTER OF THE APPLICATION FOR ENROLLMENT, as a citizen of the Chickasaw Nation, of Winona Gardner

born on the 2nd day of __October__ 190 3

Name of father Robert Gardner   a citizen of   Choctaw
Nation final enrollment No. ....
Name of mother Susie Gardner   a citizen of   Chickasaw
Nation final enrollment No. 715

Postoffice   Ti, Ind. Ter.

AFFIDAVIT OF MOTHER.

UNITED STATES OF AMERICA
INDIAN TERRITORY
  Central   DISTRICT

I   Susie Gardner   , on oath state that I am 26 years of age and a citizen by blood of the Chickasaw Nation, and as such have been placed upon the final roll of the Chickasaw Nation, by the Honorable Secretary of the Interior my final enrollment number being   3407[sic] ; that I am the lawful wife of   Robert Gardner , who is a citizen of the   Choctaw   Nation, and as such has been placed upon the final roll of said Nation by the Honorable Secretary of the Interior, his final enrollment number being   715   and that a   female   child was born to me on the 2nd day of   October   190 3; that said child has been named   Winona Gardner , and is now living.

Susie Gardner

Witnesseth.
  Must be two ⎱ Anderson Lewis
  Witnesses who ⎰
  are Citizens.   J D Chastain

Subscribed and sworn to before me this 16th day of   Jan   190 5

Wm J. Hulsey
Notary Public.

My commission expires: 1908

Applications for Enrollment of Chickasaw Newborn
Act of 1905   Volume III

BIRTH AFFIDAVIT.

DEPARTMENT OF THE INTERIOR.
COMMISSION TO THE FIVE CIVILIZED TRIBES.

IN RE APPLICATION FOR ENROLLMENT, as a citizen of the Chickasaw Nation, of Winona Gardner, born on the 2nd day of October, 1903

Name of Father: Robert Gardner   a citizen of the Choctaw Nation.
Name of Mother: Susie Gardner   a citizen of the Chickasaw Nation.

Postoffice   Ti, Ind. Ter.

AFFIDAVIT OF MOTHER.

UNITED STATES OF AMERICA, Indian Territory,
Central   DISTRICT.

I, Susie Gardner, on oath state that I am 26 years of age and a citizen by blood, of the Chickasaw Nation; that I am the lawful wife of Robert Gardner, who is a citizen, by blood of the Choctaw Nation; that a female child was born to me on 2nd day of October, 1903; that said child has been named Winona Gardner, and was living March 4, 1905.

Susie Gardner

Witnesses To Mark:

Subscribed and sworn to before me this 27th day of April, 1905.

Wm J Hulsey
Notary Public.

AFFIDAVIT OF ATTENDING PHYSICIAN OR MID-WIFE.

UNITED STATES OF AMERICA, Indian Territory,
DISTRICT.

I, _____, a _____, on oath state that I attended on Mrs. Susie Gardner, wife of Robert Gardner on the 2nd day of October, 1903; that there was born to her on said date a female child; that said child was living March 4, 1905, and is said to have been named Winona Gardner

Applications for Enrollment of Chickasaw Newborn
Act of 1905   Volume III

Witnesses To Mark:

{ ....

....

Subscribed and sworn to before me this .... day of ...., 1905.

....
Notary Public.

HARTSHORNE, INDIAN TERRITORY,
CENTRAL DISTRICT.

I, H. A. Collins, do solemnly swear that I am personally ~~and well~~ and well acquainted with Susie Gardner, a citizen of the Chickasaw Nation, and that to my personal knowledge her girl child, Winona Gardner, which is now about eighteen months old, was living on the 4th day of March, 1905, and is living now.

H.A. Collins

Subscribed and sworn to before me at Hartshorne, Indian Territory, this the 27th day of April, 1905.
Wm. J. Hulsey
My Com. Ex. 1908.   Notary Public.

HARTSHORNE, INDIAN TERRITORY,
CENTRAL DISTRICT.

I, J. D. Chastain, do solemnly swear that I am personally acquainted with Susie Gardner and her husband, Robert Gardner; that to my personal knowledge their girl child, which is now about eighteen months old, was living on the fourth day of March, 1905.

JD Chastain

Subscribed and sworn to before me at Hartshorne, Indian Territory, this the 27th day of April, 1905.
Wm. J. Hulsey
My Com. Ex. 1908.   Notary Public.

TO THE COMMISSION TO THE FIVE CIVILIZED TRIBES,
MUSKOGEE, INDIAN TERRITORY.

WE, Robert M. Gardner and Susie Gardner, father and mother of Winona Gardner whose application for enrollment is now pending before the Commission To The Five

Applications for Enrollment of Chickasaw Newborn
Act of 1905   Volume III

Civilized Tribes, do hereby certify that we wish her to be placed on the Chickasaw rolls, and we do hereby authorize you to do so.

Witness our hands and seal this 19th day of May, 1905.

Robert M. Gardner

Susie Gardner

Subscribed and sworn to before me this 19th day of May 1905.

My Com Exp Mch 9th 1909.   WR Patterson
Notary Public.

9-1143

Muskogee, Indian Territory, April 6, 1905.

Hulsey & Patterson,
    Attorneys at Law.
        Hartshorne, Indian Territory.

Gentlemen:

    Receipt is hereby acknowledged of your letter of March 30, 1905, enclosing affidavits of Susie Gardner and I. N. Carrell to the birth of Winona Gardner, daughter of Robert and Susie Gardner, October 2, 1903, and the same have been filed with our records as an application for the enrollment of said child.

    Replying to that portion of your letter in which you refer to the work of Honorable James Bower and ask if it will be approved without further proof, you are advised that it is impracticable to state whether or not application for the enrollment of infant children which may have been forwarded to this office by Mr. Bower will be approved without further proof, as you do not mention the names of the children for whom such applications were made. You are advised, however, that all applications for the enrollment of infant children under the act of Congress of March 3, 1905, should be forwarded to this office or to one of the enrolling parties of the Commission.

    That part of your letter referring to the application for the enrollment of Abel H. Johnson will be made the subject of another communication.

Respectfully,

Commissioner in Charge.

Applications for Enrollment of Chickasaw Newborn
Act of 1905   Volume III

9 N B 183

Muskogee, Indian Territory, April 15, 1905.

Robert Gardner,
    Ti, Indian Territory.

Dear Sir:

There is inclosed you herewith for execution application for the enrollment of your infant child, Winona Gardner, born October 2, 1903.

The affidavit of the mother heretofore filed with the Commission, shows the child was living on January 16, 1905. It is necessary, for the child to be enrolled, that she was living on March 4, 1905. Please insert the mother's age in space left blank for the purpose.

In having these affidavits executed care should be exercised to see that all names are written in full, as they appear in the body of the affidavit, and in the event that either of the persons signing the affidavit are unable to write, signatures by mark must be attested by two witnesses. Each affidavit must be executed before a Notary Public and the notarial seal and signature of the officer must be attached to each separate affidavit.

Respectfully,

LM 14-100   Chairman.

Chickasaw N.B. 183

MUskogee[sic], Indian Territory, May 1, 1905.

Hulsey & Patterson,
    Attorneys at Law,
        Hartshorne, Indian Territory.

Gentlemen:

Receipt is hereby acknowledged of your letter of April 27, transmitting the affidavits of Susie Gardner, J. D. Chastain and H. A. Collins to the birth of Winona Gradner[sic], daughter of Robert and Susie Gardner, October 2, 1903, and the same have been filed with our records in the matter of the enrollment of said child.

Respectfully,

Chairman.

Applications for Enrollment of Chickasaw Newborn
Act of 1905   Volume III

9-NB-183.

Muskogee, Indian Territory, May 15, 1905.

Robert Gardner,
    Ti, Indian Territory.

Dear Sir:

Referring to the application for the enrollment of your infant child, Winona Gardner, it appears that you are a citizen by blood of the Choctaw Nation, while your wife is a citizen by blood of the Chickasaw Nation.

Your attention is called to the provision of the Act of Congress approved June 28, 1898, as follows:

The several Tribes may, by agreement, determine the right of persons who for any reason may claim citizenship in two or more tribes, and to allotment of lands and distribution of moneys belonging to each tribe; but if no such agreement be made, then such claimant shall be entitled to such rights in one tribe only, and may elect in which tribe he will take such right; but if he fail or refuse to make such selection in due time, he shall be enrolled in the tribe with whom he has resided, and there be given such allotment and distributions, and not elsewhere.

It will therefore be necessary for you and your wife to appear before a Notary Public or other officer authorized to administer oaths and by affidavit elect in which nation you desires[sic] to have said child enrolled, forwarding the same, when properly executed, to the Commission.

Respectfully,

Chairman.

---

9 N.B. 183.

Muskogee, Indian Territory, May 24, 1905.

Robert M. Gardner,
    Ti, Indian Territory.

Dear Sir:

Receipt is hereby acknowledged of the joint affidavit of yourself and Susie Gardner electing to have your child, Wynona[sic] Gardner, as a citizen by blood of the Chickasaw Nation and the same has been filed with the records in this case.

Respectfully,

Chairman.

Applications for Enrollment of Chickasaw Newborn
Act of 1905 Volume III

Chic. N.B. - 184
    (Lorena E. Kemp
    Born July 21, 1903)

BIRTH AFFIDAVIT.

DEPARTMENT OF THE INTERIOR.
COMMISSION TO THE FIVE CIVILIZED TRIBES.

    IN RE APPLICATION FOR ENROLLMENT, as a citizen of the Chickasaw Nation, of Lorena E Kemp, born on the 21 day of July, 1903

Name of Father: Joe Kemp   a citizen of the Chickasaw Nation.
Name of Mother: Marilons E Kemp   a citizen of the Chickasaw Nation.

    Postoffice   Kemp Ind Ter

AFFIDAVIT OF MOTHER.

UNITED STATES OF AMERICA, Indian Territory,
    Central   DISTRICT.

    I, Marilons E Kemp, on oath state that I am 30 years of age and a citizen by Marriage, of the Chickasaw Nation; that I am the lawful wife of Joe Kemp, who is a citizen, by Birth of the Chickasaw Nation; that a Girle[sic] child was born to me on 21 day of July, 1903; that said child has been named Lorena E Kemp, and was living March 4, 1905.

                                M E Kemp

Witnesses To Mark:

    Subscribed and sworn to before me this 27 day of March, 1905

                                S.T. Johns
                                    Notary Public.

AFFIDAVIT OF ATTENDING PHYSICIAN OR MID-WIFE.

UNITED STATES OF AMERICA, Indian Territory,
    Central   DISTRICT.

    I, C.A. Kirby, a mid wife, on oath state that I attended on Mrs. Marilons E Kemp, wife of Joe Kemp on the 21 day of July, 1903;

Applications for Enrollment of Chickasaw Newborn
Act of 1905 Volume III

that there was born to her on said date a Girle child; that said child was living March 4, 1905, and is said to have been named Lorena E Kemp

her
C.A. x Kirby
mark

Witnesses To Mark:
{ *(Name Illegible)*
  Alice A Lewallen

Subscribed and sworn to before me this 27 day of March , 1905

S.T. Johns
Notary Public.

9-1158

Muskogee, Indian Territory, April 3, 1905.

Joe Kemp,
Kemp, Indian Territory.

Dear Sir:

Receipt is hereby acknowledged of the affidavits of M. E. Kemp and C. A. Kirby to the birth of Lorena E. Kemp, daughter of Joe and Marilons E. Kemp, July 21, 1903, and the same have been filed with our records as an application for the enrollment of said child.

Respectfully,

Chairman.

Chic. N.B. - 185
(Joseph E. Johnston Harper
Born March 3, 1905)

Applications for Enrollment of Chickasaw Newborn
Act of 1905   Volume III

BIRTH AFFIDAVIT.

DEPARTMENT OF THE INTERIOR.
COMMISSION TO THE FIVE CIVILIZED TRIBES.

IN RE APPLICATION FOR ENROLLMENT, as a citizen of the Chickasaw Nation, of Joseph E Johnston Harper, born on the 3" day of March, 1905

Name of Father: J. L. Harper   a citizen of the Chickasaw Nation.
Name of Mother: Mrs. Viola Harper   a citizen of the " Nation.

Postoffice Cumberland, I.T.

AFFIDAVIT OF MOTHER.

UNITED STATES OF AMERICA, Indian Territory,
Southern DISTRICT.

I, Mrs. Viola Harper, on oath state that I am 30 years of age and a citizen by intermarriage, of the Chickasaw Nation; that I am the lawful wife of J. L. Harper, who is a citizen, by blood of the Chickasaw Nation; that a male child was born to me on third day of March, 1905; that said child has been named Joseph E Johnston Harper, and was living March 4, 1905.

                         Mrs Viola x Harper
Witnesses To Mark: her mark
{ *(Name Illegible)*
   L. L. Holder

Subscribed and sworn to before me this 24 day of March, 1905

                         J. Frank Adams
                         Notary Public.

AFFIDAVIT OF ATTENDING PHYSICIAN OR MID-WIFE.

UNITED STATES OF AMERICA, Indian Territory,
Southern DISTRICT.

I, F. M. Jackman, a physician, on oath state that I attended on Mrs. Viola Harper, wife of J. L. Harper on the 3" day of March, 1905; that there was born to her on said date a male child; that said child was living March 4, 1905, and is said to have been named Joseph E Johnston Harper

                         F M Jackman

Applications for Enrollment of Chickasaw Newborn
Act of 1905   Volume III

Witnesses To Mark:
{

Subscribed and sworn to before me this 3" day of March , 1905

J. Frank Adams
Notary Public.

BIRTH AFFIDAVIT.

DEPARTMENT OF THE INTERIOR.
COMMISSION TO THE FIVE CIVILIZED TRIBES.

IN RE APPLICATION FOR ENROLLMENT, as a citizen of the Chickasaw Nation, of Joseph E Johnston Harper , born on the 3" day of March , 1905

Name of Father: Joseph Lea Harper   a citizen of the Chickasaw Nation.
Name of Mother: Viola Harper   a citizen of the Chickasaw Nation.

Postoffice Cumberland, I.T.

AFFIDAVIT OF MOTHER.

UNITED STATES OF AMERICA, Indian Territory, }
     Southern   DISTRICT. }

I, Viola Harper , on oath state that I am 30 years of age and a citizen by intermarriage , of the Chickasaw Nation; that I am the lawful wife of Joseph Lea Harper , who is a citizen, by blood of the Chickasaw Nation; that a male child was born to me on 3" day of March , 1905; that said child has been named Joseph E Johnston Harper , and was living March 4, 1905.

                      her
                Viola x Harper
Witnesses To Mark: mark
{ H. R. Inge
  John Shockey

Subscribed and sworn to before me this 22 day of April , 1905

C.M. Inge
Notary Public.

Applications for Enrollment of Chickasaw Newborn
Act of 1905   Volume III

AFFIDAVIT OF ATTENDING PHYSICIAN OR MID-WIFE.

UNITED STATES OF AMERICA, Indian Territory,
Southern   DISTRICT.

I,   F. M. Jackman   , a   M.D.   , on oath state that I attended on Mrs.   Viola Harper , wife of   Joseph Lea Harper   on the 3" day of   March , 1905; that there was born to her on said date a   male   child; that said child was living March 4, 1905, and is said to have been named   Joseph E Johnston Harper

F M Jackman

Witnesses To Mark:
{

Subscribed and sworn to before me this   22 day of   April   , 1905.

C.M. Inge
Notary Public.

Chickasaw 1159

Muskogee, Indian Territory, March 30, 1905.

J. L. Harper,
Cumberland, Indian Territory.

Dear Sir:

Receipt is hereby acknowledged of the affidavits of Mrs. Viola Harper and F. M. Jackman to the birth of Joseph E. Johnston Harper, son of J. L. and Viola Harper, March 3, 1905, and the same have been filed with our record as an application for the enrollment of said child.

Respectfully,

Chairman.

Applications for Enrollment of Chickasaw Newborn
Act of 1905   Volume III

9 N B 185

Muskogee, Indian Territory, April 14, 1905.

Joseph Lea Harper,
    Cumberland, Indian Territory.

Dear Sir:

    There is inclosed you herewith for execution application for the enrollment of your infant child, Joseph E. Johnston Harper, born March 3, 1905.

    In the affidavit of the physician heretofore filed with the Commission, it is shown that the child was living on March 3, 1905. It is necessary, for the child to be enrolled, that all affidavits show said child was living on March 4, 1905.

    In having the affidavits executed care should be exercised to see that all names are written in full, as they appear in the body of the affidavits and in the event that either of the persons signing the affidavit are unable to write, signatures by mark must be attested by two witnesses. Each affidavit must be executed before a Notary Public and the notarial seal and signature of the officer must be attached to each separate affidavit.

Respectfully,

LM 14-160.   Commissioner in Charge.

9- N B 185.

Muskogee, Indian Territory, April 26, 1905.

Joseph Lea Harper,
    Cumberland, Indian Territory.

Dear Sir:

    Receipt is hereby acknowledged of the affidavits of Viola Harper and F. M. Jackman to the birth of Joseph E. Johnston Harper, son of Joseph Lea and Viola Harper, March 3, 1905, and the same have been filed with our records in the matter of the enrollment of said child.

Respectfully,

Chairman.

Applications for Enrollment of Chickasaw Newborn
Act of 1905   Volume III

Chic. N.B. - 186
(Lee Ora or Leeora Beshirs
Born January 7, 1904)

BIRTH AFFIDAVIT.

DEPARTMENT OF THE INTERIOR.
COMMISSION TO THE FIVE CIVILIZED TRIBES.

IN RE APPLICATION FOR ENROLLMENT, as a citizen of the   Chickasaw   Nation, of   Lee Ora Beshirs , born on the 7th day of Jan , 1904

Name of Father: Aaron Beshirs   a citizen of the   Chickasaw   Nation.
Name of Mother: Laura Belle Beshirs   a citizen of the   Chickasaw   Nation.

Postoffice   Yuba, Ind. T.

AFFIDAVIT OF MOTHER.

UNITED STATES OF AMERICA, Indian Territory, }
    Central   DISTRICT.

I,   Laura Belle Beshirs , on oath state that I am   37   years of age and a citizen by   Blood , of the   Chickasaw   Nation; that I am the lawful wife of Aaron Beshirs , who is a citizen, by Blood   of the   Chickasaw   Nation; that a   Female   child was born to me on 7th day of   Jan , 1904; that said child has been named   Lee Ora Beshirs , and was living March 4, 1905.

Laura Bell Beshirs

Witnesses To Mark:
{

Subscribed and sworn to before me this 27th day of   Mar   , 1905

J.M. Reasor
Notary Public.

AFFIDAVIT OF ATTENDING PHYSICIAN OR MID-WIFE.

UNITED STATES OF AMERICA, Indian Territory, }
    Central   DISTRICT.

I,   C.O. Lively   , a   Physician   , on oath state that I attended on Mrs.   Laura Belle Beshirs   , wife of   Aaron Beshirs   on the 7th day of Jan ,

Applications for Enrollment of Chickasaw Newborn
Act of 1905   Volume III

1904; that there was born to her on said date a   Female   child; that said child was living March 4, 1905, and is said to have been named   Lee Ora Beshirs

C.O. Lively M.D.

Witnesses To Mark:

{

Subscribed and sworn to before me this 27th day of   Mar , 1905

J.M. Reasor
Notary Public.

BIRTH AFFIDAVIT.

IN RE-APPLICATION FOR ENROLLMENT, as a citizen of the   Chickasaw   Nation, of   Leeora Beshirs , born on the 7 day of January , 190 4

Name of Father: Aron C Beshirs   a citizen of the   Chickasaw   Nation.
Name of Mother: Laura Bell Beshirs   a citizen of the   Chickasaw   Nation.

Postoffice   Yuba IT

AFFIDAVIT OF MOTHER.

UNITED STATES OF AMERICA, INDIAN TERRITORY, }
          Central   District.

I, Laura Bell Beshirs , on oath state that I am 37 years of age and a citizen by Blood , of the Chickasaw Nation; that I am the lawful wife of   Aron C Beshirs , who is a citizen, by   Blood   of the   Chickasaw   Nation; that a   female   child was born to me on 7 day of January , 1904 , that said child has been named Leeora Beshirs , and is now living.

Laura Belle Beshirs

Witnesses To Mark:

{

Subscribed and sworn to before me this 28 day of   Feb   , 1905.

Chas P Walker
Notary Public.

Applications for Enrollment of Chickasaw Newborn
Act of 1905   Volume III

AFFIDAVIT OF ATTENDING PHYSICIAN OR MID-WIFE.

UNITED STATES OF AMERICA, INDIAN TERRITORY,
Central   District.

I,   M E Whisenhunt   , a   mid wife   , on oath state that I attended on Mrs.   Beshirs   , wife of   Aron C Beshirs   on the   7   day of   January , 190 4; that there was born to her on said date a   female   child; that said child is now living and is said to have been named   Leeora Beshirs
her
M E x Whisenhunt
Witnesses To Mark: mark
   Eli Perry
   (Name Illegible)

Subscribed and sworn to before me this   28   day of   Feb   , 1905.

Chas P Walker
Notary Public.

Chickasaw 1176.

Muskogee, Indian Territory, April 4, 1905.

Aaron Beshirs,
   Yuba, Indian Territory.

Dear Sir:

   Receipt is hereby acknowledged of the affidavits of Laura Bell Beshirs and C. O. Lively to the birth of Lee Ora Beshirs, daughter of Aaron and Laura Bell Beshirs, January 7, 1904, and the same have been filed with our records as an application for the enrollment of said child.

Respectfully,

Commissioner in Charge.

Chic. N.B. - 187
   (Edna May Hayward
   Born December 2, 1904)

Applications for Enrollment of Chickasaw Newborn
Act of 1905   Volume III

BIRTH AFFIDAVIT.

DEPARTMENT OF THE INTERIOR.
COMMISSION TO THE FIVE CIVILIZED TRIBES.

IN RE APPLICATION FOR ENROLLMENT, as a citizen of the Chickasaw Nation, of Edna May Hayward, born on the 2nd day of Dec, 1904

Name of Father: James L Hayward   a citizen of the .... Nation.
Name of Mother: Mona E Hayward   a citizen of the Chickasaw Nation.

Postoffice   Edwards IT

AFFIDAVIT OF MOTHER.

UNITED STATES OF AMERICA, Indian Territory, }
Central   DISTRICT.

I, Mona E Hayward, on oath state that I am 25 years of age and a citizen by Blood, of the Chickasaw Nation; that I am the lawful wife of James L Hayward, who is a citizen, by .... of the .... Nation; that a Female child was born to me on 2nd day of Dec, 1904; that said child has been named Edna May Hayward, and was living March 4, 1905.

Mrs Mona E Hayward

Witnesses To Mark:
{

Subscribed and sworn to before me this 21 day of March, 1905

(Name Illegible)
Notary Public.

AFFIDAVIT OF ATTENDING PHYSICIAN OR MID-WIFE.

UNITED STATES OF AMERICA, Indian Territory, }
Central   DISTRICT.

I, Albert Allen, a Physician, on oath state that I attended on Mrs. Mona E Hayward, wife of James L Hayward on the 2 day of Dec, 1904; that there was born to her on said date a Female child; that said child was living March 4, 1905, and is said to have been named Edna May Hayward

Albert Allen M.D.

Witnesses To Mark:
{

Applications for Enrollment of Chickasaw Newborn
Act of 1905   Volume III

Subscribed and sworn to before me this 21 day of   March   , 1905

(Name Illegible)
Notary Public.

Chic. N.B. - 188
(Nora Vena Moore
Born June 30, 1903)

BIRTH AFFIDAVIT.

DEPARTMENT OF THE INTERIOR.
COMMISSION TO THE FIVE CIVILIZED TRIBES.

IN RE APPLICATION FOR ENROLLMENT, as a citizen of the   Chickasaw   Nation, of   Nora Vena Moore , born on the 30 day of June , 1903

Name of Father: Lemmuel[sic] Capel Moore   a citizen of the   Chickasaw   Nation.

Name of Mother: Nora Moore   a ~~citizen~~ *non citizen* of the   Choctaw   Nation.

Postoffice   Sterrett I.T.

AFFIDAVIT OF MOTHER.

UNITED STATES OF AMERICA, Indian Territory,
Central Judicial   DISTRICT.

non

I,   Nora Moore , on oath state that I am 35   years of age and a citizen by .... , of the   Choctaw   Nation; that I am the lawful wife of   Lemmuel Caple Moore , who is a citizen, by Blood   of the   Chickasaw   Nation; that a   Female   child was born to me on   the 30th day of June   , 1903; that said child has been named   Nora Vena Moore , and was living March 4, 1905.

Nora Moore

Witnesses To Mark:
{

Applications for Enrollment of Chickasaw Newborn
Act of 1905   Volume III

Subscribed and sworn to before me this 27th day of March , 1905

GW Goodwin
Notary Public.

AFFIDAVIT OF ATTENDING PHYSICIAN OR MID-WIFE.

UNITED STATES OF AMERICA, Indian Territory,
Central Judicial   DISTRICT.

I, J.R. Keller , a Phycian[sic] , on oath state that I attended on Mrs. Nora Moore , wife of Lemmuel Caple Moore on the 30th day of June , 1903; that there was born to her on said date a Female child; that said child was living March 4, 1905, and is said to have been named Nora Vena Moore

J.R. Keller M.D.

Witnesses To Mark:

Subscribed and sworn to before me this 27th day of March , 1905

G.W. Goodwin
Notary Public.

Chickasaw 1182

Muskogee, Indian Territory, March 31, 1905.

Lemuel Capel Moore,
  Sterrett, Indian Territory.

Dear Sir:

Receipt is hereby acknowledged of the affidavits of Nora Moore and J. R. Keller to the birth of Nora Vena Moore, daughter of Lemuel Capel and Nora Moore, June 30, 1903, and the same have been filed with our records as an application for the enrollment of said child.

Respectfully,

Chairman.

Applications for Enrollment of Chickasaw Newborn
Act of 1905 Volume III

Chic. N.B. - 189
(Hester Pruitt
June 21, 1903)

BIRTH AFFIDAVIT.

DEPARTMENT OF THE INTERIOR.
COMMISSION TO THE FIVE CIVILIZED TRIBES.

IN RE APPLICATION FOR ENROLLMENT, as a citizen of the Chickasaw Nation, of Hester Pruitt , born on the 21st day of June , 1903

Name of Father: Willis Pruitt   a citizen of the Chickasaw Nation.
Name of Mother: Allice[sic] Pruitt   a citizen of the Chickasaw Nation.

Postoffice   Utica I.T.

AFFIDAVIT OF MOTHER.

UNITED STATES OF AMERICA, Indian Territory,
Central   DISTRICT.

     I, Allice Pruitt , on oath state that I am 39 years of age and a citizen by Blood , of the Chickasaw Nation; that I am the lawful wife of Willis Pruitt , who is a citizen, by Intermarriage of the Chickasaw Nation; that a Female child was born to me on 21st day of June , 1903; that said child has been named Hester Pruitt , and was living March 4, 1905.

                             Alice Pruitt

Witnesses To Mark:

Subscribed and sworn to before me this 28th day of March , 1905

                         W.J. O'Donley
                         Notary Public.

AFFIDAVIT OF ATTENDING PHYSICIAN OR MID-WIFE.

UNITED STATES OF AMERICA, Indian Territory,
Central   DISTRICT.

     I, A.J. Wells , a Physician , on oath state that I attended on Mrs. Allice Pruitt , wife of Willis Pruitt on the 21st day of June ,

Applications for Enrollment of Chickasaw Newborn
Act of 1905   Volume III

1903; that there was born to her on said date a Female child; that said child was living March 4, 1905, and is said to have been named Hester Pruitt

A.J. Wells, M.D.

Witnesses To Mark:
{

Subscribed and sworn to before me this 28th day of March , 1905

W.J. O'Donley
Notary Public.

Chic. N.B. - 190
    (Peter P. Pitchlynn
    Born March 17, 1904)

BIRTH AFFIDAVIT.

DEPARTMENT OF THE INTERIOR.
COMMISSION TO THE FIVE CIVILIZED TRIBES.

IN RE APPLICATION FOR ENROLLMENT, as a citizen of the Chickasaw Nation, of Peter P. Pitchlynn , born on the 17th day of March , 1904

Name of Father: Edward E. Pitchlynn   a citizen of the Choctaw Nation.
Name of Mother: Sudie Pitchlynn   a citizen of the Chickasaw Nation.

Postoffice   Caddo I.T.

AFFIDAVIT OF MOTHER.

UNITED STATES OF AMERICA, Indian Territory, }
    Central   **DISTRICT.**

    I, Sudie Pitchlynn , on oath state that I am 22 years of age and a citizen by Blood , of the Chickasaw Nation; that I am the lawful wife of Edward E. Pitchlynn , who is a citizen, by Blood of the Choctaw Nation; that a Male child was born to me on 17th day of March , 1904; that said child has been named Peter P. Pitchlynn , and was living March 4, 1905.

Sudie Pitchlynn

Applications for Enrollment of Chickasaw Newborn
Act of 1905   Volume III

Witnesses To Mark:

{

    Subscribed and sworn to before me this 20th day of   March   , 1905

                              C.H. Elting
                              Notary Public.

AFFIDAVIT OF ATTENDING PHYSICIAN OR MID-WIFE.

UNITED STATES OF AMERICA, Indian Territory, }
    Central   DISTRICT.

    I,   W.J. Melton   , a Physician   , on oath state that I attended on Mrs. Sudie Pitchlynn   , wife of   Edward E. Pitchlynn   on the 17th day of March   , 1904; that there was born to her on said date a   male   child; that said child was living March 4, 1905, and is said to have been named   Peter P. Pitchlynn

                              W.J. Melton M.D.

Witnesses To Mark:

{

    Subscribed and sworn to before me this 20th day of   March   , 1905

                              C.H. Elting
                              Notary Public.

(The affidavit below typed as given.)

                    DEPARTMENT OF THE INTERIOR.

            COMMISSION TO THE FIVE CIVILIZED TRIBES.

In the Matter   of the

Application of   Peter P.Pitchlynn,

to Be Enrolled   as Member Of   Chickasaw Tribe.

    Before Me C.H.Elting ,aNotary Public In and for the Central District of the Indian Territory,This day Personally Appeared Edward E.Pitchlynn and Sudie Pitchlynn,Husband and and Wife,And Father and Mother of   Peter P.Pitchlynn,And They State Upon Their oaths That They are 45 years of Age and 22--- Years Respectively,and Reside At Caddo,I.T.

Applications for Enrollment of Chickasaw Newborn
Act of 1905   Volume III

xxxxxxxxxxxxxxxxxxxxxxxxxxxxxxxxxxxxxxxxxxxxxxxxxxxxxxxxxxxxxxxxxxx
xxxxxxxx   That they elect to have the said Peter P.Pitchlynn enrolled as a citizen by Blood of the Chickasaw Nation.

Witness our hands this 17th.day of May A.D.19o5.

         Edward E. Pitchlynn
         Sudie Pitchlynn

Subscribed and Sworn to before me this 17th.day of May A.D.19o5.

         C.H. Elting
         Notary Public.

9-1242

Muskogee, Indian Territory, March 24, 1905.

Edward E. Pitchlynn,
  Caddo, Indian Territory.

Dear Sir:

  Receipt is hereby acknowledged of your letter of March 20, 1905, enclosing affidavits of Sudie Pitchlynn and W. J. Melton to the birth of Peter P. Pitchlynn, son of Edward E. Pitchlynn and Sudie Pitchlynn, March 17, 1904, and the same have been filed with our records as an application for the enrollment of said child.

        Respectfully,

              Chairman.

9-NB-190.

Muskogee, Indian Territory, May 15, 1905.

Edward E. Pitchlynn,
  Caddo, Indian Territory.

Dear Sir:

  Referring to the application for the enrollment of your infant child, Peter P. Pitchlynn, it appears that you are a citizen by blood of the Choctaw Nation, while your wife is a citizen by blood of the Chickasaw Nation.

Applications for Enrollment of Chickasaw Newborn
Act of 1905   Volume III

Your attention is called to the provision of the Act of Congress approved June 28, 1898, as follows:

The several Tribes may, by agreement, determine the right of persons who for any reason may claim citizenship in two or more tribes, and to allotment of lands and distribution of moneys belonging to each tribe; but if no such agreement be made, then such claimant shall be entitled to such rights in one tribe only, and may elect in which tribe he will take such right; but if he fail or refuse to make such selection in due time, he shall be enrolled in the tribe with whom he has resided, and there be given such allotment and distributions, and not elsewhere.

It will therefore be necessary for you and your wife to appear before a Notary Public or other officer authorized to administer oaths and by affidavit elect in which nation you desire to have said child enrolled, forwarding same, when properly executed, to the Commission.

Respectfully,

[sic]

9 NB 190

Muskogee, Indian Territory, May 19, 1905.

Edward E. Pitchlyn[sic],
    Caddo, Indian Territory.

Dear Sir:

Receipt is hereby acknowledged of your letter of May 17, 1905, enclosing joint affidavit of yourself and your wife Sudie Pitchlyn electing to have your child Peter Pitchlyn enrolled as a citizen by blood of the Chickasaw Nation and the same have been filed with the record in the matter of the enrollment of said child.

Respectfully,

Chairman.

Chic. N.B. - 191
    (Easmon Pusley
    Born July 16, 1903)

Applications for Enrollment of Chickasaw Newborn
Act of 1905   Volume III

BIRTH AFFIDAVIT.

DEPARTMENT OF THE INTERIOR,
COMMISSION TO THE FIVE CIVILIZED TRIBES.

IN RE Application for Enrollment, as a citizen of the Chickasaw Nation, of Easmon Pusley, born on the 16 day of July, 1903

Name of Father: James Pusley   a citizen of the Chickasaw Nation.
Name of Mother: Mary J. Pusley   a citizen of the Chickasaw Nation.

Post-Office: Indianola I.T.

AFFIDAVIT OF MOTHER.

UNITED STATES OF AMERICA,
    INDIAN TERRITORY.
    Western   District.

I, Mary J Pusley, on oath state that I am 26 years of age and a citizen by intermarriage, of the Chickasaw Nation; that I am the lawful wife of James Pusley, who is a citizen, by Blood of the Chickasaw Nation; that a male child was born to me on 16 day of July, 1903, that said child has been named Easmon Pusley, and is now living.

            her
          Mary J x Pusley
WITNESSES TO MARK: mark
 John Taylor
 J.C. Wooten

Subscribed and sworn to before me this 29 *day of* March, 1905.

          T.J. Rice
          NOTARY PUBLIC.

AFFIDAVIT OF ATTENDING PHYSICIAN OR MID-WIFE.

UNITED STATES OF AMERICA,
    INDIAN TERRITORY.
    Central Judicial   District.

I, W.J. Maniss, a Physician, on oath state that I attended on Mrs. Mary J Pusley, wife of James S Pusley on the 16 day of July, 1903; that there was born to her on said date a male child; that said child is now living and is said to have been named Easmon Pusley

Applications for Enrollment of Chickasaw Newborn
Act of 1905 Volume III

WITNESSES TO MARK:

W.J. Maniss M.D.

Subscribed and sworn to before me this 18th *day of* March , 1905.

L.T. Jones

NOTARY PUBLIC.

Chickasaw 1243.

Muskogee, Indian Territory, April 4, 1905.

James Pusley,
    Indianola, Indian Territory.

Dear Sir:

    Receipt is hereby acknowledged of the affidavits of Mary J. Pusley and W. J. Maniss to the birth of Easmon Pusley, son of James and Mary J. Pusley, July 16, 1903, and the same have been filed with our records as an application for the enrollment of said child.

Respectfully,

Commissioner in Charge.

Chic. N.B. - 192
    (Mattie Thomas Duckworth
    Born March 11, 1903)

BIRTH AFFIDAVIT.

DEPARTMENT OF THE INTERIOR.
COMMISSION TO THE FIVE CIVILIZED TRIBES.

IN RE APPLICATION FOR ENROLLMENT, as a citizen of the Chickasaw Nation, of Mattie Thomas Duckworth , born on the 11 day of March , 1903

Name of Father: Thomas Duckworth   a citizen of the Chickasaw Nation.
Name of Mother: Josephine Duckworth   a citizen of the Chickasaw Nation.

Applications for Enrollment of Chickasaw Newborn
Act of 1905   Volume III

Postoffice   Kemp Ind Ter

AFFIDAVIT OF MOTHER.

UNITED STATES OF AMERICA, Indian Territory, }
Central DISTRICT. }

I, Josephine Duckworth, on oath state that I am 22 years of age and a citizen by Marriage, of the Chickasaw Nation; that I am the lawful wife of Thomas Duckworth, who is a citizen, by Birth of the Chickasaw Nation; that a female child was born to me on 11 day of March, 1903; that said child has been named Mattie Thomas Duckworth, and was living March 4, 1905.

Josephine Duckworth

Witnesses To Mark:
{

Subscribed and sworn to before me this 29 day of March, 1905

S.T. Johns
Notary Public.

AFFIDAVIT OF ATTENDING PHYSICIAN OR MID-WIFE.

UNITED STATES OF AMERICA, Indian Territory, }
Central DISTRICT. }

I, Mrs C A Kirby, a Mid wife, on oath state that I attended on Mrs. Josephine Duckworth, wife of Thomas Duckworth on the 11 day of March, 1903; that there was born to her on said date a female child; that said child was living March 4, 1905, and is said to have been named Mattie Thomas Duckworth

C A Kirby

Witnesses To Mark:
{ A.J. Turner
  Alice A Lewallen

Subscribed and sworn to before me this 29 day of March, 1905

S.T. Johns
Notary Public.

Applications for Enrollment of Chickasaw Newborn
Act of 1905   Volume III

Chic. N.B. - 193
    (Virginia Louise Atkinson
    Born January 27, 1903)

BIRTH AFFIDAVIT.

DEPARTMENT OF THE INTERIOR.
COMMISSION TO THE FIVE CIVILIZED TRIBES.

IN RE APPLICATION FOR ENROLLMENT, as a citizen of the   Chickasaw   Nation, of   Virginia Louise Atkinson , born on the 27th   day of January , 1903

Name of Father: Clarence E Atkinson   a citizen of the Chickasaw Nation.
Name of Mother: Mattie Atkinson   a citizen of the Chickasaw Nation.

    Postoffice   Chickasha, I.T.

AFFIDAVIT OF MOTHER.

UNITED STATES OF AMERICA, Indian Territory, }
    Southern   DISTRICT.

    I, Mattie Atkinson , on oath state that I am 28   years of age and a citizen by   Blood , of the   Chickasaw   Nation; that I am the lawful wife of Clarence E Atkinson , who is a citizen, by   Marriage   of the   Chickasaw   Nation; that a   female   child was born to me on 27th   day of January , 1903, that said child has been named Virginia Louise , and is now living.

    Mattie Atkinson

Witnesses To Mark:
  { B.P. Smith
    Lanay Maxey

    Subscribed and sworn to before me this 11th day of March , 1905.

    E.A.F. Johns
        Notary Public.

Applications for Enrollment of Chickasaw Newborn
Act of 1905 Volume III

AFFIDAVIT OF ATTENDING PHYSICIAN OR MID-WIFE.

UNITED STATES OF AMERICA, Indian Territory,
Southern DISTRICT.

I, Jno. E. Stinson, a Physician, on oath state that I attended on Mrs. Mattie Atkinson, wife of Clarence E Atkinson on the 27th day of January, 1903; that there was born to her on said date a female child; that said child is now living and is said to have been named Virginia Louise Atkinson

Jno. E. Stinson M.D.

Witnesses To Mark:
{ *(Name Illegible)*
{ *(Name Illegible)*

Subscribed and sworn to before me this 18th day of March, 1905.

E.A.F. Johns
Notary Public.

Chic. N.B. - 194
(Blanche Percival
Born October 11, 1904)

Indian Territory,
Southern District.

I, C. M. Campbell, Clerk of the United States Court, Southern District, Indian Territory, do hereby certify that the above and foregoing is a true and correct copy of the Marriage License and Certificate of Marriage, filed for record in my office at Ardmore on the 17th day of Feb., 1904 and duly recorded in Book H, page 72 of Marriage Records.

IN TESTIMONY WHEREOF, I have hereunto set my hand and affixed the seal of said Court at my office in Ardmore, Indian Territory this 5th day of July, 1905.

C. M. Campbell, Clerk,

By NH McCoy Chief Deputy.

Applications for Enrollment of Chickasaw Newborn
Act of 1905   Volume III

CERTIFICATE OF
RECORD OF MARRIAGE

UNITED STATES OF AMERICA,
INDIAN TERRITORY,   } sct.
SOUTHERN DISTRICT.

I, C. M. CAMPBELL, Clerk of the United States Court, in the Territory and District aforesaid Do HEREBY CERTIFY, that the License for and Certificate of Marriage of

Mr   Edward H. Percival   and

M   Alta Kimzey

were filed in my office in said Territory and District the   17th   day of Feb.   A.D., 190 4 and duly recorded in Book   H.   of Marriage Record, Page   77

WITNESS my hand and Seal of said Court, at Ardmore, this   17th   day of   Feb.   A.D. 190 4

C. M. Campbell
CLERK.

DEPARTMENT OF THE INTERIOR,
COMMISSION TO THE FIVE CIVILIZED TRIBES.
FILED
JUL 1 1905
Tams Bixby CHAIRMAN.

Return this license to the United States Clerk at Ardmore, that it may be recorded, when it will be mailed to the proper address.

Texas Printing Company, Fort Worth.

No person is authorized to perform the Marriage Ceremony in the Indian Territory unless the proper credentials have first been recorded in the Clerk's office.

MARRIAGE LICENSE.
No. 274

UNITED STATES OF AMERICA,
INDIAN TERRITORY,   } SS.   To Any Person Authorized by Law to Solemnize
SOUTHERN DISTRICT.   Marriage, Greeting:

YOU ARE HEREBY COMMANDED to solemnize the Rite and publish the Banns of Matrimony between Mr.   Edward H. Percival
of   Marlow   in the Indian Territory, aged   22   years, and
M   Alta Kimzey   of   Marlow

Applications for Enrollment of Chickasaw Newborn
Act of 1905 Volume III

in the Indian Territory, aged 18 years, according to law; and do you officially sign and return this license to the parties therein named.

WITNESS my hand and official Seal, this 10th day of February A. D. 190 4

C. M. Campbell
Clerk of the United States Court.
By J. W. Speake, Deputy.

Certificate of Marriage.

UNITED STATES OF AMERICA,
INDIAN TERRITORY, } SS.
SOUTHERN DISTRICT.

I, D.W. Garrison Minister of the Gospel do hereby certify that on the 14th day of February A. D. 190 4 , I did duly and according to law, as commanded in the foregoing License, solemnize the Rite and publish the Banns of Matrimony between the parties therein named.

WITNESS my hand this 15th day of February A. D. 190 4

My credentials are recorded in the office of the Clerk of the United States Court, Indian Territory, Southern District, at Ardmore, Book C. , Page 12

D. W. Garrison
Marlow, I.T.

NOTE. (a)- This License and Certificate of Marriages must be returned to the office of the Clerk of the United States Court in the Indian Territory, at Ardmore, within sixty days from the date thereof, or the party to whom the License was issued will be liable in the amount of ONE HUNDRED DOLLARS ($100).

BIRTH AFFIDAVIT.

DEPARTMENT OF THE INTERIOR.
COMMISSION TO THE FIVE CIVILIZED TRIBES.

IN RE APPLICATION FOR ENROLLMENT, as a citizen of the Chickasaw Nation, of Blanche Percival , born on the 11 day of October , 1904

Name of Father: Edward H. Percival a citizen of the Chickasaw Nation.
Name of Mother: Alta Percival a citizen of the Nation.

Postoffice Marlow, I. T.

Applications for Enrollment of Chickasaw Newborn
Act of 1905   Volume III

AFFIDAVIT OF MOTHER.

UNITED STATES OF AMERICA, Indian Territory,
Southern District   DISTRICT.

I, Alta Percival, on oath state that I am 19 years of age and a citizen by xxx, of the United States Nation; that I am the lawful wife of Edward H. Percival, who is a citizen, by blood of the Chickasaw Nation; that a female child was born to me on 11 day of October, 1904; that said child has been named Blanche Percival, and was living March 4, 1905.

Alta Percival

Witnesses To Mark:
{

Subscribed and sworn to before me this 17 day of March, 1905

Geo.T. Putty
Notary Public.

AFFIDAVIT OF ATTENDING PHYSICIAN OR MID-WIFE.

UNITED STATES OF AMERICA, Indian Territory,
Southern   DISTRICT.

I, T. C. Barnes, a physician, on oath state that I attended on Mrs. Alta Percival, wife of Edward H. Percival on the 11 day of October, 1904; that there was born to her on said date a female child; that said child was living March 4, 1905, and is said to have been named Blanche Percival

T C Barnes, M.D.

Witnesses To Mark:
{

Subscribed and sworn to before me this 17 day of March, 1905

Geo.T. Putty
Notary Public.

Applications for Enrollment of Chickasaw Newborn
Act of 1905   Volume III

9-1277

Muskogee, Indian Territory, March 23, 1905.

Edward H. Percival,
    Marlow, Indian Territory.

Dear Sir:

    Receipt is hereby acknowledged of the affidavits of Alta Percival and T. C. Barnes to the birth of Blanche Percival, daughter of Edward H. and Alta Percival, October 11, 1904, and the same have been filed with our records as an application for the enrollment of said child.

        Respectfully,

        Chairman.

---

9 N.B. 194

Muskogee, Indian Territory April 14, 1905.

Edward H. Percival,
    Marlow, Indian Territory.

Dear Sir:

    You are hereby advised that before the application for the enrollment of your infant child, Blanche Percival, can be finally disposed of, it will be necessary for you to furnish the Commission either the original or a certified copy of the license and certificate of your marriage to her mother, Alta Percival.

    Please attend to this matter at once.

        Respectfully,

        Commissioner in Charge.

Applications for Enrollment of Chickasaw Newborn
Act of 1905   Volume III

9-NB-194.

Muskogee, Indian Territory, June 29, 1905.

Edward H. Percival,
    Marlow, Indian Territory.

Dear Sir:

    Referring to the application for the enrollment of your infant child, Blanche Percival, your attention is called to the Commission's letter of April 14, 1905, in which you were requested to furnish evidence of your marriage to the applicant's mother, Alta Percival, to which you have failed to reply.

    Before any further action can be taken in this matter it will be necessary for you to file with the Commission either the original or a certified copy of the license and certificate of your marriage to Alta Percival.

Respectfully,

Chairman.

Chic. N.B. - 195
    (Tandy J. Miller
    Born April 23, 1904)

BIRTH AFFIDAVIT.

DEPARTMENT OF THE INTERIOR.
COMMISSION TO THE FIVE CIVILIZED TRIBES.

IN RE APPLICATION FOR ENROLLMENT, as a citizen of the Chickasaw Nation, of Tandy J. Miller, born on the 23 day of April, 1904

Name of Father: Jno. M. Miller   a citizen of the Chickasaw Nation.
Name of Mother: Virginia P. Miller   a citizen of the Chickasaw Nation.

Postoffice   Bailey, I.T.

Applications for Enrollment of Chickasaw Newborn
Act of 1905   Volume III

AFFIDAVIT OF MOTHER.

UNITED STATES OF AMERICA, Indian Territory, }
Southern   DISTRICT.

I, Virginia P. Miller, on oath state that I am 27 years of age and a citizen by Inter marriage, of the Chickasaw Nation; that I am the lawful wife of Jno. M. Miller, who is a citizen, by blood of the Chickasaw Nation; that a male child was born to me on 23 day of April, 1904, that said child has been named Tandy J. Miller, and is now living.

                            Virginia P. Miller

Witnesses To Mark:
{

Subscribed and sworn to before me this 18 day of March, 1905.

                        (Name Illegible)
                        Notary Public.

AFFIDAVIT OF ATTENDING PHYSICIAN OR MID-WIFE.

UNITED STATES OF AMERICA, Indian Territory, }
Southern   DISTRICT.

I, J.W. Tucker, a Physician, on oath state that I attended on Mrs. V.P. Miller, wife of Jno. M. Miller on the 23 day of April, 1904; that there was born to her on said date a male child; that said child is now living and is said to have been named Tandy J. Miller

                        J.W. Tucker, M.D.

Witnesses To Mark:
{

Subscribed and sworn to before me this 16 day of march, 1905.

                        V. Smith
                        Notary Public.

Applications for Enrollment of Chickasaw Newborn
Act of 1905   Volume III

Chickasaw 1278.

Muskogee, Indian Territory, April 4, 1905.

Clayton & Brainard, Attorney,
    Muskogee, Indian Territory.

Gentlemen:

    Receipt is hereby acknowledged of your letter of March 31, enclosing the affidavits of Virginia P. Miller and J. W. Tucker to the birth of Tandy J. Miller, son of John M. and Virginia P. Miller, April 23, 1904, and the same have been filed with our records as an application for the enrollment of said child.

                  Respectfully,

                                Commissioner in Charge.

                                      Chickasaw N.B. 195.

Muskogee, Indian Territory, April 12, 1905.

John M. Miller,
    Bailey, Indian Territory.

Dear Sir:

    Receipt is hereby acknowledged of your letter of April 3, and replying to that portion thereof in which you ask if application has been made for the enrollment of your infant child, Tandy J. Miller, son of John M. and Virginia P. Miller, April 23, 1904, have been filed with our records as an application for the enrollment of said child.

                  Respectfully,

                                Commissioner in Charge.

<u>Chic. N.B. - 196</u>
    (Jewel Esther Leftwich
    Born October 9, 1904)

Applications for Enrollment of Chickasaw Newborn
Act of 1905 Volume III

BIRTH AFFIDAVIT.

DEPARTMENT OF THE INTERIOR.
COMMISSION TO THE FIVE CIVILIZED TRIBES.

IN RE APPLICATION FOR ENROLLMENT, as a citizen of the Chickasaw Nation, of Jewel Esther Leftwich , born on the 9" day of Oct , 1904

Name of Father: James Leftwich   a citizen of the Chickasaw Nation.
Name of Mother: Minnie C Leftwich   a citizen of the Chickasaw Nation.

Postoffice   Loco Ind Ter

AFFIDAVIT OF MOTHER.

UNITED STATES OF AMERICA, Indian Territory,
     Southern   DISTRICT.

I, Minnie C Leftwich , on oath state that I am 29 years of age and a citizen by Blood , of the Chickasaw Nation; that I am the lawful wife of James Leftwich , who is a citizen, by Marriage of the Chickasaw Nation; that a female child was born to me on 9" day of October , 1904; that said child has been named Jewel Esther Leftwich , and was living March 4, 1905.

                                                 Minnie C Leftwich

Witnesses To Mark:
{

Subscribed and sworn to before me this 22nd day of March , 1905

                                 N N Hightower
                                        Notary Public.

AFFIDAVIT OF ATTENDING PHYSICIAN OR MID-WIFE.

UNITED STATES OF AMERICA, Indian Territory,
     Southern   DISTRICT.

I, W.C. Thagard , a M.D. , on oath state that I attended on Mrs. Minnie C Leftwich , wife of James Leftwich on the 9" day of October , 1904; that there was born to her on said date a female child; that said child was living March 4, 1905, and is said to have been named Jewel Esther Leftwich

                                   W.C. Thagard MD

Witnesses To Mark:
{

Applications for Enrollment of Chickasaw Newborn
Act of 1905 Volume III

Subscribed and sworn to before me this 22nd day of March , 1905

N N Hightower
Notary Public.

9-1281

Muskogee, Indian Territory, March 29, 1905.

James Leftwich,
 Loco, Indian Territory.

Dear Sir:

Receipt is hereby acknowledged of the affidavits of Minnie C. Leftwich and W. C. Thagard to the birth of Jewel Esther Leftwich, daughter of James and Minnie C. Leftwich, October 9, 1904, and the same have been filed with our records as an application for the enrollment of said child.

Respectfully,

Chairman.

Chic. N.B. - 197
 (Eddie Leroy Reynolds
 Born December 15, 1904)

Applications for Enrollment of Chickasaw Newborn
Act of 1905   Volume III

Certificate of Record of Marriage

United States of America,
   Indian Territory,   } sct.
      Southern District.

I, C. M. CAMPBELL, Clerk of the United States Court, in the Territory and District aforesaid Do HEREBY CERTIFY, that the License for and Certificate of Marriage of

MR   B. F. Reynolds   and

M   Tennie Brisher

were filed in my office in said Territory and District the   16"   day of   March   A.D., 190 3   and duly recorded in Book   G   of Marriage Record, Page   195

WITNESS my hand and Seal of said Court, at Ardmore, this   16"   day of March   A.D. 190 3

C. M. Campbell
                CLERK.

DEPARTMENT OF THE INTERIOR,
COMMISSION TO THE FIVE CIVILIZED TRIBES.
FILED
APR 2*6* 1905
Tams Bixby CHAIRMAN.

FILED
AT ARDMORE.
MAR 16 1903 8AM
**C. M. CAMPBELL, Clerk and Exofficio Recorder.
District No 21 Ind. Ter.**

  MARRIAGE LICENSE

UNITED STATES OF AMERICA,
   INDIAN TERRITORY, } ss:
     SOUTHERN DISTRICT.

To Any Person Authorized by Law to Solemnize Marriage, Greeting:

𝔜ou are hereby commanded to solemnize the Rite and publish the Banns of Matrimony between Mr.   B. F. Reynolds   of   Mill Creek   in the Indian Territory, aged   30   years, and M iss Tennie Brisher   of   Mill Creek   in the Indian Territory, aged   17   years, according to law; and do you officially sign and return this License to the parties therein named.

𝔚itness my hand and official Seal, this   5"   day of   Mch   A. D. 190 3

Applications for Enrollment of Chickasaw Newborn
Act of 1905   Volume III

C.M. Campbell
Clerk of the United States Court.

Certificate of Marriage.

UNITED STATES OF AMERICA,
  INDIAN TERRITORY,   } ss:
  SOUTHERN DISTRICT.   I,   L. W. Wright   a minister

of the gospel   do hereby certify that on the   8   day of   March   , A. D. 1903, I did duly according to law, as commanded in the foregoing License, solemnize the Rite and publish the Banns of Matrimony between the parties therein named.

    Witness my hand this   8   day of   March   A. D. 1903

    My credentials are recorded in the office of the Clerk of the United States Court, Indian Territory, ~~Southern District~~, at ~~Ardmore~~, Book A , Page 186
        (NOTE-The person officiating should fill in the   2nd Judicial (Illegible) Muskogee
        spaces for book and page and sign here.)☞
                                L W Wright
                                a Minister of the gospel

NOTE (a)-The License and Certificate of Marriage must be returned to the office of the Clerk of the United States Court in the Indian Territory, at Ardmore, within sixty days from the date thereof, or the party to whom the License was issued will be liable in the amount of One Hundred Dollars ($100).

NOTE (b)-No person is authorized to perform the Marriage Ceremony in the Southern District unless the proper credentials have first been recorded in the Clerk's office.

BIRTH AFFIDAVIT.
            DEPARTMENT OF THE INTERIOR.
            COMMISSION TO THE FIVE CIVILIZED TRIBES.

        IN RE APPLICATION FOR ENROLLMENT, as a citizen of the   Chickasaw   Nation,
of   Eddie Leroy Reynolds   , born on the 15   day of   December , 1904

Name of Father: Bengeman[sic] F Reynolds   a citizen of the   Chickasaw   Nation.
Name of Mother: Tinnie[sic] L. Reynolds   a citizen of the   U. S.   Nation.

                        Postoffice   Mill Creek I.T.

Applications for Enrollment of Chickasaw Newborn
Act of 1905   Volume III

AFFIDAVIT OF MOTHER.

UNITED STATES OF AMERICA, Indian Territory,
Southern   DISTRICT.

I, Tennie L Reynolds, on oath state that I am 19 years of age and a citizen ~~by~~_____, of the U. S. Nation; that I am the lawful wife of Bengaman F Reynolds, who is a citizen, by Blood of the Chickasaw Nation; that a male child was born to me on 15 day of Dec , 1904; that said child has been named Eddie Leroy Reynolds, and was living March 4, 1905.

Tennie L Reynolds

Witnesses To Mark:

Subscribed and sworn to before me this 14 day of March , 1905

S.W. Frost
Notary Public.

AFFIDAVIT OF ATTENDING PHYSICIAN OR MID-WIFE.

UNITED STATES OF AMERICA, Indian Territory,
Southern   DISTRICT.

I, J H Simmons, a Practicing Physician, on oath state that I attended on Mrs. Tinnie[sic] Reynols[sic], wife of Ben F Reynolds on the 15 day of December , 1904; that there was born to her on said date a male child; that said child was living March 4, 1905, and is said to have been named Ed Reynolds

J.H. Simmons M.D.

Witnesses To Mark:

Subscribed and sworn to before me this 13 day of March , 1905

S.W. Frost
Notary Public.

Applications for Enrollment of Chickasaw Newborn
Act of 1905   Volume III

9-1283

Muskogee, Indian Territory, March 21, 1905.

Walter & Frost,
    Attorneys at Law.
        Millcreek, Indian Territory.

Gentlemen:

    Receipt is hereby acknowledged of your letter of March 16, 1905, enclosing affidavits of Tennie L. Reynolds and J. H. Simmons to the birth of Eddie Leroy Reynolds, son of B. F. and Tennie L. Reynolds, December 15, 1904, and the same have been filed as an application for the enrollment of said child.

        Respectfully,

                Chairman.

---

9 N.B. 197

Muskogee, Indian Territory, April 13, 1905.

Benjamin F. Reynolds,
    Millcreek, Indian Territory.

Dear Sir:

    You are hereby advised that before the application for the enrollment of your infant child, Eddie Leroy Reynolds, can be finally disposed of, it will be necessary for you to furnish the Commission either the original or a certified copy of the license and certificate of your marriage to his mother, Tennie L. Reynolds.

    Please give this matter your immediate attention.

        Respectfully,

                Commissioner in Charge.

Applications for Enrollment of Chickasaw Newborn
Act of 1905 Volume III

9 NB 197

Muskogee, Indian Territory, April 27, 1905.

Walter & Frost,
    Attorneys at Law,
        Millcreek, Indian Territory.

Gentlemen:

    Receipt is hereby acknowledged of your letter of April 22, 1905, enclosing marriage license and certificate between B. F. Reynolds and Tennie Brishers which you offer in support of the application for the enrollment of Eddie Leroy Reynolds and the same have been filed with the record in this case.

        Respectfully,

            Chairman.

Chic. N.B. - 198
    (Alice Marzie Burney
    Born November 10, 1904)

BIRTH AFFIDAVIT.
DEPARTMENT OF THE INTERIOR.
COMMISSION TO THE FIVE CIVILIZED TRIBES.

    IN RE APPLICATION FOR ENROLLMENT, as a citizen of the   Chickasaw   Nation, of   Alice Marzie Burney   , born on the 10th   day of   November   , 1904

Name of Father: Edward Sehon Burney   a citizen of the   Chickasaw   Nation.
                                            By Inter-marriage
Name of Mother: Ada Burney   a citizen of the   Chickasaw Nation.

            Postoffice   Chickasha, Ind. Ter.

Applications for Enrollment of Chickasaw Newborn
Act of 1905   Volume III

AFFIDAVIT OF MOTHER.

UNITED STATES OF AMERICA, Indian Territory, }
Southern   DISTRICT. }

I,   Ada Burney , on oath state that I am Thirty-nine (39)   years of age and a citizen by   Inter-marriage   , of the   Chickasaw   Nation; that I am the lawful wife of   Edward Sehon Burney   , who is a citizen, by   Blood   of the Chickasaw   Nation; that a   Female   child was born to me on   10th   day of   November , 1904, that said child has been named Alice Marzie Burney , and is now living.

Ada Burney

Witnesses To Mark:
{

Subscribed and sworn to before me this 23rd day of March , 1905.

R M Cochran
Notary Public.

AFFIDAVIT OF ATTENDING PHYSICIAN OR MID-WIFE.

UNITED STATES OF AMERICA, Indian Territory, }
Southern   DISTRICT. }

I, W. L. Peters   , a   Physician   , on oath state that I attended on Mrs. Ada Burney , wife of   Edward Sehon Burney   on the   10th   day of November , 1904; that there was born to her on said date a   Female   child; that said child is now living and is said to have been named   Alice Marzie Burney

W.L. Peters M.D.

Witnesses To Mark:
{

Subscribed and sworn to before me this 23rd day of   March , 1905.

R M Cochran
Notary Public.

Applications for Enrollment of Chickasaw Newborn
Act of 1905 Volume III

9-1297

Muskogee, Indian Territory, March 29, 1905.

Edward Sehon Burney,
    Chickasha, Indian Territory.

Dear Sir:

    Receipt is hereby acknowledged of your letter of March 23, 1905, enclosing affidavits of Ada Burney and W. L. Peters to the birth of Alice Marzie Burney, daughter of Edward Sehon and Ada Burney, November 10, 1904, and the same have been filed with our records as an application for the enrollment of said child.

Respectfully,

Chairman.

Chic. N.B. - 199
    (Gracie Walthall
    Born November 25, 1904)

Applications for Enrollment of Chickasaw Newborn
Act of 1905 Volume III

DEPARTMENT OF THE INTERIOR,
COMMISSION TO THE FIVE CIVILIZED TRIBES.
FILED
MAY 3 1905
Tams Bixby CHAIRMAN.

Certificate of Record of Marriage.

UNITED STATES OF AMERICA, }
INDIAN TERRITORY, } sct.
SOUTHERN DISTRICT. }

I, C. M. CAMPBELL, Clerk of the United States Court, in the Territory and District aforesaid do hereby certify, that the License for and Certificate of Marriage of

MR.   Nicklous Walthall
AND
M   A Lena Fitzpatrick

were filed in my office in said Territory and District the 21" day of August A.D., 190 2 and duly recorded in Book F. of Marriage Record, Page 460

WITNESS my hand and Seal of said Court, at Ardmore, this 21" day of Aug A.D. 190 2

C. M. Campbell
CLERK.

☞ Return this License to the United States Clerk at Ardmore, that it may be recorded, when it will be mailed to the proper address.

FILED

AUG 21 1902 8 AM

C. M. CAMPBELL Clerk.
Southern Dist. Ind. Ter.

MARRIAGE LICENSE

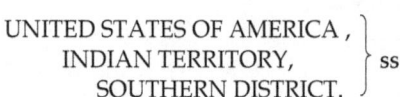

UNITED STATES OF AMERICA, }
INDIAN TERRITORY, } ss:
SOUTHERN DISTRICT. }

To Any Person Authorized by Law to Solemnize Marriage --- Greeting:

You are hereby commanded to solemnize the Rite and publish the Banns of Matrimony between Mr. Nicklous Walthall *of* Ireton *, in the Indian Territory, aged* 18 *years and M* iss A. Lena Fitzpatrick *of* Dibble, I.T. *in the Indian Territory aged* 16 *years according to law, and do you officially sign and return this License to the parties therein named.*

136

Applications for Enrollment of Chickasaw Newborn
Act of 1905 Volume III

Witness *my hand and official seal this* 13th *day of* August *A.D. 190* 2

CM Campbell
Clerk of the United States Court

J W Speake *Deputy*

Certificate of Marriage.

United States of America, } ss. I, J. H. Wilburn
Indian Territory, a minister of the gospel
Southern District.

do hereby certify, that on the 17th day of August , A. D. 190__ , I did duly and according to law, as commanded in the foregoing License, solemnize the Rite and publish the Banns of Matrimony between the parties therein named.

Witness my hand, this 18 day of August , A. D. 190__

My credentials are recorded in the office of the Clerk of the United States Court, Indian Territory, Southern District, at Ardmore, Indian Territory Book____ , Page____

South McAlester

NOTE:-The person officiating should fill in the spaces for book and page and sign here

a _____

NOTE (a)-The License and Certificate of Marriage must be returned to the office of the Clerk of the United States Court in the Indian Territory, at Ardmore, within sixty days from the date thereof, or the party to whom the License was issued will be liable in the amount of One Hundred Dollars ($100).

NOTE (b)-No person is authorized to perform the Marriage Ceremony in the Southern District unless the proper credentials have first been recorded in the Clerk's office.

BIRTH AFFIDAVIT.

IN RE-APPLICATION FOR ENROLLMENT, as a citizen of the Chickasaw Nation, of Gracie Walthall , born on the 25 day of Nov , 190 4

Name of Father: Nicholas M Walthall a citizen of the Chickasaw Nation.
Name of Mother: Lena Walthall a citizen of the ~~Chickas~~ Nation.
 United States

Postoffice Ireton I.T.

Applications for Enrollment of Chickasaw Newborn
Act of 1905   Volume III

AFFIDAVIT OF MOTHER.

UNITED STATES OF AMERICA, INDIAN TERRITORY,
Southern   District.

I,   Lena Walthall   , on oath state that I am   18   years of age and a citizen by _____ , of the   United States   ~~Nation~~; that I am the lawful wife of   Nicholas M Walthall   , who is a citizen, by   Blood   of the   Chickasaw   Nation; that a   Female   child was born to me on   25   day of   November   , 1904 , that said child has been named   Gracie Walthall   , and is now living.

Lena Walthall

Witnesses To Mark:
{

Subscribed and sworn to before me this   17th   day of   March   , 1905.

Ado Melton
Notary Public.

AFFIDAVIT OF ATTENDING PHYSICIAN OR MID-WIFE.

UNITED STATES OF AMERICA, INDIAN TERRITORY,
Southern   District.

I,   J.B. McBride   , a   physician   , on oath state that I attended on Mrs.   Lena Walthall   , wife of   Nicholas M Walthall   on the   25   day of   Nov   , 190 4; that there was born to her on said date a   female   child; that said child is now living and is said to have been named   Gracie Walthall

J.B. McBride, M.D.

Witnesses To Mark:
{

Subscribed and sworn to before me this   17th   day of   Feb   , 1905.

A Melton
Notary Public.

Applications for Enrollment of Chickasaw Newborn
Act of 1905   Volume III

BIRTH AFFIDAVIT.

DEPARTMENT OF THE INTERIOR.
COMMISSION TO THE FIVE CIVILIZED TRIBES.

IN RE APPLICATION FOR ENROLLMENT, as a citizen of the Chickasaw Nation, of Gracie Walthall, born on the 25 day of November, 1904

Name of Father: Nicholas Mondavis Walthall   a citizen of the Chickasaw Nation.
Name of Mother: Lena Walthall   a citizen of the United States Nation.

Postoffice   Ireton I.T.

AFFIDAVIT OF MOTHER.

UNITED STATES OF AMERICA, Indian Territory,
.... DISTRICT.

I, Lena Walthall, on oath state that I am 18 years of age and a citizen by ———, of the United States Nation; that I am the lawful wife of Nicholas Mondavis Walthall, who is a citizen, by blood of the Chickasaw Nation; that a female child was born to me on 25" day of November, 1904; that said child has been named Gracie Walthall, and was living March 4, 1905.

Lena Walthall

Witnesses To Mark:

Subscribed and sworn to before me this 28th day of April, 1905

J.D. Armstrong
Notary Public.
my commission expires Feb 25-1909

AFFIDAVIT OF ATTENDING PHYSICIAN OR MID-WIFE.

UNITED STATES OF AMERICA, Indian Territory,
Southern   DISTRICT.

I, J. B. McBride, a Physician, on oath state that I attended on Mrs. Lena Walthall, wife of Nicholas Mondavis Walthall on the 25" day of November, 1904; that there was born to her on said date a female child; that said child was living March 4, 1905, and is said to have been named Gracie Walthall

J.B. McBride

Applications for Enrollment of Chickasaw Newborn
Act of 1905   Volume III

Witnesses To Mark:
{

Subscribed and sworn to before me this   26   day of   Apr   , 1905

J.D. Armstrong
Notary Public.
my commission expires Feb 25-1909

9-1299

Muskogee, Indian Territory, March 24, 1905.

Bond & Melton,
    Attorneys at Law.
        Chickasha, Indian Territory.

Gentlemen:

    Receipt is hereby acknowledged of your letter of March 17, 1905, enclosing affidavits of Lena Walthall and J. B. McBride to the birth of Gracie Walthall daughter of Nicholas M. and Lena Walthall, November 25, 1904, and the same have been filed with our records as an application for the enrollment of said child.

Respectfully,

Chairman.

Muskogee, Indian Territory, April 15, 1905.

Nicholas Mondavis Walthall,
    Ireton, Indian Territory.

Dear Sir:

    There is inclosed you herewith for execution application for the enrollment of your infant child, Gracie Walthall, born November 25, 1904.

    The affidavit of the physician heretofore filed with the Commission shows the child was living on February 17, 1905. It is necessary, for the child to be enrolled, that all the affidavits show she was living on March 4, 1905.

    You are further advised that before the application can be finally disposed of, it will be necessary for you to furnish the license and certificate of your marriage to the

Applications for Enrollment of Chickasaw Newborn
Act of 1905   Volume III

applicant's mother, Lena Walthall, forwarding same with the return of the inclosed application.

In having these affidavits executed care should be exercised to see that all names are written in full, as they appear in the body of the affidavit, and in the event that either of the persons signing the affidavit are unable to write, signatures by mark must be attested by two witnesses. Each affidavit must be executed before a Notary Public and the notarial seal and signature of the officer must be attached to each separate affidavit.

Respectfully,

LM 15-115   Chairman.

9 N.B. 199.

Muskogee, Indian Territory, May 4, 1905.

Nicholas Mondavis Walthall,
   Ireton, Indian Territory.

Dear Sir:

Receipt is hereby acknowledged of the affidavits of Lena Walthall and J. B. McBride to the birth of Gracie Walthall, daughter of Nicholas Mondavis and Lena Walthall, November 25, 1904; also the marriage license and certificate between Nicklous Walthall and A. Lena Fitzpatrick and the same have been filed with our records in the matter of the enrollment of said child.

Respectfully,

Chairman.

(The letter below does not belong with the current applicant. See NB-194.)

9-NB-196[sic].

Muskogee, Indian Territory, July 14, 1905.

Edward H. Percival,
   Marlow, Indian Territory.

Dear Sir:

Receipt is hereby acknowledged of your letter without date enclosing certified copy of the marriage license and certificate between Edward H. Percival and Alta

Applications for Enrollment of Chickasaw Newborn
Act of 1905 Volume III

Kimzey which you offer in support of the application for the enrollment of your child Blanch[sic] Percival and the same has been filed with the record in this case.

                Respectfully,

                              Commissioner.

Chic. N.B. - 200
    (Alpha Thomas
    Born March 15, 1904)
    (Alma Thomas
    Born March 15, 1904)

BIRTH AFFIDAVIT.

DEPARTMENT OF THE INTERIOR,
COMMISSION TO THE FIVE CIVILIZED TRIBES.

In Re Application for Enrollment, as a citizen of the Chickasaw Nation, of Alpha Thomas, born on the 15th day of March, 1904

Name of Father: Charles Thomas   a citizen of the Chickasaw Nation.
Name of Mother: Nancy Thomas   a citizen of the Choctaw Nation.

                Post-office   Lindsay Ind Territory

AFFIDAVIT OF MOTHER.

UNITED STATES OF AMERICA, }
    INDIAN TERRITORY,
    Southern   District.

    I, Nancy Thomas, on oath state that I am Thirty-nine years of age and a citizen by blood, of the Choctaw Nation; that I am the lawful wife of Charles Thomas, who is a citizen, by Blood of the Chickasaw Nation; that a *twin* female child was born to me on 15th day of March, 1904, that said child has been named Alpha Thomas, and is now living.

                              her
                       Nancy x Thomas
                             mark

Applications for Enrollment of Chickasaw Newborn
Act of 1905   Volume III

WITNESSES TO MARK:
{ A Reeves
{ GH Penn

Subscribed and sworn to before me this 14th day of May , 1904

F.E. Rice
NOTARY PUBLIC.
Southern Dist Ind Ty

AFFIDAVIT OF ATTENDING PHYSICIAN OR MID-WIFE.

UNITED STATES OF AMERICA,
INDIAN TERRITORY,
Southern   District.

I, Benj W Ralston M.D. , a Physician , on oath state that I attended on Mrs. Nancy Thomas , wife of Charles Thomas on the fifteenth day of March , 1904 ; that there was born to her on said date a twin female child; that said child is now living and is said to have been named Alpha Thomas

Benj. W. Ralston M.D.

WITNESSES TO MARK:
{

Subscribed and sworn to before me this 20th day of May , 1904

My commission expires Dec 4" 1907   F.E. Rice
NOTARY PUBLIC.
Southern Dist Ind Terr

BIRTH AFFIDAVIT.

DEPARTMENT OF THE INTERIOR,
COMMISSION TO THE FIVE CIVILIZED TRIBES.

In Re Application for Enrollment, as a citizen of the Chickasaw Nation, of Alma Thomas , born on the 15 day of March , 1904

Name of Father: Charles Thomas   a citizen of the Chickasaw Nation.
Name of Mother: Nancy Thomas   a citizen of the Choctaw Nation.

Post-office   Lindsay Ind Territory

Applications for Enrollment of Chickasaw Newborn
Act of 1905 Volume III

AFFIDAVIT OF MOTHER.

UNITED STATES OF AMERICA, }
INDIAN TERRITORY,
Southern District.

I, Nancy Thomas , on oath state that I am Thirty-nine years of age and a citizen by blood , of the Choctaw Nation; that I am the lawful wife of Charles Thomas , who is a citizen, by blood of the Chickasaw Nation; that a *Twin* female child was born to me on fifteenth day of March, 1904 , that said child has been named Alma Thomas , and is now living.

her
Nancy x Thomas
mark

WITNESSES TO MARK:
{ A Reeves
{ GH Penn

Subscribed and sworn to before me this 14th day of May , 1904

F.E. Rice
NOTARY PUBLIC.
Southern Dist Ind Ty.

AFFIDAVIT OF ATTENDING PHYSICIAN OR MID-WIFE.

UNITED STATES OF AMERICA, }
INDIAN TERRITORY,
Southern District.

I, Benj W Ralston M.D. , a Physician , on oath state that I attended on Mrs. Nancy Thomas , wife of Charles Thomas on the fifteenth day of March , 1904 ; that there was born to her on said date a twin Female child; that said child is now living and is said to have been named Alma Thomas

Benj. W. Ralston M.D.

WITNESSES TO MARK:
{

Subscribed and sworn to before me this 20th day of May , 1904

My commission expires Dec 4"1907 F.E. Rice
NOTARY PUBLIC.
Southern Dist Ind Terr

Applications for Enrollment of Chickasaw Newborn
Act of 1905   Volume III

BIRTH AFFIDAVIT.

DEPARTMENT OF THE INTERIOR.
COMMISSION TO THE FIVE CIVILIZED TRIBES.

IN RE APPLICATION FOR ENROLLMENT, as a citizen of the Chickasaw Nation, of Alma Thomas, born on the 15th day of March, 1904

Name of Father: Charley Thomas   a citizen of the Chickasaw Nation.
                                      Intermarried
Name of Mother: Nancy Thomas   a citizen of the Chickasaw Nation.

                          Postoffice   Lindsay, Indian Territory

AFFIDAVIT OF MOTHER.

UNITED STATES OF AMERICA, Indian Territory,
    Southern   DISTRICT.

I, Nancy Thomas, on oath state that I am 39 years of age and a citizen by Intermarriage, of the Chickasaw Nation; that I am the lawful wife of Charley Thomas, who is a citizen, by Blood of the Chickasaw Nation; that a female child was born to me on fifteenth day of March, 1904; that said child has been named Alma Thomas, and was living March 4, 1905.

                                        her
                               Nancy x Thomas
Witnesses To Mark: mark
    C L McArthur
    L S Burch

Subscribed and sworn to before me this 24th day of March, 1905

                                 F. E. Rice
                                      Notary Public.

AFFIDAVIT OF ATTENDING PHYSICIAN OR MID-WIFE.

UNITED STATES OF AMERICA, Indian Territory,
    Southern   DISTRICT.

I, Benj. W. Ralston M.D., a Physician, on oath state that I attended on Mrs. Nancy Thomas, wife of Charley Thomas on the 15th day of March, 1904; that there was born to her on said date a female (twin) child; that said child was living March 4, 1905, and is said to have been named Alma Thomas

                              Benj. W. Ralston M.D.

Applications for Enrollment of Chickasaw Newborn
Act of 1905   Volume III

Witnesses To Mark:
{

Subscribed and sworn to before me this 24th day of   March   , 1905

F. E. Rice
Notary Public.

BIRTH AFFIDAVIT.

DEPARTMENT OF THE INTERIOR.
COMMISSION TO THE FIVE CIVILIZED TRIBES.

IN RE APPLICATION FOR ENROLLMENT, as a citizen of the   Chickasaw   Nation, of   Alpha Thomas   , born on the   15th   day of   March   , 1904

Name of Father: Charley Thomas   a citizen of the   Chickasaw   Nation.
                                        Intermarried
Name of Mother: Nancy Thomas   a citizen of the   Chickasaw   Nation.

Postoffice   Lindsay, Indian Territory

AFFIDAVIT OF MOTHER.

UNITED STATES OF AMERICA, Indian Territory, }
    Southern   DISTRICT.   }

I,   Nancy Thomas   , on oath state that I am   39   years of age and a citizen by   Intermarriage   , of the   Chickasaw   Nation; that I am the lawful wife of   Charley Thomas   , who is a citizen, by Blood   of the   Chickasaw Nation; that a   female   child was born to me on fifteenth   day of   March   , 1904; that said child has been named   Alpha Thomas   , and was living March 4, 1905.

her
                        Nancy x Thomas
Witnesses To Mark: mark
{ C L McArthur
{ L S Burch

Subscribed and sworn to before me this 24th   day of   March   , 1905

F. E. Rice
Notary Public.

Applications for Enrollment of Chickasaw Newborn
Act of 1905 Volume III

AFFIDAVIT OF ATTENDING PHYSICIAN OR MID-WIFE.

UNITED STATES OF AMERICA, Indian Territory, }
Southern   DISTRICT.

I, Benj. W. Ralston M.D. , a Physician , on oath state that I attended on Mrs. Nancy Thomas , wife of Charley Thomas on the 15th day of March, 1904; that there was born to her on said date a female (twin) child; that said child was living March 4, 1905, and is said to have been named Alpha Thomas

Benj. W. Ralston M.D.

Witnesses To Mark:
{

Subscribed and sworn to before me this 24th day of March , 1905

F. E. Rice
Notary Public.

107

BIRTH AFFIDAVIT.

DEPARTMENT OF THE INTERIOR,
COMMISSION TO THE FIVE CIVILIZED TRIBES.

In Re Application for Enrollment, as a citizen of the Chickasaw Nation, of Alpha Thomas , born on the 15th day of March , 1904

Name of Father: Charley Thomas   a citizen of the Chickasaw Nation.
                                         by Intermarriage
Name of Mother: Nancy Thomas   a citizen of the Chickasaw Nation.

Post-office   Lindsay Ind Territory

AFFIDAVIT OF MOTHER.

UNITED STATES OF AMERICA, }
  INDIAN TERRITORY,
Southern   District.

I, Nancy Thomas , on oath state that I am 39 years of age and a citizen by Intermarriage , of the Chickasaw Nation; that I am the lawful wife of Charley Thomas , who is a citizen, by Blood of the Chickasaw Nation; that a female child was born to me on 15th day of March , 1904 , that said child has been named Alpha Thomas , and is now living.

147

Applications for Enrollment of Chickasaw Newborn
Act of 1905 Volume III

her
Nancy x Thomas
mark

WITNESSES TO MARK:
{ WO Batts
{ W.A. Carlton

Subscribed and sworn to before me this 23rd day of February , 1905

My commission expires　　　　　　　　　F.E. Rice
Dec 4 1907
　　　　　　　　　　　　　　　　　　　　　　NOTARY PUBLIC.

AFFIDAVIT OF ATTENDING PHYSICIAN OR MID-WIFE.

UNITED STATES OF AMERICA,
　INDIAN TERRITORY,
　Southern　　　District.

I, Benj W Ralston , a Practicing Physician , on oath state that I attended on Mrs. Nancy Thomas , wife of Charley Thomas on the 15th day of March , 1904 ; that there was born to her on said date a female *(Twins)* child; that said child is now living and is said to have been named Alpha Thomas

Benj. W. Ralston M.D.

WITNESSES TO MARK:
{

Subscribed and sworn to before me this 23rd day of February , 1905

My commission expires　　　　　　　　　F.E. Rice
Dec 4 1907
　　　　　　　　　　　　　　　　　　　　　　NOTARY PUBLIC.

Applications for Enrollment of Chickasaw Newborn
Act of 1905   Volume III

#108

BIRTH AFFIDAVIT.

DEPARTMENT OF THE INTERIOR,
COMMISSION TO THE FIVE CIVILIZED TRIBES.

In Re Application for Enrollment, as a citizen of the Chickasaw Nation, of   Alma Thomas   , born on the 15th day of March , 1904

Name of Father: Charley Thomas   a citizen of the Chickasaw Nation.
                                        Intermarried
Name of Mother: Nancy Thomas   a citizen of the Chickasaw Nation.

Post-office   Lindsay Indian Territory

AFFIDAVIT OF MOTHER.

UNITED STATES OF AMERICA, ⎫
   INDIAN TERRITORY,   ⎬
  Southern   District. ⎭

I,   Nancy Thomas   , on oath state that I am 39 years of age and a citizen by Intermarriage , of the Chickasaw Nation; that I am the lawful wife of Charley Thomas   , who is a citizen, by Blood of the Chickasaw Nation; that a female child was born to me on 15th day of March , 1904 , that said child has been named   Alma Thomas   , and is now living.

                            her
                      Nancy x Thomas
                          mark

WITNESSES TO MARK:
   { WO Batts
     W.A. Carlton

Subscribed and sworn to before me this 23rd day of February , 1905

My commission expires
Dec 4 1907   F.E. Rice
                                NOTARY PUBLIC.

Applications for Enrollment of Chickasaw Newborn
Act of 1905 Volume III

AFFIDAVIT OF ATTENDING PHYSICIAN OR MID-WIFE.

UNITED STATES OF AMERICA,
   INDIAN TERRITORY,
Southern   District.

I, Benj W Ralston , a Practicing Physician , on oath state that I attended on Mrs. Nancy Thomas , wife of Charley Thomas on the 15th day of March , 1904 ; that there was born to her on said date a female *(Twins)* child; that said child is now living and is said to have been named Alma Thomas

Benj. W. Ralston M.D.

WITNESSES TO MARK:

Subscribed and sworn to before me this 23rd day of February , 1905

My commission expires
Dec 4 1907

F.E. Rice

NOTARY PUBLIC.

Chickasaw N.B.
200.

Muskogee, Indian Territory, April 18, 1905.

F. E. Rice,
   Lindsey, Indian Territory.

Dear Sir:

Receipt is hereby acknowledged of your letter of April 13, asking if affidavits to the birth of Alma and Alpha Thomas had been received.

in reply to your letter you are advised that the affidavits heretofore forwarded to the birth of Alma Thomas and Alpha Thomas, children or Charley and Nancy Thomas, have been filed with our records in support of the application for the enrollment of said children.

Respectfully,

Chairman.

Applications for Enrollment of Chickasaw Newborn
Act of 1905 Volume III

Chic. N.B. - 201
  (Mary Emma Baker
  Born December 2, 1904)

BIRTH AFFIDAVIT.

DEPARTMENT OF THE INTERIOR.
COMMISSION TO THE FIVE CIVILIZED TRIBES.

IN RE APPLICATION FOR ENROLLMENT, as a citizen of the   Chickasaw   Nation, of   Mary Emma Baker , born on the 2nd day of   Dec , 1904

Name of Father: Frank Elmer Baker   a citizen of the   Chickasaw Nation.
Name of Mother: Mary V Baker   a citizen of the   Chickasaw Nation.

Postoffice   Chickasha Ind. Ter.

AFFIDAVIT OF MOTHER.

UNITED STATES OF AMERICA, Indian Territory,
  Southern   DISTRICT.

I,   Mary V. Baker , on oath state that I am   30   years of age and a citizen by   Blood , of the   Chickasaw   Nation; that I am the lawful wife of   Frank Elmer Baker , who is a citizen, by   Intermarriage   of the   Chickasaw   Nation; that a   Female   child was born to me on   2nd day of   December , 1904, that said child has been named   Mary Emma Baker , and is now living.

                                         Mary V. Baker
Witnesses To Mark:

Subscribed and sworn to before me this   20th   day of   March , 1905.

                                         JD Carmichael
                                              Notary Public.

AFFIDAVIT OF ATTENDING PHYSICIAN OR MID-WIFE.

UNITED STATES OF AMERICA, Indian Territory,
  Southern   DISTRICT.

I,   R.P. Tye M.D. , a   Physician , on oath state that I attended on Mrs.   Mary V. Baker , wife of   Frank Elmer Baker   on the   2nd   day of

Applications for Enrollment of Chickasaw Newborn
Act of 1905 Volume III

December , 1904; that there was born to her on said date a Female child; that said child is now living and is said to have been named Mary Emma Baker

R.P. Tye M.D.

Witnesses To Mark:
{

Subscribed and sworn to before me this 20th day of March , 1905.

B.B. (Illegible)
Notary Public.

Chic. N.B. - 202
    (Elizabeth Johnson
    Born October 21, 1902)

BIRTH AFFIDAVIT.

DEPARTMENT OF THE INTERIOR,
COMMISSION TO THE FIVE CIVILIZED TRIBES.

IN RE Application for Enrollment, as a citizen of the Chickasaw Nation, of Elizabeth Johnson , born on the 21 day of October , 1902

Name of Father: Henry B Johnson   a citizen of the Chickasaw Nation.
Name of Mother: Effie M Johnson   a citizen of the " Nation.

Post-Office: Chickasha, I.T.

AFFIDAVIT OF MOTHER.

UNITED STATES OF AMERICA, ⎫
    INDIAN TERRITORY.   ⎬
  Southern   District. ⎭

    I, Effie M Johnson , on oath state that I am 29 years of age and a citizen by inter-marriage , of the Chickasaw Nation; that I am the lawful wife of HB Johnson , who is a citizen, by blood of the Chickasaw Nation; that a female child was born to me on 21 day of October , 1902 , that said child has been named Elizabeth Johnson , and is now living.

Applications for Enrollment of Chickasaw Newborn
Act of 1905 Volume III

Effie M Johnson

WITNESSES TO MARK:

{

Subscribed and sworn to before me this 5th *day of* November , 1902

JH Melton Notary Public
Tarrant Co Texas

AFFIDAVIT OF ATTENDING PHYSICIAN OR MID-WIFE.

UNITED STATES OF AMERICA,
INDIAN TERRITORY.
Tarrant Co Texas District.

I, I.L. Van Zandt , a Physician , on oath state that I attended on Mrs. Effie Johnson , wife of H.B. Johnson on the 21st day of October , 1902 ; that there was born to her on said date a female child; that said child is now living and is said to have been named Elizabeth

I.L. Van Zandt M.D.

WITNESSES TO MARK:

{

Subscribed and sworn to before me this 4th *day of* November , 1902

JH Melton Notary Public
Tarrant Co Texas

BIRTH AFFIDAVIT.

DEPARTMENT OF THE INTERIOR.
COMMISSION TO THE FIVE CIVILIZED TRIBES.

IN RE APPLICATION FOR ENROLLMENT, as a citizen of the Chickasaw Nation, of Elizabeth Johnson , born on the 21st day of October , 1902

Name of Father: Henry Belton Johnson a citizen of the Chickasaw Nation.
Name of Mother: Effie M. Johnson a citizen of the Chickasaw Nation.

Postoffice Chickasha Ind Ter

Applications for Enrollment of Chickasaw Newborn
Act of 1905   Volume III

AFFIDAVIT OF MOTHER.

State of Missouri
UNITED STATES OF AMERICA, ~~Indian Territory~~,
Jackson County   ~~DISTRICT.~~

I, Effie M. Johnson , on oath state that I am 29 years of age and a citizen by intermarriage , of the Chickasaw Nation; that I am the lawful wife of Henry Belton Johnson , who is a citizen, by blood of the Chickasaw Nation; that a female child was born to me on 21 day of October , 1902; that said child has been named Elizabeth Johnson , and was living March 4, 1905.

                        Effie M Johnson

Witnesses To Mark:
{ (Name Illegible)
{ Mary M Embry

Subscribed and sworn to before me this 21st day of April , 1905

                        Hughes Bryant
                        Notary Public.

AFFIDAVIT OF ATTENDING PHYSICIAN OR MID-WIFE.

State of Texas
UNITED STATES OF AMERICA, ~~Indian Territory~~,
Tarrant County   ~~DISTRICT.~~

                        affirmation
I, I.L. Van Zandt , a physician , on ~~oath~~ state that I attended on Mrs. Effie M Johnson , wife of Henry Belton Johnson on the 21 day of October , 1902; that there was born to her on said date a _____ child; that said child ~~was living March 4, 1905, and is~~ said to have been named Elizabeth Johnson
Have heard and believe the child was living Mar 4, 05
Witnesses To Mark: I.L. Van Zandt M.D.
{ CE Gillham
{ K M Van Zandt
       affirmed
Subscribed and ~~sworn~~ to before me this 24th day of April , 1905

                        (Name Illegible)
                        Notary Public.

Applications for Enrollment of Chickasaw Newborn
Act of 1905   Volume III

9 N B 202

Muskogee, Indian Territory, April 17, 1905.

Henry Bilton[sic] Johnson,
  Chickasha, Indian Territory.

Dear Sir:

There is inclosed you herewith for execution application for the enrollment of your infant child, Elizabeth Johnson, born October 21, 1902.

The affidavits heretofore filed with the Commission show the child was living on November 4, 1902. It is necessary, for the child to be enrolled, that she was living on March 4, 1905.

In having these affidavits executed care should be exercised to see that all names are written in full, as they appear in the body of the affidavit, and in the event that either of the persons signing the affidavit are unable to write, signatures by mark must be attested by two witnesses. Each affidavit must be executed before a Notary Public and the notarial seal and signature of the officer must be attached to each separate affidavit.

Respectfully,

LM 17-125.   Chairman.

Chickasaw N.B. 202

Muskogee, Indian Territory, May 1, 1905.

H. B. Johnson,
  Chickasha, Indian Territory.

Dear Sir:

Receipt is hereby acknowledged of the affidavits of Effie M. Johnson and I. L. Van Zandt to the birth of Elizabeth Johnson, daughter of Henry Belton and Effie M. Johnson, October 21, 1902, and the same have been filed with our records in the matter of the enrollment of said child.

Respectfully,

Chairman.

Applications for Enrollment of Chickasaw Newborn
Act of 1905   Volume III

Chic. N.B. - 203
(Josephine Keno
Born April 22, 1904)

It appearing from the within affidavits that Josephine Keno, for enrollment application was made under the Act of Congress approved March 3, 1905 (33 Stat. 1060), died prior to March 4, 1905, I am of the opinion that the application for her enrollment as a citizen by blood of the Chickasaw Nation, should be and the same is, dismissed.

Tams Bixby
Commissioner.

Muskogee, Indian Territory.
FEB 18 1907

DEPARTMENT OF THE INTERIOR.
COMMISSION TO THE FIVE CIVILIZED TRIBES.

N.B.   In the matter of the death of   application pending   Josephine Keno a^citizen of the   Chickasaw   Nation, ^ who formerly resided at or near   Chickasha , Ind. Ter., and died on the   17th day of   February   , 1905

AFFIDAVIT OF RELATIVE.

UNITED STATES OF AMERICA, Indian Territory,
Southern   DISTRICT.

husband of

I, B.W. Holt   , on oath state that I am 23   years of age and^a citizen by blood , of the Chickasaw Nation; that my postoffice address is   Ninnekah   , Ind. Ter.; that I am the husband of a Sister   of   Josephine Keno   who was a citizen, by blood   , of the Chickasaw   Nation and that said   Josephine Keno   died on the .... day of   February   , 1905

B W Holt

Witnesses To Mark:

Subscribed and sworn to before me this   1st day of   February   , 1907

(Name Illegible)
Notary Public.

Applications for Enrollment of Chickasaw Newborn
Act of 1905 Volume III

Father
AFFIDAVIT OF ~~ACQUAINTANCE~~.

UNITED STATES OF AMERICA, Indian Territory, }
Southern   DISTRICT.   }

I, M. Keno   , on oath state that I am about 58 years of age, and a citizen ~~by~~ ——— of the   U.S.A. (?) Nation; that my postoffice address is   Lucile   , Ind. Ter.; that I ~~was personally acquainted with~~ am the father of Josephine Keno   who was a citizen, by blood , of the Chickasaw Nation; and that said Josephine Keno   died on the 17th   day of February , 1905   His
                                                M + Keno
Witnesses To Mark: mark
{ Jacob Homer
{ (Name Illegible)

Subscribed and sworn to before me this 2nd   day of   February   , 1907

(Name Illegible)
Notary Public.

M. Keno a Mexican by birth has lived continuously in U.S.A for past forty years but has no naturalization papers.   L.P.B.

BIRTH AFFIDAVIT.
DEPARTMENT OF THE INTERIOR.
COMMISSION TO THE FIVE CIVILIZED TRIBES.

IN RE APPLICATION FOR ENROLLMENT, as a citizen of the   Chickasaw   Nation, of Josaphine[sic] Keno , born on the 22 day of April , 1904

Name of Father: M Keno   a citizen of the United States Nation.
Name of Mother: Emily Keno   a citizen of the   Chickasaw Nation.

Postoffice   Tulsa I.T.

AFFIDAVIT OF MOTHER.

UNITED STATES OF AMERICA, Indian Territory, }
Western   DISTRICT.   }

I, Emily Keno   , on oath state that I am about 36   years of age and a citizen by   blood   , of the   Chickasaw   Nation; that I am the lawful wife of M Keno   , who is a citizen, by .... of the   United States   ~~Nation~~; that a

157

Applications for Enrollment of Chickasaw Newborn
Act of 1905   Volume III

female   child was born to me on   22   day of   April   , 1904, that said child has been named   Josaphine   , and is now living.

her
Emily x Keno
mark

Witnesses To Mark:
{ B.M. *(Illegible)*
  W.D. Abbott

    Subscribed and sworn to before me this 24th day of   October   , 1904

My Com expires Oct. 11, 1906.   Walter I Reneau
                                                    Notary Public.

AFFIDAVIT OF ATTENDING PHYSICIAN OR MID-WIFE.

UNITED STATES OF AMERICA, Indian Territory, }
     Western   DISTRICT.

    I,   J.W. Hensley   , a   Physician   , on oath state that I attended on Mrs.   Emily Keno   , wife of   M Keno   on the   22   day of April 1904 , 1........; that there was born to her on said date a   female   child; that said child is now living and is said to have been named Josaphine

                                      J W Hensley MD

Witnesses To Mark:
{ WD Rowell
  EP Stamp

    Subscribed and sworn to before me this   26th day of   Oct , 1904

                                  (Name Illegible)
                                    Notary Public.

Applications for Enrollment of Chickasaw Newborn
Act of 1905   Volume III

COMMISSIONERS:
TAMS BIXBY,
THOMAS B. NEEDLES,
C.R. BRECKINBRIDGE.

WM. O. BEALL
Secretary

DEPARTMENT OF THE INTERIOR,
COMMISSIONER TO THE FIVE CIVILIZED TRIBES.

W^{m}O.B.

REFER IN REPLY TO THE FOLLOWING:

9 N B 203

ADDRESS ONLY THE
COMMISSION TO THE FIVE CIVILIZED TRIBES.

Muskogee, Indian Territory, April 15, 1905.

M. Keno,
    Tulsa, Indian Territory.

Dear Sir:

    There is inclosed you herewith for execution application for the enrollment of your infant child, Josephine Keno, born April 22, 1904.

    The affidavits heretofore filed with the Commission show the child was living on October 26, 1904. It is necessary, for the child to be enrolled, that she was living on March 4, 1905.

    In having these affidavits executed care should be exercised to see that all names are written in full, as they appear in the body of the affidavit, and in the event that either of the persons signing the affidavit are unable to write, signatures by mark must be attested by two witnesses. Each affidavit must be executed before a Notary Public and the notarial seal and signature of the officer must be attached to each separate affidavit.

                       Respectfully,
                         Tams Bixby

LM 15-170   Chairman.

Applications for Enrollment of Chickasaw Newborn
Act of 1905   Volume III

aP

COMMISSIONERS:
TAMS BIXBY,
THOMAS B. NEEDLES,
C.R. BRECKINBRIDGE.
WM. O. BEALL
Secretary

DEPARTMENT OF THE INTERIOR,
COMMISSIONER TO THE FIVE CIVILIZED TRIBES.

REFER IN REPLY TO THE FOLLOWING:

9 N B 203

ADDRESS ONLY THE
COMMISSION TO THE FIVE CIVILIZED TRIBES.

Muskogee, Indian Territory, June 29, 1905.

Emily Keno,
   Tulsa, Indian Territory.

Dear Madam:

    There is enclosed herewith for execution application for the enrollment of your infant child, Josephine Keno, born April 22, 1904. The affidavits heretofore filed with the Commission show that the child was living on October 26, 1904. It is necessary, for the child to be enrolled, that she was living on March 4, 1905.

    In having these affidavits executed care should be exercised to see that all names are written in full, as they appear in the body of the affidavit, and if either of the persons signing the affidavits is unable to write, signature by mark must be attested by two witnesses. Each affidavit must be executed before a Notary Public and the notarial seal and signature of the officer must be attached to each separate affidavit.

    You are requested to give this matter your immediate attention, as no further action can be taken until these affidavits are filed with the Commission.

                         Respectfully,
                           Tams Bixby
DeB--6/29.   Chairman.

Applications for Enrollment of Chickasaw Newborn
Act of 1905   Volume III

REFER IN REPLY TO THE FOLLOWING:

9-NB-203

DEPARTMENT OF THE INTERIOR,
COMMISSIONER TO THE FIVE CIVILIZED TRIBES.

Muskogee, Indian Territory, August 16, 1905.

Emily Keno,
    Tulsa, Indian Territory.

Dear Madam:

    On April 15, 1905, and June 29, 1905, letters were addressed to you by the Commission to the Five Civilized Tribes requesting you to furnish this Office with proof of birth of your minor daughter, Josephine Keno, and with each letter a blank for proof of her birth, properly filled out, was enclosed.

    You are again requested to furnish such proof, and you are advised that until the same is filed with this Office, nothing further can be done in the matter of the enrollment of said Josephine Keno as a citizen by blood of the Chickasaw Nation.

                               Respectfully,
SEP 30 1905   W^m.O.Beall
                                          Acting Commissioner.

9-NB-203

Muskogee, Indian Territory, February 13, 1905.

Emily Keno,
    Ninnekah, Indian Territory.

Dear Madam:

    Letters have heretofore been addressed to you and your husband, M. Keno, requesting proof of the birth of your minor child, Josephine Keno, and with each letter a proof of birth was inclosed.

    You are now requested to have one of the blanks previously inclosed you executed and returned this office at once, in order that disposition may be made of the application for the enrollment of your child, Josephine Keno.

                                   Respectfully,

                                  Acting Commissioner.

Applications for Enrollment of Chickasaw Newborn
Act of 1905 Volume III

aP

REFER IN REPLY TO THE FOLLOWING:
9-NB-203

DEPARTMENT OF THE INTERIOR,
COMMISSIONER TO THE FIVE CIVILIZED TRIBES.

Muskogee, Indian Territory, February 27, 1907.

M. Keno,
    Tulsa, Indian Territory.

Dear Sir:

    You are hereby advised that it appearing from the records of this office that your minor child Josephine Keno, died prior to March 4, 1905, the Commissioner to the Five Civilized Tribes, on February 18, 1907, dismissed the application for her enrollment as a citizen by blood of the Chickasaw Nation.

                  Respectfully,
                  Tams Bixby
                        Commissioner.

<u>Chic. N.B. - 204</u>
    (Edgar Ray Jordan
    Born January 7, 1905)

BIRTH AFFIDAVIT.

DEPARTMENT OF THE INTERIOR.
COMMISSION TO THE FIVE CIVILIZED TRIBES.

    IN RE APPLICATION FOR ENROLLMENT, as a citizen of the Chickasaw Nation, of Edgar Ray Jordan, born on the 7th day of January, 1905.

Name of Father: William Gaston Jordan   a citizen of the Chickasaw Nation.
Name of Mother: Ethel Jordan   a citizen of the Chickasaw Nation.

                  Postoffice   Sulphur, Indian Territory

Applications for Enrollment of Chickasaw Newborn
Act of 1905 Volume III

AFFIDAVIT OF MOTHER.

UNITED STATES OF AMERICA, Indian Territory, }
Southern DISTRICT. }

I, Ethel Jordan, on oath state that I am 31 years of age and a citizen by Blood, of the Chickasaw Nation; that I am the lawful wife of William Gaston Jordan, who is a citizen, by Marriage of the Chickasaw Nation; that a Male child was born to me on 7th day of January, 1905; that said child has been named Edgar Ray Jordan, and was living March 4, 1905.

Ethel Jordan

Witnesses To Mark:
{

Subscribed and sworn to before me this 21 day of January, 1905

My Commission Expires June 27, 1907   AD Goodenough
Notary Public.

AFFIDAVIT OF ATTENDING PHYSICIAN OR MID-WIFE.

UNITED STATES OF AMERICA, Indian Territory, }
Southern DISTRICT. }

I, G.W. Slover, a Physician, on oath state that I attended on Mrs. Ethel Jordan, wife of William Gaston Jordan on the 7th day of January, 1905; that there was born to her on said date a Male child; that said child was living March 4, 1905, and is said to have been named Edgar Ray Jordan

G.W. Slover M.D.

Witnesses To Mark:
{

Subscribed and sworn to before me this 23 day of March, 1905

My Commission Expires June 27, 1907   AD Goodenough
Notary Public.

Applications for Enrollment of Chickasaw Newborn
Act of 1905 Volume III

BIRTH AFFIDAVIT.

DEPARTMENT OF THE INTERIOR.
COMMISSION TO THE FIVE CIVILIZED TRIBES.

IN RE APPLICATION FOR ENROLLMENT, as a citizen of the Chickasaw Nation, of Edgar Ray Jordan, born on the 7th day of January, 1905

Name of Father: Willis Gaston Jordan   a citizen of the Chickasaw Nation.
Name of Mother: Ethel Jordan   a citizen of the Chickasaw Nation.

Postoffice   Sulphur, Ind Ter

AFFIDAVIT OF MOTHER.

UNITED STATES OF AMERICA, Indian Territory,
Southern DISTRICT.

I, Ethel Jordan, on oath state that I am 31 years of age and a citizen by blood, of the Chickasaw Nation; that I am the lawful wife of Willis Gaston Jordan, who is a citizen, by intermarriage of the Chickasaw Nation; that a male child was born to me on 7th day of January, 1905; that said child has been named Edgar Ray Jordan, and was living March 4, 1905.

Ethel Jordan

Witnesses To Mark:

Subscribed and sworn to before me this 19th day of May, 1905

My Commission Expires June 27, 1907   AD Goodenough
Notary Public.

AFFIDAVIT OF ATTENDING PHYSICIAN OR MID-WIFE.

UNITED STATES OF AMERICA, Indian Territory,
Southern DISTRICT.

I, G.W. Slover, a Physician, on oath state that I attended on Mrs. Ethel Jordan, wife of Willis Gaston Jordan on the 7th day of January, 1905; that there was born to her on said date a Male child; that said child was living March 4, 1905, and is said to have been named Edgar Ray Jordan

G.W. Slover M.D.

Witnesses To Mark:

Applications for Enrollment of Chickasaw Newborn
Act of 1905   Volume III

Subscribed and sworn to before me this 22 day of May , 1905

My Commission Expires June 27, 1907   AD Goodenough
                                            Notary Public.

BIRTH AFFIDAVIT.

DEPARTMENT OF THE INTERIOR.
COMMISSION TO THE FIVE CIVILIZED TRIBES.

IN RE APPLICATION FOR ENROLLMENT, as a citizen of the   Chickasaw   Nation, of   Edgar Ray Jordan   , born on the 7th   day of   January , 1905

Name of Father: William Gaston Jordan   a citizen of the   Chickasaw   Nation.
Name of Mother: Ethel Jordan   a citizen of the   Chickasaw   Nation.

Postoffice   **SULPHUR, I. T.**

AFFIDAVIT OF MOTHER.

UNITED STATES OF AMERICA, Indian Territory,}
    Southern   DISTRICT.

I,   Ethel Jordan   , on oath state that I am   31   years of age and a citizen by blood   , of the   Chickasaw   Nation; that I am the lawful wife of   William Gaston Jordan   , who is a citizen, by intermarriage   of the   Chickasaw   Nation; that a   Male   child was born to me on   7th   day of   January   , 1905; that said child has been named   Edgar Ray Jordan   , and was living March 4, 1905.

                                            Ethel Jordan

Witnesses To Mark:
{

Subscribed and sworn to before me this 19th day of May , 1905

My Commission Expires June 27, 1907   AD Goodenough
                                            Notary Public.

AFFIDAVIT OF ATTENDING PHYSICIAN OR MID-WIFE.

UNITED STATES OF AMERICA, Indian Territory,}
    Southern   DISTRICT.

I,   G.W. Slover   , a   Physician   , on oath state that I attended on Mrs. Ethel Jordan   , wife of   William Jordan   on the 7th   day of   January   ,

165

Applications for Enrollment of Chickasaw Newborn
Act of 1905   Volume III

1905; that there was born to her on said date a   male   child; that said child was living March 4, 1905, and is said to have been named Edgar Ray Jordan

G.W. Slover M.D.

Witnesses To Mark:

{

Subscribed and sworn to before me this 22   day of   May   , 1905

My Commission Expires June 27, 1907   AD Goodenough
                                              Notary Public.

9-1365

Muskogee, Indian Territory, March 30, 1905.

A. D. Goodenough,
    Sulphur, Indian Territory.

Dear Sir:

   Receipt is hereby acknowledged of your letter of March 22, 1905, enclosing affidavits of Ethel Jordan and G. W. Slover to the birth of Edgar Roy[sic] Jordan, son of William Gaston and Ethel Jordan, January 7, 1905, and the same have been filed with our records as an application for the enrollment of said child.

Respectfully,

Chairman.

9-NB-204.

Muskogee, Indian Territory, May 13, 1905.

Willis Gaston Jordan,
    Sulpher[sic], Indian Territory.

Dear Sir:

   There is enclosed you herewith for execution application for the enrollment of your infant child, Edgar Ray Jordan, born January 7, 1905.

   The affidavits heretofore filed with the Commission show the child was living January 21, 1904. It is necessary, for the child to be enrolled, that he was living on March 4, 1905.

Applications for Enrollment of Chickasaw Newborn
Act of 1905   Volume III

In having these affidavits executed care should be exercised to see that all names are written in full, as they appear in the body of the affidavit, and in the event that either of the persons signing the affidavit are unable to write, signatures by mark must be attested by two witnesses. Each affidavit must be executed before a Notary Public and the notarial seal and signature of the officer must be attached to each separate affidavit.

Respectfully,

Chairman.

V. 13/5.

9-N.B. 204.

Muskogee, Indian Territory, May 26, 1905.

A. D. Goodenough,
    Sulphur, Indian Territory.

Dear Sir:

Receipt is hereby acknowledged of the affidavits of Ethel Jordan and G. W. Slover to the birth of Edgar Ray Jordan, son of William Gaston Jordan, January 7, 1905, and the same have been filed with the record in the matter of the enrollment of this child.

Respectfully,

Chairman.

Chic. N.B. - 205
    (Roland Jack
    Born July 22, 1903)

Applications for Enrollment of Chickasaw Newborn
Act of 1905 Volume III

BIRTH AFFIDAVIT.

DEPARTMENT OF THE INTERIOR.
COMMISSION TO THE FIVE CIVILIZED TRIBES.

IN RE APPLICATION FOR ENROLLMENT, as a citizen of the Chickasaw Nation, of Roland Jack, born on the 22 day of July, 1903

Name of Father: J.T. Jack   a citizen of the United States Nation.
Name of Mother: Mary Jack   a citizen of the Chickasaw Nation.

Postoffice   Sulphur I.T.

AFFIDAVIT OF MOTHER.

UNITED STATES OF AMERICA, Indian Territory,
Southern   DISTRICT.

I, Mary Jack, on oath state that I am 27 years of age and a citizen by Blood, of the Chickasaw Nation; that I am the lawful wife of J.T. Jack, who is a citizen, by Birth of the United States Nation; that a Male child was born to me on 22nd day of July, 1903; that said child has been named Roland Jack, and was living March 4, 1905.

                             Mary Jack

Witnesses To Mark:
{

Subscribed and sworn to before me this 6th day of April, 1905.

                         Eugene E. White
                             Notary Public.

AFFIDAVIT OF ATTENDING PHYSICIAN OR MID-WIFE.

UNITED STATES OF AMERICA, Indian Territory,
.... DISTRICT.

I, Jesse Bird, a Physician, on oath state that I attended on Mrs. Mary Jack, wife of J.T. Jack on the 22nd day of July, 1903; that there was born to her on said date a Male child; that said child was living March 4, 1905, and is said to have been named Roland Jack

                         Jesse Bird, M.D.

Witnesses To Mark:
{

Applications for Enrollment of Chickasaw Newborn
Act of 1905   Volume III

Subscribed and sworn to before me this 1 day of   April   , 1905

W.S. Partain
Notary Public.

9-1360

Muskogee, Indian Territory, January 21, 1904.

Mary Jack,
    Drake, Indian Territory.

Dear Madam:

    Receipt is hereby acknowledged of your letter of the 15th inst., enclosing the certificate of Jesse Bird, a physician, relative to the birth of your infant child Rolan[sic] Jack, July 22, 1903, and you state you desire to make application for the enrollment of said child.

    You are informed that under the provisions of the Act of Congress approved July 1, 1902 (32 Stats., 641), the Commission is now without authority to receive or consider the original application for enrollment of any person whomsoever as a citizen of the Choctaw or Chickasaw Nation.

Respectfully,

Commissioner in Charge.

Daugherty, I.T
Jan 14th

To Whom it may concern

This is to certify that Roland Jack was born of Mary Jack on the 22nd Day of July 1903. I was the attending physician.

    signed.   Jesse Bird M.D.

Applications for Enrollment of Chickasaw Newborn
Act of 1905   Volume III

Chic. N.B. - 206
   (Ruby Leah Cooper
   Born October 23, 1903)

DEPARTMENT OF THE INTERIOR,
COMMISSION TO THE FIVE CIVILIZED TRIBES.

Record in the matter of the application for enrollment as a citizen by blood of the Chickasaw [sic] of:

RUBY LEAH COOPER   9-NB-206.

W.J.
9-NB-206.

DEPARTMENT OF THE INTERIOR,
COMMISSION TO THE FIVE CIVILIZED TRIBES.

In the matter of the application for the enrollment of Ruby Leah Cooper as a citizen by blood of the Chickasaw Nation.

---oOo---

It appears from the record herein that on March 4, 1905 there was filed with the Commission application for the enrollment of Ruby Leah Cooper as a citizen by blood of the Chickasaw Nation.

It further appears from the record in this case and the records of the Commission that the applicant was born on October 3, 1903; that she is a daughter of Demis Mattie Cooper, a recognized and enrolled citizen by blood of the Chickasaw Nation whose name appears as number 3852 upon the final roll of citizens by blood of the Chickasaw Nation, approved by the Secretary of the Interior December 12, 1902, and William W. Cooper, a recognized and enrolled citizen by intermarriage of the Chickasaw Nation; and that said applicant died October 20, 1904.

The Act of Congress approved March 3, 1905, (Public No. 212) among other things provides:

"That the Commission to the Five Civilized Tribes is authorized for sixty days after the date of the approval of this act to receive and consider applications for enrollment of children born subsequent to September twenty-fifth, nineteen hundred and two, and prior to March fourth, nineteen hundred and five, and who were living on said latter date, to citizens by blood of the Choctaw and Chickasaw tribes of Indians whose enrollment has been approved by the Secretary of the Interior prior to the date of the approval of this act; and to enroll and make allotments to such children."

It is, therefore, hereby ordered that the application for the enrollment of Ruby Leah Cooper as a citizen by blood of the Chickasaw Nation be dismissed in accordance with the order of the Commission of March 31, 1905.

Applications for Enrollment of Chickasaw Newborn
Act of 1905 Volume III

COMMISSION TO THE FIVE CIVILIZED TRIBES,

Tams Bixby
Chairman.

Muskogee, Indian Territory.
JUN 16 1905

BIRTH AFFIDAVIT.

DEPARTMENT OF THE INTERIOR.
COMMISSION TO THE FIVE CIVILIZED TRIBES.

IN RE APPLICATION FOR ENROLLMENT, as a citizen of the Chickasaw Nation, of Ruby Leah Cooper, born on the 23 day of Oct, 1903

Name of Father: William W Cooper   a citizen of the Chickasaw Nation.
Name of Mother: Demis M Cooper   a citizen of the " "   Nation.

Postoffice   Roff I.T.

AFFIDAVIT OF MOTHER.

UNITED STATES OF AMERICA, Indian Territory,
Southern   DISTRICT.

I, Demis M Cooper, on oath state that I am 39 years of age and a citizen by Blood, of the Chickasaw Nation; that I am the lawful wife of William W Cooper, who is a citizen, by marriage of the Chickasaw Nation; that a Female child was born to me on 23 day of Oct, 1903, that said child has been named Ruby Leah Cooper, and is now ~~living~~. *dead*

Demis M Cooper

Witnesses To Mark:

Subscribed and sworn to before me this 2 day of March, 1905.

My Commission Expires Mar. 12, 1908.   AJ Turner
Notary Public.

Applications for Enrollment of Chickasaw Newborn
Act of 1905 Volume III

AFFIDAVIT OF ATTENDING PHYSICIAN OR MID-WIFE.

UNITED STATES OF AMERICA, Indian Territory, }
Southern   DISTRICT.

I, Dr J A Deen , a Doctor , on oath state that I attended on Mrs. Demis M Cooper , wife of William W Cooper on the 23 day of Oct, 1903; that there was born to her on said date a Female child; that said child is now ~~living~~ and is said to have been named Ruby Leah Cooper
dead

J.A. Deen, M.D.

Witnesses To Mark:
{

Subscribed and sworn to before me this 2 day of March , 1905.

AJ Turner
Notary Public.

10.F.
9-NB-206.

DEPARTMENT OF THE INTERIOR,
COMMISSION TO THE FIVE CIVILIZED TRIBES.

In the matter of the application for the enrollment of Ruby Leah Cooper as a citizen by blood of the Chickasaw Nation.

---oOo---

It appears from the record herein that on March 4, 1905 there was filed with the Commission application for the enrollment of Ruby Leah Cooper as a citizen by blood of the Chickasaw Nation.

It further appears from the record in this case and the records of the Commission that the applicant was born on October 3, 1903; that she is a daughter of Demis Mattie Cooper, a recognized and enrolled citizen by blood of the Chickasaw Nation whose name appears as number 3852 upon the final roll of citizens by blood of the Chickasaw Nation, approved by the Secretary of the Interior December 12,1902, and William W. Cooper, a recognized and enrolled citizen by intermarriage of the Chickasaw Nation; and that said applicant died October 20, 1904.

The Act of Congress approved March 3, 1905, (Public No. 212) among other things provides:

"That the Commission to the Five Civilized Tribes is authorized for sixty days after the date of the approval of this act to receive and consider applications for enrollment of children born subsequent to September twenty-fifth, nineteen hundred and two, and prior to March fourth, nineteen hundred and five, <u>and who were living on said latter date,</u> to citizens by blood of the Choctaw and

Applications for Enrollment of Chickasaw Newborn
Act of 1905   Volume III

Chickasaw tribes of Indians whose enrollment has been approved by the Secretary of the Interior prior to the date of the approval of this act; and to enroll and make allotments to such children."

It is, therefore, hereby ordered that the application for the enrollment of Ruby Leah Cooper as a citizen by blood of the Chickasaw Nation be dismissed in accordance with the order of the Commission of March 31, 1905.

COMMISSION TO THE FIVE CIVILIZED TRIBES,

Tams Bixby
Chairman.

Muskogee, Indian Territory.
JUN 16 1905

9-NB-206

Muskogee, Indian Territory, June 16, 1905.
COPY

William W. Cooper,
Roff, Indian Territory.

Dear Sir:

Inclosed herewith you will find a copy of the order of this Commission, dated June 16, 1905, dismissing the application for the enrollment of Ruby Leah Cooper as a citizen by blood of the Chickasaw Nation.

Respectfully,
SIGNED

Tams Bixby
Chairman.

Registered.
Incl. 9-NB-206.

9-NB-206

Muskogee, Indian Territory, June 16, 1905.

Mansfield, McMurray & Cornish,   **COPY**
    Attorneys for Choctaw and Chickasaw Nations,
        South McAlester, Indian Territory.

Gentlemen:

Inclosed herewith you will find a copy of the order of this Commission, dated June 16, 1905, dismissing the application for the enrollment of Ruby Leah Cooper as a citizen by blood of the Chickasaw Nation.

Applications for Enrollment of Chickasaw Newborn
Act of 1905 Volume III

Respectfully,
SIGNED

Tams Bixby

Incl. 9-NB-206. Chairman.

9-1363

Muskogee, Indian Territory, March 8, 1905.

William W. Cooper,
    Roff, Indian Territory.

Dear Sir:

    Receipt is hereby acknowledged of the affidavits of Demis M. Cooper and J. A. Deen to the birth of Ruby Leah Cooper, infant daughter of William W. and Demis M. Cooper, October 23, 1903, and that said child is now dead.

    You are advised that the act of Congress approved March 3, 1905, provides as follows:

    "That the Commission to the Five Civilized Tribes is authorized for sixty days after the date of the approval of this act to receive and consider applications for enrollment of children born subsequent to September twenty-fifth, nineteen hundred and two, and prior to March fourth, nineteen hundred and five, <u>and who were living on said latter date</u>, to citizens by blood of the Choctaw and Chickasaw tribes of Indians whose enrollment has been approved by the Secretary of the Interior prior to the date of the approval of this act; and to enroll and make allotments to such children."

    Under the above legislation the Commission is without authority to enroll children born subsequent to September 25, 1902 who are not living on March 4, 1905.

Respectfully,

[sic]

Applications for Enrollment of Chickasaw Newborn
Act of 1905 Volume III

9 N B 206

Muskogee, Indian Territory, April 17, 1905.

William W. Cooper,
    Roff, Indian Territory.

Dear Sir:

    There is inclosed you herewith for execution application for the enrollment of your infant child, Ruby Leah Cooper, born October 23, 1903.

    The affidavits heretofore filed with the Commission show the child was living on March 2, 1905. It is necessary, for the child to be enrolled, that she was living on March 4, 1905.

    In having these affidavits executed care should be exercised to see that all names are written in full, as they appear in the body of the affidavit, and in the event that either of the persons signing the affidavit are unable to write, signatures by mark must be attested by two witnesses. Each affidavit must be executed before a Notary Public and the notarial seal and signature of the officer must be attached to each separate affidavit.

        Respectfully,

        SIGNED *Tams Bixby*
LM 17-120.   Chairman.

(The letter below typed as given.)

9 N. B. 206

Holdenville, I. T., April 21, 1905.

Commission to the Five Civilized Tribes
    Honl Commission

        Yours dated 17th at hand   You will pardon me for correcting an arror you are under   You claim the affidavit made out and filed with the Commission shows the child was living on March 2nd 1905   If you will examine closely the affidavit you will find the child was born Oct 23rd 1903 and died October 20th 1904 and was not living on March the 2nd 1905 as stated in your communication to me dated April 17th 1905.

        Respect
            W W Cooper
                Roff, I. T.

Applications for Enrollment of Chickasaw Newborn
Act of 1905   Volume III

9 NB 206

Muskogee, Indian Territory, April 26, 1905.

W. W. Cooper,
  Roof[sic], Indian Territory,

Dear Sir:

Receipt is hereby acknowledged of your letter of April 21, 1905, in which you state that you child, Ruby Leah Cooper, died October 20, 1904. Your information has been made a matter of record in this case.

You are advised that under the provisions of the act of Congress approved March 3, 1905, the Commission is authorized for sixty days from that date to receive applications for the enrollment of children born to enrolled citizens by blood of the Choctaw and Chickasaw Nations, between September 25, 1902, and March 4, 1905, and living on the latter date. You will, therefore, see the Commission is without authority to enroll your child.

Respectfully,

SIGNED   *Tams Bixby*
Chairman.

Chic. N.B. - 207
  (Oscar Emmett Lowrance
  Born April 2, 1904)

BIRTH AFFIDAVIT.
DEPARTMENT OF THE INTERIOR.
COMMISSION TO THE FIVE CIVILIZED TRIBES.

IN RE APPLICATION FOR ENROLLMENT, as a citizen of the   Chickasaw   Nation, of   Oscar Emmett Lowrance   , born on the 2nd day of April , 1904

Name of Father: Robert H Lowrance   a citizen of the   Chickasaw   Nation.
Name of Mother: Sophia A.E. Lowrance   a citizen of the   Chickasaw   Nation.

Postoffice   Buckhorn, Indian Territory

Applications for Enrollment of Chickasaw Newborn
Act of 1905   Volume III

AFFIDAVIT OF MOTHER.

UNITED STATES OF AMERICA, Indian Territory,
Southern   DISTRICT.

I,   Sophia A.E. Lowrance   , on oath state that I am   21   years of age and a citizen by   intermarriage   , of the   Chickasaw   Nation; that I am the lawful wife of   Robert H Lowrance   , who is a citizen, by   blood   of the   Chickasaw   Nation; that a   male   child was born to me on   2nd day of   April   , 1904; that said child has been named   Oscar Emmett Lowrance   , and was living March 4, 1905.

Sophia A.E. Lowrance

Witnesses To Mark:
{   E White

Subscribed and sworn to before me this 24th day of   March   , 1905

Eugene E. White
Notary Public.

AFFIDAVIT OF ATTENDING PHYSICIAN OR MID-WIFE.

UNITED STATES OF AMERICA, Indian Territory,
Southern   DISTRICT.

I,   Dr Geo. W. Slover   , a   physician   , on oath state that I attended on Mrs.   Sophia A. E. Lowrance   , wife of   Robert H. Lowrance   on the   2nd day of   April   , 1904; that there was born to her on said date a   male   child; that said child was living March 4, 1905, and is said to have been named   Oscar Emmett Lowrance

G.W. Slover M.D.

Witnesses To Mark:
{

Subscribed and sworn to before me this 24th day of   March   , 1905

Eugene E. White
Notary Public.

Applications for Enrollment of Chickasaw Newborn
Act of 1905   Volume III

9-1377

Muskogee, Indian Territory, March 31, 1905.

Robert H. Lowrance,
    Buckhorn, Indian Territory.

Dear Sir:

Receipt is hereby acknowledged of the affidavits of Sophia A. E. Lowrance and G. W. Slover to the birth of Oscar Emmett Lowrance son of Robert H. and Sophia A. E. Lowrance, April 2, 1904 and the same have been filed with our records as an application for the enrollment of said child.

Respectfully,

Chairman.

Chic. N.B. - 208
    (Winnefred Clem Myers
    Born September 27, 1903)

BIRTH AFFIDAVIT.
DEPARTMENT OF THE INTERIOR.
COMMISSION TO THE FIVE CIVILIZED TRIBES.

IN RE APPLICATION FOR ENROLLMENT, as a citizen of the   Chickasaw   Nation, of   Winnefred Clem Myers   , born on the 27" day of September , 1903

Name of Father: Winfield S. Myers   a citizen of the   Chickasaw   Nation.
Name of Mother: Alice Magnolia Myers   a citizen of the   Chickasaw   Nation.

Postoffice   Arbuckle, Ind. Ter.

AFFIDAVIT OF MOTHER.

UNITED STATES OF AMERICA, Indian Territory,
    Southern   DISTRICT.

I, Alice Magnolia Myers   , on oath state that I am 23   years of age and a citizen by   blood   , of the   Chickasaw   Nation; that I am the lawful wife of Winfield S Myers   , who is a citizen, by Intermarriage   of the   Chickasaw Nation; that a   Female   child was born to me on 27th day of September ,

178

Applications for Enrollment of Chickasaw Newborn
Act of 1905   Volume III

1903; that said child has been named Winnefred Clem Myers   , and was living March 4, 1905.

Alice Magnolia Myers

Witnesses To Mark:

{

Subscribed and sworn to before me this 29" day of   March   , 1905

Ire Adler
Notary Public.

AFFIDAVIT OF ATTENDING PHYSICIAN OR MID-WIFE.

UNITED STATES OF AMERICA, Indian Territory, }
Southern   DISTRICT.

I,   Mary Jane Myers   , a mid wife   , on oath state that I attended on Mrs. Alice Magnolia Myers   , wife of   Winfield S Myers   on the   27" day of September   , 1903; that there was born to her on said date a   Female   child; that said child was living March 4, 1905, and is said to have been named Winnefred Clem Myers

Mary J Myers

Witnesses To Mark:

{

Subscribed and sworn to before me this 29" day of   March   , 1905

Ire Adler
Notary Public.

Chickasaw 1384.

Muskogee, Indian Territory, April 4, 1905.

Winfield S. Myers,
  Arbuckle, Indian Territory.

Dear Sir:

Receipt is hereby acknowledged of the affidavits of Alice Magnolia Myers and Mary J. Myers to the birth of Winnefred Clem Myers, daughter of Winfield S. and Alice Magnolia Myers, September 27, 1903, and the same have been filed with our records as an application for the enrollment of said child.

Applications for Enrollment of Chickasaw Newborn
Act of 1905 Volume III

Respectfully,

Commissioner in Charge.

9 NB 208

Muskogee, Indian Territory, June 26, 1905.

W. S. Myers,
Arbuckles[sic], Indian Territory.

Dear Sir:

Receipt is hereby acknowledged of your letter of June 21, 1905, asking if land may be reserved for your child and when its enrollment will be approved.

In reply to your letter you are advised that the name of your child Winnifred[sic] Clem Myers has been placed upon a schedule of citizens by blood of the Chickasaw Nation prepared for forwarding to the Secretary of the Interior and you will be notified when her enrollment is approved. You are advised, however, that no reservation of land or selection of allotment can be made for children enrolled under the provisions of the act of Congress approved March 3, 1905, until their enrollment has been approved by the Secretary of the Interior.

Respectfully,

Chairman.

Chic. N.B. - 209
*(Mary King
Born October 16, 1904)*

9 NB 208
BIRTH AFFIDAVIT.

DEPARTMENT OF THE INTERIOR.
COMMISSION TO THE FIVE CIVILIZED TRIBES.

IN RE APPLICATION FOR ENROLLMENT, as a citizen of the Chickasaw Nation, of Mary King, born on the 16 day of Oct, 1904

Name of Father: Phillip King   a citizen of the Chickasaw freedman Nation.
Name of Mother: Cornelia King   a citizen of the Chickasaw Nation.

Applications for Enrollment of Chickasaw Newborn
Act of 1905 Volume III

Postoffice   Coleman I.T.

AFFIDAVIT OF MOTHER.

UNITED STATES OF AMERICA, Indian Territory,
.... DISTRICT.

I, ..., on oath state that I am .... years of age and a citizen by ...., of the .... Nation; that I am the lawful wife of ...., who is a citizen, by .... of the .... Nation; that a .... child was born to me on .... day of ...., 1........, that said child has been named ...., and was living March 4, 1905.

Witnesses To Mark:
{ ....
  .... }

Subscribed and sworn to before me this   29   day of   July   , 1905.

my commission expires   David A. Bailey
Jan 11-1909   Notary Public.

AFFIDAVIT OF ATTENDING PHYSICIAN OR MID-WIFE.

UNITED STATES OF AMERICA, Indian Territory,
     Central   DISTRICT.

we are personally acquainted with
WE,   J.F Nelson , and   Emma Nelson , on oath state that ~~I attended on~~ Mrs.   Cornelia King , wife of   Philip[sic] King *and*   on the 16 day of Oct , 1904; that there was born to her on said date a   female   child; that said child was living March 4, 1905, and is said to have been named   Mary King   *and that we are not related to the applicant*

                                              J.F. Nelson
Witnesses To Mark: Emma Nelson
{

Subscribed and sworn to before me this   29   day of   July   , 1905.

                                              David A. Bailey
my Commission Expires Jan 11-1909   Notary Public.

Applications for Enrollment of Chickasaw Newborn
Act of 1905   Volume III

BIRTH AFFIDAVIT.

DEPARTMENT OF THE INTERIOR.
COMMISSION TO THE FIVE CIVILIZED TRIBES.

IN RE APPLICATION FOR ENROLLMENT, as a citizen of the Chickasaw Nation, of Mary King , born on the 16th day of October , 1904

Choctaw[sic] *freedman*
Name of Father: Phillip King   ~~a citizen of the~~   ~~Nation~~.
Name of Mother: Cornelia King   a citizen of the Chickasaw Nation.

Postoffice   Craig, I.T.

Child present WF

AFFIDAVIT OF MOTHER.

UNITED STATES OF AMERICA, Indian Territory, }
    Central   DISTRICT.

I, Cornelia King , on oath state that I am about 35 years of age and a citizen by blood , of the Chickasaw Nation; that I am the lawful wife of Phillip King , who is a ~~citizen, by~~ Choctaw ~~of the~~ freedman Nation; that a female child was born to me on 16th day of October , 1904; that said child has been named Mary King , and was living March 4, 1905. *and that no physician or midwife attended me at the birth of said child.*

                                            her
Witnesses To Mark: Cornelia x King
  { Silas D. Folsom   mark
    Alfred W McClure

Subscribed and sworn to before me this 20th day of March , 1905

                                      Wirt Franklin
                                      Notary Public.

AFFIDAVIT OF ATTENDING PHYSICIAN OR MID-WIFE.

UNITED STATES OF AMERICA, Indian Territory, }
    Central   DISTRICT.

I, Phillip King , a ...., on oath state that I attended on Mrs. Cornelia King , ~~wife of~~ my wife on the 16th day of October , 1904; that there was born to her on said date a female child; that said child was living March 4, 1905, and ~~is said to have~~ *has* been named Mary King *and that no other person was present at the time of said birth*

Applications for Enrollment of Chickasaw Newborn
Act of 1905 Volume III

his
Phillip x King
mark

Witnesses To Mark:
   { Alfred W McClure
    Silas D. Folsom

Subscribed and sworn to before me this 20th day of March , 1905

Wirt Franklin
Notary Public.

9 N B 209

Muskogee, Indian Territory, April 15, 1905.

Phillip King,
    Craig, Indian Territory.

Dear Sir:

    Referring to the affidavits heretofore filed with the Commission relative to the birth of your infant children, Arthur King and Mary King, it is stated therein that there was no one in attendance at the birth of said children, excepting yourself. It will be necessary, for them to be enrolled, that you secure the affidavits of two persons who have actual knowledge of the fact, that the children were born, were living on March 4, 1905, the dates of their birth, and that Cornelia King is their mother.

Respectfully,

Chairman.

9-NB-209

Muskogee, Indian Territory, July 25, 1905.

Phillip King,
    Coleman, Indian Territory.

Dear Sir:

    Referring to the application for the enrollment of your infant child, Mary King, it is noted from the affidavits heretofore filed in this office, that you were the only one in attendance upon your wife at the time of the birth of this child.

Applications for Enrollment of Chickasaw Newborn
Act of 1905   Volume III

Before her right to enrollment can be finally determined, it will be necessary for you to tile the affidavits of two persons who have actual knowledge of the facts, that the child was born, the date of her birth, that she was living March 4, 1905, and that Cornelia King is her mother.

There is inclosed you herewith affidavit to be executed by two disinterested witnesses who are not realted[sic] to the applicant, which you will have properly executed and return to this office as soon as possible as no further action can be taken relative to the enrollment of said child, until the evidence requested is supplied.

Respectfully,

LM 25/2

Commissioner.

9-NB-209

Muskogee, Indian Territory, August 4, 1905.

Phillip King,
    Coleman, Indian Territory.

Dear Sir:

Receipt is hereby acknowledged of the affidavit of Cornelia King and the joint affidavit of J. F. Nelson and Emma Nelson to the birth of Arthur King, son of Phillip and Cornelia King, September 30, 1901; and also the joint affidavit of J. F. Nelson and Emma Nelson to the birth of Mary King, daughter of Phillip and Cornelia King, October 16, 1904, and the same have been filed with the records of this office in the matter of the enrollment of said children.

Respectfully,

Commissioner.

Chic. N.B. - 210
    (Henry Clay Nash
    Born September 5, 1904)

Applications for Enrollment of Chickasaw Newborn
Act of 1905   Volume III

BIRTH AFFIDAVIT.

DEPARTMENT OF THE INTERIOR.
COMMISSION TO THE FIVE CIVILIZED TRIBES.

IN RE APPLICATION FOR ENROLLMENT, as a citizen of the   Chickasaw   Nation, of   Henry Clay Nash   , born on the   5th   day of   Sept   , 1904

Name of Father: Henry C. Nash   a citizen of the   Chickasaw   Nation.
Name of Mother: Lizzie Nash   a citizen of the   Chickasaw   Nation.

Postoffice   Antlers Ind. Tery.

AFFIDAVIT OF MOTHER.

UNITED STATES OF AMERICA, Indian Territory, }
  Central   DISTRICT.   }
Territory of New Mexico, County of San Miguel

I,   Lizzie Nash   , on oath state that I am   thirty   years of age and a citizen by   blood   , of the   Chickasaw   Nation; that I am the lawful wife of   Henry C. Nash   , who is a citizen, by   intermarriage   of the   Chickasaw   Nation; that a   male   child was born to me on   fifth   day of   Sept.   , 1904, that said child has been named   Henry Clay Nash   , and is now living.

Lizzie Nash

Witnesses To Mark:
{ S E Mills
{ T M Ganard

Subscribed and sworn to before me this   23^d day of   September   , 1904

W. G. Koogler
Notary Public.

AFFIDAVIT OF ATTENDING PHYSICIAN OR MID-WIFE.

UNITED STATES OF AMERICA, Indian Territory, }
.... DISTRICT. }
Territory of New Mexico, County of San Miguel

I,   E.B. Shaw   , a   physician   , on oath state that I attended on Mrs.   Lizzie Nash   , wife of   Henry C. Nash   on the   5th day of Sept , 1904; that there was born to her on said date a   male   child; that said child is now living and is said to have been named   Henry Clay Nash

Edwin B. Shaw

185

Applications for Enrollment of Chickasaw Newborn
Act of 1905   Volume III

Witnesses To Mark:
{

Subscribed and sworn to before me this 23^d day of September , 1904

W. G. Koogler & Co.
Notary Public.

BIRTH AFFIDAVIT.

DEPARTMENT OF THE INTERIOR.
COMMISSION TO THE FIVE CIVILIZED TRIBES.

IN RE APPLICATION FOR ENROLLMENT, as a citizen of the   Chickasaw   Nation, of   Henry Clay Nash   , born on the 5th   day of September , 1904

Name of Father: Henry C. Nash   a citizen of the   Chickasaw   Nation.
Name of Mother: Lizzie Nash   a citizen of the   Chickasaw   Nation.

Postoffice   Antlers, Ind. Ter.

AFFIDAVIT OF MOTHER.

UNITED STATES OF AMERICA, Indian Territory, }
.... DISTRICT.

I, Lizzie Nash   , on oath state that I am 30   years of age and a citizen by Blood , of the   Chickasaw   Nation; that I am the lawful wife of   Henry C. Nash , who is a citizen, by Intermarriage   of the   Chickasaw   Nation; that a   male   child was born to me on 5th   day of   September   , 1904; that said child has been named   Henry Clay Nash   , and was living March 4, 1905.

Lizzie Nash

Witnesses To Mark:
{

Subscribed and sworn to before me this 22^d day of   May   , 1905

AJ Arnote
Notary Public.

Applications for Enrollment of Chickasaw Newborn
Act of 1905   Volume III

AFFIDAVIT OF ATTENDING PHYSICIAN OR MID-WIFE.

UNITED STATES OF AMERICA, Indian Territory,
.... DISTRICT.

  I, ..., a ...., on oath state that I attended on Mrs. Lizzie Nash , wife of Henry C Nash on the 5th day of September, 1904; that there was born to her on said date a male child; that said child was living March 4, 1905, and is said to have been named Henry Clay Nash

                 ....

Witnesses To Mark:

{ ....

 ....

  Subscribed and sworn to before me this .... day of ...., 1905.

             ....

             Notary Public.

Central District,

Indian Territory.

I' Nettie G. Harris on oath state that I am 31 years of age that I am not related to, nor interested in the enrollment of the applicant herein, Henry Clay Nash, that I am acquainted with Henry C. Nash a citizen by intermarriage of the Chickasaw Nation and his wife Lizzie Nash a citizen by blood of the Chickasaw Nation. I know that a male child was born to them on the 5th day of September, 1904, and was named Henry Clay Nash, and that said child was living on the 4th day of March, 1905 and that said child is now living, that I was living near them at the time of the birth of said Henry Clay Nash and am living near them now, and know the father and mother and child.

            Nettie G. Harris

Subscribed and sworn to before me this the 20 day of May, 1905.

            Erasmus A. Ingle
              Notary Public.

My commission expires Feby 190 9

Applications for Enrollment of Chickasaw Newborn
Act of 1905   Volume III

Central District,

Indian Territory.

I' Cyrus L. Harris, on oath state that I am 37 years of age that I am not related to, nor interested in the enrollment of the applicant herein, Henry Clay Nash, that I am acquainted with Henry C. Nash a citizen by intermarriage of the Chickasaw Nation and his wife Lizzie Nash a citizen by blood of the Chickasaw Nation. I know that a male child was born to them on the 5th day of September, 1904, and was named Henry Clay Nash, and that said child was living on the 4th day of March, 1905 and that said child is now living, that I was living near them at the time of the birth of said Henry Clay Nash and am living near them now, and know the father and mother and child.

Cyrus L. Harris

Subscribed and sworn to before me this the 20 day of May, 1905.

Erasmus A. Ingle
Notary Public.

My commission expires   Feby   190 9

Central District,

Indian Territory.

I, Lizzie Nash, mother of Henry Clay Nash, state on oath that the physician who attended me at the time of the birth of my child Henry Clay Nash, lives in New Mexico and can not know that said child was living on the 4th day of March, 1905, and that his affidavit as to the birth of said child has been heretofore filed with the commission[sic].

Lizzie Nash

Subscribed and sworn to before me, this the   22"   day of May, 1905.

AJ Arnote
Notary Public.

My commission expires May 16" 1907.

Applications for Enrollment of Chickasaw Newborn
Act of 1905 Volume III

9-1427

Muskogee, Indian Territory, January 21, 1905.

Henry C. Nash,
    Antlers, Indian Territory.

Dear Sir:

    Receipt is hereby acknowledged of your letter of January 16, 1905, asking that the birth certificate of Henry Clay Nash, son of Henry C. and Lizzie Nash which was forwarded by you some months ago, be returned in order that you may file it with the Choctaw enrolling Commission.

    In reply to you letter you are informed that on September 30, 1904, the affidavits of Lizzie Nash and Edwin B. Shaw to the birth of Henry Clay Nash, son of Henry C. and Lizzie Nash, September 5, 1904, were received.

    In as much as the affidavits above referred to have been forwarded to the Commission it is not deemed advisable at present to return the same.

                        Respectfully,

                                          Chairman.

9-1427

Muskogee, Indian Territory, January 28, 1905.

H. C. Nash,
    Antlers, Indian Territory.

Dear Sir:

    Receipt is hereby acknowledged of your letter of January 24, 1905, in which you have requested the return of the affidavits of Lizzie Nash and Edward[sic] Shaw to the birth of your son Henry Clay nash[sic], September 5, 1904, and state that in as much as you have been advised by the Commission that it is without authority to receive or consider the same, you desire to file it with the Choctaw enrolling Commission created by an act of the Choctaw Council requesting the enrollment of children born to citizens subsequent to September 25, 1902.

    In reply to your letter you are advised that the affidavits referred to in your letter have been filed with the Commission to the Five Civilized Tribes and as this Commission has nothing what ever to do with the Choctaw enrolling Commission to which you refer it

Applications for Enrollment of Chickasaw Newborn
Act of 1905 Volume III

is not deemed advisable at this time to return the affidavits relative to the birth of your son Henry Clay Nash.

Respectfully,

Chairman.

---

9 N B 210

Muskogee, Indian Territory, April 17, 1905.

H. C. Nash,
    Antlers, Indian Territory.

Dear Sir:

    Receipt is hereby acknowledged of your letter of April 9, 1905, stating that sometime since you forwarded a certificate as to the birth of your child on September 5, 1904 and you ask that the same be returned to you or forwarded to the enrolling Commission as you cannot comply with the requirements in order to secure another certificate the child having been born in Los Vegas, New Mexico.

    In reply to your letter you are informed that the affidavits heretofore forwarded to the birth of your child Henry Clay Nash have been filed with our records as an application for the enrollment of said child. In event further evidence is necessary to enable the Commission to determine his right to enrollment you will be duly advised.

Respectfully,

Chairman.

9-NB-210.

Muskogee, Indian Territory, May 13, 1905.

Henry C. Nash,
    Antlers, Indian Territory.

Dear Sir:

    There is enclosed you herewith for execution application for the enrollment of your infant child, Henry Clay Nash, born September 5, 1904.

    The affidavits heretofore filed with the Commission show the child was living on September 23, 1904. It is necessary, for the child to be enrolled, that he was living on March 4, 1905.

Applications for Enrollment of Chickasaw Newborn
Act of 1905 Volume III

In the event that you cannot secure the affidavit of the attending physician, it will be necessary for you to file with the Commission the affidavits of two disinterested persons who have actual knowledge of the facts that the child was born, the date of its birth; that he was living on March 4, 1905, and that Lizzie Nash is his mother.

In having these affidavits executed care should be exercised to see that all names are written in full, as they appear in the body of the affidavit, and in the event that either of the persons signing the affidavit are unable to write, signatures by mark must be attested by two witnesses. Each affidavit must be executed before a Notary Public and the notarial seal and signature of the officer must be attached to each separate affidavit.

Respectfully,

Chairman.

---

9 N.B. 210.

Muskogee, Indian Territory, May 26, 1905.

H. C. Nash,
Antlers, Indian Territory.

Dear Sir:

Receipt is hereby acknowledged of the affidavits of Lizzie Nash, Cyrus L. Harris and Nettie G. Harris to the birth of your child, Henry Clay Nash, and the same have been filed in the matter of the enrollment of said child.

Respectfully,

Chairman.

9-NB-210

Muskogee, Indian Territory, August 1, 1905.

H. C. Nash,
Antlers, Indian Territory.

Dear Sir:

Replying to that portion of your letter of July 23, 1905, in which you ask if your child Henry Clay Nash has been approved by the Secretary of the Interior, you are advised that the name of your child Henry Clay Nash has been placed upon a schedule of

Applications for Enrollment of Chickasaw Newborn
Act of 1905   Volume III

citizens by blood of the Chickasaw Nation which has been forwarded the Secretary of the Interior and you will be notified when his enrollment is approved by the Department.

Respectfully,

Commissioner.

Chic. N.B. - 211
    (Darcey Deshan
    Born July 31, 1903)

BIRTH AFFIDAVIT.

DEPARTMENT OF THE INTERIOR,
COMMISSION TO THE FIVE CIVILIZED TRIBES.

IN RE Application for Enrollment, as a citizen of the   Chickasaw   Nation, of   Dorsey Deshan , born on the   31   day of   July   , 1903

Name of Father: Albert Deshan   a citizen of the Choctaw   Nation.
Name of Mother: Rilla Deshan   a citizen of the white   Nation.

Post-Office: Tamaha I.T.

AFFIDAVIT OF MOTHER.

UNITED STATES OF AMERICA,
    INDIAN TERRITORY.
    Central   District.

I,   Rilla Deshan   , on oath state that I am   23   years of age and a citizen by   Intermarriage   , of the   Choctaw   Nation; that I am the lawful wife of   Albert Deshan , who is a citizen, by   Blood   of the Choctaw Nation; that a   Girl   child was born to me on   31   day of   July   , 1903 , that said child has been named   Dorsey Deshan , and is now living.

                                      her
                            Iva Rilla x Deshan
WITNESSES TO MARK: mark
    { L.L Banner
    { W^mB Davidson

Applications for Enrollment of Chickasaw Newborn
Act of 1905 Volume III

Subscribed and sworn to before me this 12 *day of* March , *1904*

My Commission Expires W^m. B. Davidson
11 May 1907 NOTARY PUBLIC.

AFFIDAVIT OF ATTENDING PHYSICIAN OR MID-WIFE.

UNITED STATES OF AMERICA,
  INDIAN TERRITORY.
  Central   District.

I, C.D. Dale , a physician , on oath state that I attended on Mrs. Rilla Deshan , wife of Albert Deshan on the 31 day of July , 1903 ; that there was born to her on said date a Female child; that said child is now living and is said to have been named Dorsey Deshan

Dr C.D. Dale

WITNESSES TO MARK:
{

Subscribed and sworn to before me this 3 *day of* March , *1904*

My Commission Expires W^m. B. Davidson
11 May 1907 NOTARY PUBLIC.

---

9 - 65   9 - 3915
BIRTH AFFIDAVIT.

DEPARTMENT OF THE INTERIOR.
COMMISSION TO THE FIVE CIVILIZED TRIBES.

IN RE APPLICATION FOR ENROLLMENT, as a citizen of the Chickasaw Nation, of Darcey Deshan , born on the 31st day of July , 1903

Name of Father: Albert Deshan   a citizen of the Chickasaw Nation.
Name of Mother: Iva A. Deshan   a citizen of the Chickasaw Nation.

Postoffice   Tamaha, Ind. Ter.

Applications for Enrollment of Chickasaw Newborn
Act of 1905   Volume III

AFFIDAVIT OF MOTHER.

UNITED STATES OF AMERICA, Indian Territory, }
    Central   DISTRICT.

    I, Iva A. Deshan, on oath state that I am 24 years of age and a citizen by intermarriage, of the Choctaw Nation; that I am the lawful wife of Albert Deshan, who is a citizen, by blood of the Chickasaw Nation; that a female child was born to me on 31st day of July, 1903; that said child has been named Darcey Deshan, and was living March 4, 1905.

                                              her
                                    Iva x A. Deshan
Witnesses To Mark: mark
  { J R Williamson
    H. Williamson

    Subscribed and sworn to before me this 8 day of April, 1905

                              W^m.B. Davidson
                                  Notary Public.

AFFIDAVIT OF ATTENDING PHYSICIAN OR MID-WIFE.

UNITED STATES OF AMERICA, Indian Territory, }
    Central   DISTRICT.

    I, Chas D Dale, a physician, on oath state that I attended on Mrs. Iva A. Deshan, wife of Albert Deshan on the 31st day of July, 1903; that there was born to her on said date a female child; that said child was living March 4, 1905, and is said to have been named Darcey Deshan

                                  Chas.D. Dale M.D.
Witnesses To Mark:
  {

    Subscribed and sworn to before me this 8 day of April, 1905

                              W^m.B. Davidson
                                  Notary Public.

Applications for Enrollment of Chickasaw Newborn
Act of 1905   Volume III

9-1448

Muskogee, Indian Territory, April 11, 1905.

Albert Deshan,
    Tamaha, Indian Territory.

Dear Sir:

Receipt is hereby acknowledged of the affidavits of Iva A. Deshan and Charles D. Dale, to the birth of Darcey Deshan, daughter of Albert and Iva A. Deshan, July 31, 1903, and the same have been filed with our records as an application for the enrollment of said child.

Respectfully,

Commissioner in Charge.

Chic. N.B. - 212
    (Douglas E. Owens
    Born April 29, 1904)

BIRTH AFFIDAVIT.

IN RE-APPLICATION FOR ENROLLMENT, as a citizen of the   Chickasaw   Nation, of   Duglas E Owens   , born on the   29   day of   April   , 190 4

Name of Father: Lafayette Owens   a citizen of the   Chickasaw   Nation.
Name of Mother: Minnie Owens   a citizen of the   Chickasaw   Nation.

Postoffice   Nebo I.T.

AFFIDAVIT OF MOTHER.

UNITED STATES OF AMERICA, INDIAN TERRITORY,
    21   District.

I,   Minnie Owens   , on oath state that I am   24   years of age and a citizen by Blood   , of the   Chickasaw   Nation; that I am the lawful wife of   Laffayett[sic] Owens , who is a citizen, by   Marriage   of the   Chickasaw   Nation; that a   Male   child was born to me on   29   day of   April   , 1904 , that said child has been named   Duglas Elihu Owens   , and is now living.

Minnie Owens

Applications for Enrollment of Chickasaw Newborn
Act of 1905 Volume III

Witnesses To Mark:
- Mrs J B Cleveland
- N N Barksdale

    Subscribed and sworn to before me this 22 day of March , 1905.

                                C C Smith   Notary Public.

AFFIDAVIT OF ATTENDING PHYSICIAN OR MID-WIFE.

UNITED STATES OF AMERICA, INDIAN TERRITORY,
    Southern   District.

    I, G.M. Cambert , a Physician , on oath state that I attended on Mrs. Minnie Owens , wife of L.F. Owens on the 29 day of April , 190 4; that there was born to her on said date a male child; that said child is now living and is said to have been named Douglas[sic] Elihu

                              G.M. Cambert M.D.

Witnesses To Mark:

    Subscribed and sworn to before me this 16 day of March , 1905.

                                L.R. Teny
                                   Notary Public.

                                9-1484

            Muskogee, Indian Territory, March 29, 1905.

Lafayette Owens,
    Nebo, Indian Territory.

Dear Sir:

    Receipt is hereby acknowledged of the affidavits of Minnie Owens and G. M. Cambert to the birth of Duglas Elihu Owens, son of Lafayette and Minnie Owens April 29, 1904, and the same have been filed with our records as an application for the enrollment of said child.

                      Respectfully,

                                      Chairman.

Applications for Enrollment of Chickasaw Newborn
Act of 1905   Volume III

Chic. N.B. - 213
  (Vivian Hayes
  Born June 21, 1904)

Department of the Interior
Commission to the five civilized Tribes

In Re Application for Enrollment as a citizen of the Chickasaw Nation of Vivian Hayes born on the 21st day of June 1904
Name of Father   John Benjamin Hayes a citizen of the Chickasaw Nation
Name of Mother   Annie E. Hayes a citizen of the United States
                                Post Office Willis Ind Ter

United States of America
  Indian Territory   I, Annie E Hayes on oath state that I am 23
  Southern District   years of age that I am the lawful wife of John B Hayes who is a citizen by blood of the Chickasaw Nation that a female child was born to me on the 21st day of June 1904 that said child has been named Vivian Hayes and is now living

                                Annie Hayes

Subscribed and sworn to before me this 25th day of March 1905
                                C. H. Thomes
Southern District Ind. Ter.   Notary Public

I, J. P. Collins a Physician on oath state that I attended on Mrs. Annie Hayes, wife of John Benjamin Hayes on the 21st day of June 1904 that there was born to her on said date a female child; that said child is now living and is said to have been named Vivian Hayes   J. P. Collins
Subscribed and sworn to before me this 25th day of March 1905
                                C. H. Thomes Notary Public

Applications for Enrollment of Chickasaw Newborn
Act of 1905   Volume III

Chickasaw-1499.

Muskogee, Indian Territory, April 3, 1905.

C. H. Thomas[sic],
    Willis, Indian Territory.

Dear Sir:

    Receipt is hereby acknowledged of your letter of March 26, 1905, enclosing the affidavits of Annie Hayes and J. P. Collins to the birth of Vivian Hayes, daughter of John Benjamin and Annie Hayes, June 21, 1904, and the same have been filed with our records as an application for the enrollment of said child.

                Respectfully,

                            Chairman.

Chic. N.B. - 214
    (Nellie Hawley
    Born September 18, 1904)
    Daisy Hawley
    Born January 18, 1903)

BIRTH AFFIDAVIT.

DEPARTMENT OF THE INTERIOR.
COMMISSION TO THE FIVE CIVILIZED TRIBES.

    IN RE APPLICATION FOR ENROLLMENT, as a citizen of the Chickasaw Nation, of Nellie Hawley, born on the 18 day of Sept, 1904

Name of Father: Arthur E. Hawley   a citizen of the Chickasaw Nation.
Name of Mother: Lizzie Hawley   a citizen of the Chickasaw Nation.

                Postoffice   Tupelo, Ind. Ter.

Applications for Enrollment of Chickasaw Newborn
Act of 1905 Volume III

AFFIDAVIT OF MOTHER.

UNITED STATES OF AMERICA, Indian Territory,
    Central   DISTRICT.

   I, Lizzie Hawley   , on oath state that I am   21   years of age and a citizen by   Blood   , of the   Chickasaw   Nation; that I am the lawful wife of   Arthur E Hawley   , who is a citizen, by Intermarriage   of the   Chickasaw   Nation; that a   female   child was born to me on   18th   day of   September   , 1904; that said child has been named   Nellie Hawley   , and was living March 4, 1905.

                              Lizzie Hawley
Witnesses To Mark:
{
   Subscribed and sworn to before me this 27th day of   March   , 1905

                              W.H. Angell
                                   Notary Public.

AFFIDAVIT OF ATTENDING PHYSICIAN OR MID-WIFE.

UNITED STATES OF AMERICA, Indian Territory,
    Central   DISTRICT.

   I,   Annie Butcher   , a   Mid-wife   , on oath state that I attended on Mrs.   Lizzie Hawley   , wife of   Arthur E Hawley   on the   18th day of Sept   , 1904; that there was born to her on said date a   female   child; that said child was living March 4, 1905, and is said to have been named Anna Butcher[sic]

Witnesses To Mark:
{
   Subscribed and sworn to before me this 27th day of   March   , 1905

                              W.H. Angell
                                   Notary Public.

Applications for Enrollment of Chickasaw Newborn
Act of 1905 Volume III

BIRTH AFFIDAVIT.

DEPARTMENT OF THE INTERIOR.
COMMISSION TO THE FIVE CIVILIZED TRIBES.

IN RE APPLICATION FOR ENROLLMENT, as a citizen of the Chickasaw Nation, of Daisy Hawley , born on the 18 day of January , 1903

Name of Father: Arthur E. Hawley   a citizen of the Chickasaw Nation.
Name of Mother: Lizzie Hawley   a citizen of the Chickasaw Nation.

Postoffice   Tupelo, Indian Territory

AFFIDAVIT OF MOTHER.

UNITED STATES OF AMERICA, Indian Territory, }
     Central   DISTRICT.

I, Lizzie Hawley , on oath state that I am 21 years of age and a citizen by Blood , of the Chickasaw Nation; that I am the lawful wife of Arthur E Hawley , who is a citizen, by Intermarriage of the Chickasaw Nation; that a female child was born to me on 18th day of January , 1903; that said child has been named Daisy Hawley , and was living March 4, 1905.

                       Lizzie Hawley

Witnesses To Mark:
{

Subscribed and sworn to before me this 27th day of March , 1905

                       W.H. Angell
                       Notary Public.

AFFIDAVIT OF ATTENDING PHYSICIAN OR MID-WIFE.

UNITED STATES OF AMERICA, Indian Territory, }
     Central   DISTRICT.

I, Annie Butcher , a Mid wife , on oath state that I attended on Mrs. Lizzie Hawley , wife of Arthur E Hawley on the 18th day of January , 1903; that there was born to her on said date a female child; that said child was living March 4, 1905, and is said to have been named Daisy Hawley

                       Anna Butcher

Witnesses To Mark:
{

Applications for Enrollment of Chickasaw Newborn
Act of 1905 Volume III

Subscribed and sworn to before me this 27th day of March, 1905

W.H. Angell
Notary Public.

Chic. N.B. - 215
   *(Norma Elizibeth Miller
   Born May 23, 1904)*

BIRTH AFFIDAVIT.   No 17

DEPARTMENT OF THE INTERIOR.
COMMISSION TO THE FIVE CIVILIZED TRIBES.

IN RE APPLICATION FOR ENROLLMENT, as a citizen of the Chickasaw Nation, of Norma Elizibeth Miller, born on the 23^{d} day of May, 1904

Name of Father: Norman Miller   a citizen of the Chickasaw Nation.
Name of Mother: Sophia E. Miller   a citizen of the Chickasaw Nation.

Postoffice   Emet Ind. T.

AFFIDAVIT OF MOTHER.

UNITED STATES OF AMERICA, Indian Territory,
So   DISTRICT.

I, Sophia E Miller, on oath state that I am 23 years of age and a citizen by Blood, of the Chickasaw Nation; that I am the lawful wife of Norman Miller, who is a citizen, by Inter Marriage of the Chickasaw Nation; that a Female child was born to me on 23^{d} day of May, 1904, that said child has been named Norma Elizebeth Miller, and is now living.

Sophia Miller

Witnesses To Mark:
   { Idell Turk
   { Norah E. *(Illegible)*

Applications for Enrollment of Chickasaw Newborn
Act of 1905   Volume III

Subscribed and sworn to before me this   30 day of   Jan , 1905.

> John H Dobson
> Notary Public.

AFFIDAVIT OF ATTENDING PHYSICIAN OR MID-WIFE.

UNITED STATES OF AMERICA, Indian Territory, }
   So   DISTRICT.   }

I,   A. H. Seeley   , a   Physician   , on oath state that I attended on Mrs.   Sophia Miller   , wife of   Norman Miller   on the 23^d day of May, 1904; that there was born to her on said date a   Female   child; that said child is now living and is said to have been named   Norma Elizibeth Miller

> A.H. Seeley M.D.

Witnesses To Mark:
 { L.J. Horton
 { *(Name Illegible)*

Subscribed and sworn to before me this   30 day of   Jan , 1905.

> John H Dobson
> Notary Public.

BIRTH AFFIDAVIT.

DEPARTMENT OF THE INTERIOR.
COMMISSION TO THE FIVE CIVILIZED TRIBES.

IN RE APPLICATION FOR ENROLLMENT, as a citizen of the   Chickasaw   Nation, of   Norma Elizibeth Miller   , born on the 23^d day of   May, 1904

Name of Father: Norman Miller   a citizen of the   Chickasaw   Nation.
Name of Mother: Sophia E. Miller   a citizen of the   Chickasaw   Nation.

> Postoffice   Emet Ind. T.

AFFIDAVIT OF MOTHER.

UNITED STATES OF AMERICA, Indian Territory, }
   So   DISTRICT.   }

I,   Sophia E Miller   , on oath state that I am   23   years of age and a citizen by   Blood   , of the   Chickasaw   Nation; that I am the lawful wife of

Applications for Enrollment of Chickasaw Newborn
Act of 1905 Volume III

Norman Miller, who is a citizen, by Inter Marriage of the Chickasaw Nation; that a Female child was born to me on 23^d day of May, 1904, that said child has been named Norma Elizibeth Miller, and is now living.

Sophia Miller

Witnesses To Mark:
- Idell Turk
- *(Name Illegible)*

Subscribed and sworn to before me this 22 day of March, 1905.

John H Dobson
Notary Public.

AFFIDAVIT OF ATTENDING PHYSICIAN OR MID-WIFE.

UNITED STATES OF AMERICA, Indian Territory,
So   DISTRICT.

I, A. H. Seeley, a Physician, on oath state that I attended on Mrs. Sophia Miller, wife of Norman Miller on the 23^d day of May, 1904; that there was born to her on said date a Female child; that said child is now living and is said to have been named Norma Elizibeth Miller

A.H. Seeley M.D.

Witnesses To Mark:
- L.J. Horton
- Lee Thompson

Subscribed and sworn to before me this 22 day of March, 1905.

John H Dobson
Notary Public.

9-1581

Muskogee, Indian Territory, March 28, 1905.

Norman Miller,
    Emet, Indian Territory.

Dear Sir:

Receipt is hereby acknowledged of the affidavits of Sophia Miller and A. H. Seeley to the birth of Norma Elizabeth[sic] Miller, daughter of Norman and Sophia

Applications for Enrollment of Chickasaw Newborn
Act of 1905 Volume III

Miller, May 23, 1904, and the same have been filed with the records as an application for the enrollment of said child.

Respectfully,

Chairman.

Chic. N.B. - 216
    (R. Miller Francis
    Born October 31, 1904)

9 - 1583

BIRTH AFFIDAVIT.

DEPARTMENT OF THE INTERIOR.
COMMISSION TO THE FIVE CIVILIZED TRIBES.

    IN RE APPLICATION FOR ENROLLMENT, as a citizen of the Chickasaw Nation, of R. Miller Francis, born on the 31 day of Oct., 1904

Name of Father: B. L. Francis   a citizen of the Chickasaw Nation.
Name of Mother: Katie Francis   a citizen of the Chickasaw Nation.

Postoffice   Owl, I T

AFFIDAVIT OF MOTHER.

UNITED STATES OF AMERICA, Indian Territory, }
    Central   DISTRICT. }

    I, Katie Francis, on oath state that I am 30 years of age and a citizen by Blood, of the Chickasaw Nation; that I am the lawful wife of B L Francis, who is a citizen, by Marriage of the Chickasaw Nation; that a male child was born to me on 31 day of October, 1904; that said child has been named R. Miller Francis, and was living March 4, 1905.

                         Kate A Francis

Witnesses To Mark:

Applications for Enrollment of Chickasaw Newborn
Act of 1905 Volume III

Subscribed and sworn to before me this 15 day of March , 1905

D A Spears
Notary Public.

AFFIDAVIT OF ATTENDING PHYSICIAN OR MID-WIFE.

UNITED STATES OF AMERICA, Indian Territory, }
   Central   DISTRICT. }

I, J H Arnold , a Physician , on oath state that I attended on Mrs. Katie Francis , wife of B L Francis on the 31 day of Oct , 1904; that there was born to her on said date a male child; that said child was living March 4, 1905, and is said to have been named ....

Dr J.H. Arnold

Witnesses To Mark:
{

Subscribed and sworn to before me this 16 day of Mch , 1905

D A Spears
Notary Public.

BIRTH AFFIDAVIT.

DEPARTMENT OF THE INTERIOR.
COMMISSION TO THE FIVE CIVILIZED TRIBES.

IN RE APPLICATION FOR ENROLLMENT, as a citizen of the Chickasaw Nation, of R. Miller Francis , born on the 31 day of October , 1904

Name of Father: B. L.Francis   a citizen of the Chickasaw Nation.
Name of Mother: Katie Francis   a citizen of the Chickasaw Nation.

Postoffice Owl, Ind Ter

AFFIDAVIT OF MOTHER.

UNITED STATES OF AMERICA, Indian Territory, }
   Central   DISTRICT. }

I, Katie Francis , on oath state that I am 30 years of age and a citizen by Blood , of the Chickasaw Nation; that I am the lawful wife of B L Francis , who is a citizen, by marriage of the Chickasaw Nation; that a male

Applications for Enrollment of Chickasaw Newborn
Act of 1905 Volume III

child was born to me on 31st day of October , 1904; that said child has been named R. Miller Francis , and was living March 4, 1905.

Katie Francis

Witnesses To Mark:
{

Subscribed and sworn to before me this 26 day of April , 1905

D A Spears
Notary Public.

AFFIDAVIT OF ATTENDING PHYSICIAN OR MID-WIFE.

UNITED STATES OF AMERICA, Indian Territory,
Central DISTRICT.

I, J H Arnold , a Physician , on oath state that I attended on Mrs. Katie Francis , wife of B L Francis on the 31st day of October , 1904; that there was born to her on said date a male child; that said child was living March 4, 1905, and is said to have been named R. Miller Francis

Dr J.H. Arnold

Witnesses To Mark:
{

Subscribed and sworn to before me this 26 day of April , 1905

D A Spears
Notary Public.

9-1583

Muskogee, Indian Territory, March 21, 1905.

B. L. Francis,
    Owl, Indian Territory.

Dear Sir:

    Receipt is hereby acknowledged of the affidavits of Kate A. Francis and J. H. Arnold to the birth of R. Miller Francis son of B. L. and Kate A. Francis, October 31, 1904, and the same have been filed with our records as an application for the enrollment of said child.

Respectfully,

Chairman.

Applications for Enrollment of Chickasaw Newborn
Act of 1905   Volume III

9 N B 216

Muskogee, Indian Territory, April 17, 1905.

B. L. Francis,
    Owl, Indian Territory.

Dear Sir:

    There is inclosed you herewith for execution application for the enrollment of your infant child, R. Miller Francis, born October 31, 1904.

    In the affidavit of the physician heretofore filed with the Commission the Notary Public failed to attach his seal. It is therefore, necessary for you to have the application re-executed.

    In having these affidavits executed care should be exercised to see that all names are written in full, as they appear in the body of the affidavit, and in the event that either of the persons signing the affidavit are unable to write, signatures by mark must be attested by two witnesses. Each affidavit must be executed before a Notary Public and the notarial seal and signature of the officer must be attached to each separate affidavit.

                          Respectfully,

LM 17-140   Chairman.

Chickasaw N.B.
216.

Muskogee, Indian Territory, May 2, 1905.

B. L. Francis,
    Owl, Indian Territory.

Dear Sir:

    Receipt is hereby acknowledged of the affidavits of Katie Francis and Dr. J. H. Arnold to the birth of R. Miller Francis, son of B. L. and Katie Francis, October 31, 1904, and the same have been filed with our records in the matter of the enrollment of said child.

                          Respectfully,

                                                                Chairman.

Applications for Enrollment of Chickasaw Newborn
Act of 1905 Volume III

Chic. N.B. - 217
(Rubie Rhoener James
Born May 15, 1903)

No. 1613

Certificate of Record of Marriages.

UNITED STATES OF AMERICA,
INDIAN TERRITORY,   SCT:
Central   DISTRICT.

DEPARTMENT OF THE INTERIOR,
Commission to the Five Civilized Tribes.
FILED
APR 27 1905
Tams Bixby CHAIRMAN.

I, E.J. Fannin , Clerk of the United States Court in the Indian Territory and District aforesaid, do hereby CERTIFY, that the License for and Certificate of the Marriage of

Mr.   Ben James   and

Miss Bertie Hawkins   was

filed in my office in said Territory and District the 24 day of Oct A.D., 190 2 and duly recorded in Book 2 of Marriage Record, Page 189

WITNESS my hand and seal of said Court, at   Atoka   , this 25 day of   Oct   , A.D. 190 2

E.J. Fannin
Clerk.
By   JD Cotton   *Deputy.*

Applications for Enrollment of Chickasaw Newborn
Act of 1905 Volume III

No. 1613

FORM NO. 598.

MARRIAGE LICENSE.

UNITES STATES OF AMERICA,
THE INDIAN TERRITORY, } ss:
Central   DISTRICT.

To any Person Authorized by Law to Solemnize Marriage—Greeting:

You are hereby commanded to solemnize the Rite and publish the Banns of Matrimony between Mr. Ben James of Byrne in the Indian Territory, aged 18 years, and Miss Bertie Hawkins of Byrne in the Indian Territory, aged 23 years, according to law, and do you officially sign and return this License to the parties therein named.

WITNESS my hand and official seal, this 1 day of October A. D. 190 2

E J Fannin
Clerk of the United States Court.

JD Cotton   Deputy

CERTIFICATE OF MARRIAGE.

UNITES STATES OF AMERICA,
THE INDIAN TERRITORY, } ss:
Central   DISTRICT.

I, H.C. Wilson a Minister of the Gospel

do hereby CERTIFY, that on the 5th day of October A, D. 190 2 ; I did duly and according to law, as commanded in the foregoing License, solemnize the Rite and publish the BANNS OF MATRIMONY between the parties therein named.

Witness my hand this 5th day of October , A. D. 190 2

My credentials are recorded in the office of the Clerk of the United States Court in the Indian Territory, Central District, Book   Page 166

H.C. Wilson
a Minister of the Gospel

Applications for Enrollment of Chickasaw Newborn
Act of 1905 Volume III

BIRTH AFFIDAVIT.

DEPARTMENT OF THE INTERIOR.
COMMISSION TO THE FIVE CIVILIZED TRIBES.

IN RE APPLICATION FOR ENROLLMENT, as a citizen of the Chickasaw Nation, of Rubie Rhoener , born on the 15th day of May , 1903

Name of Father: Benjamin David James a citizen of the Chickasaw Nation.
Name of Mother: Birdie Stuard James a citizen of the .... Nation.

Postoffice Byrne, I.T.

AFFIDAVIT OF MOTHER.

UNITED STATES OF AMERICA, Indian Territory, }
Central   DISTRICT.

I, Birdie Stuard James , on oath state that I am 25 years of age and a citizen by .... , of the .... Nation; that I am the lawful wife of Benjamin David James , who is a citizen, by blood of the Chickasaw Nation; that a female child was born to me on 15th day of May , 1903; that said child has been named Rubie Rhoener , and was living March 4, 1905.

Mrs. Birdie Stuard James
Witnesses To Mark:
{

Subscribed and sworn to before me this 31st day of March , 1905

S.L. Barnes
My Commission expires January 6th, 1909   Notary Public.

AFFIDAVIT OF ATTENDING PHYSICIAN OR MID-WIFE.

UNITED STATES OF AMERICA, Indian Territory, }
Central   DISTRICT.

I, Rhoener James , a mid-wife , on oath state that I attended on Mrs. Birdie James , wife of Benjamin David James on the 15th day of May , 1903; that there was born to her on said date a female child; that said child was living March 4, 1905, and is said to have been named Rubie Rhoener

Rhoener James
Witnesses To Mark:
{

Applications for Enrollment of Chickasaw Newborn
Act of 1905 Volume III

Subscribed and sworn to before me this 31st day of March, 1905.

S.L. Barnes
Notary Public.

My Commission expires January 6th, 1909

9-1588

Muskogee, Indian Territory, April 5, 1905.

Benjamin David James,
    Byrne, Indian Territory.

Dear Sir:

    Receipt is hereby acknowledged of the affidavits of Mrs. Birdie Stuard James and Rhoener James to the birth of Rubie Rhoener James, daughter of Benjamin David and Birdie Stuard James, May 15, 1903, and the same have been filed with our records as an application for the enrollment of said child.

Respectfully,

Commissioner in Charge.

---

9 N B 217

Muskogee, Indian Territory, April 15, 1905.

Benjamin David James,
    Byrne, Indian Territory.

Dear Sir:

    You are hereby advised that before the application for the enrollment of your infant child, Rubie Rhoener James, can be finally disposed of, it will be necessary for you to furnish the Commission with either the original or a certified copy of the license and certificate of your marriage to her mother, Birdie Stuard James.

    Please give this matter your immediate attention.

Respectfully,

Chairman.

Applications for Enrollment of Chickasaw Newborn
Act of 1905 Volume III

Chickasaw N.B.
217.

Muskogee, Indian Territory, April 28, 1905.

Benjamin D. James,
    Byrne, Indian Territory.

Dear Sir:

    Receipt is hereby acknowledged of your letter of April 25, in which you enclosed marriage license and certificate between Ben James and Bertie Hawkins, which you offer in support of the application for the enrollment of your child and the same have been filed in the matter of the application for the enrollment of Rubie Rhoener James.

Respectfully,

Chairman.

Chic. N.B. - 218
    (Mary Ruth Hamblin
    Born October 4, 1902)
    (Lela Mildred Beatrice Hamblin
    Born May 7, 1904)

Indian Territory,
Southern District.

    I, C. M. Campbell, Clerk of the United States Court, Southern District, Indian Territory, do hereby certify that the above and foregoing is a true and correct copy of the Marriage License and Certificate of Marriage, filed for record in my office at Ardmore, and duly recorded in Vol. F, page 162 of Marriage Records.
    IN TESTIMONY WHEREOF, I have hereunto set my hand and affixed the seal of said Court, at my office in Ardmore, this 27th day of April, A.D. 1905.

C. M. Campbell, Clerk,

By NH McCoy   Chief Deputy.

Applications for Enrollment of Chickasaw Newborn
Act of 1905   Volume III

CERTIFICATE OF
RECORD OF MARRIAGE

UNITED STATES OF AMERICA,
  INDIAN TERRITORY, } sct.
    SOUTHERN DISTRICT.

I, C. M. CAMPBELL, Clerk of the United States Court, in the Territory and District aforesaid DO HEREBY CERTIFY, that the License for and Certificate of Marriage of

Mr   C. M. Hamblin   and

M   Nina Lawson

were filed in my office in said Territory and District the   28th   day of
Dec.   A.D., 190 1
and duly recorded in Book F   of Marriage Record, Page 162

WITNESS my hand and Seal of said Court, at Ardmore, this   28th   day of   Dec.   A.D. 190 1

C. M. Campbell
                    CLERK.

Return this license to the United States Clerk at Ardmore, that it may be recorded, when it will be mailed to the proper address.

Texas Printing Company, Fort Worth.

DEPARTMENT OF THE INTERIOR,
COMMISSION TO THE FIVE CIVILIZED TRIBES.
FILED
MAY 3 1905
Tams Bixby CHAIRMAN.

Applications for Enrollment of Chickasaw Newborn
Act of 1905 Volume III

No person is authorized to perform the Marriage Ceremony in the Indian Territory unless the proper credentials have first been recorded in the Clerk's office.

MARRIAGE LICENSE.

No. 1879

UNITED STATES OF AMERICA,
INDIAN TERRITORY, } SS.   To Any Person Authorized by Law to Solemnize
SOUTHERN DISTRICT.   Marriage, Greeting:

YOU ARE HEREBY COMMANDED to solemnize the Rite and publish the Banns of Matrimony between Mr. C. M. Hamblin of Purcell in the Indian Territory, aged 25 years, and M Nina Lawson of Purcell in the Indian Territory, aged 18 years, according to law; and do you officially sign and return this license to the parties therein named.

WITNESS my hand and official Seal, this 15th day of Dec. A. D. 190 1

C. M. Campbell
Clerk of the United States Court.
By T. F. Green, Deputy.

Certificate of Marriage.

UNITED STATES OF AMERICA,
INDIAN TERRITORY, } SS.
SOUTHERN DISTRICT.   I,   W. B. Crocker

Minister of the Gospel do hereby certify that on the 15th day of December A. D. 190 1, I did duly and according to law, as commanded in the foregoing License, solemnize the Rite and publish the Banns of Matrimony between the parties therein named.

WITNESS my hand this 15th day of December A. D. 190 1

My credentials are recorded in the office of the Clerk of the United States Court, Indian Territory, Southern District, at Ardmore, Book I , Page 23-24

W. B. Crocker
Minister of the Gospel

NOTE. (a)- This License and Certificate of Marriages must be returned to the office of the Clerk of the United States Court in the Indian Territory, at Ardmore, within sixty days from the date thereof, or the party to whom the License was issued will be liable in the amount of ONE HUNDRED DOLLARS ($100).

Applications for Enrollment of Chickasaw Newborn
Act of 1905   Volume III

BIRTH AFFIDAVIT.

DEPARTMENT OF THE INTERIOR,
COMMISSION TO THE FIVE CIVILIZED TRIBES.

In Re Application for Enrollment, as a citizen of the   Chickasaw   Nation, of   Mary Ruth Hamblin   , born on the   4"   day of   October, 1902.   , 1........

Name of Father: C.M. Hamblin   a citizen of the   Chickasaw Nation.
Name of Mother: Nina Hamblin   a citizen of the   White woman   Nation.

Post-office   Purcell.

AFFIDAVIT OF MOTHER.

UNITED STATES OF AMERICA, }
  INDIAN TERRITORY,
  Southern   District.

I,   Nina Hamblin   , on oath state that I am   19   years of age and a citizen by   non-citizen   , of the .... Nation; that I am the lawful wife of   C.M. Hamblin   , who is a citizen, by blood of the   Chickasaw   Nation; that a   female   child was born to me on   4"   day of   October, 1902   , 1......., that said child has been named   Mary Ruth Hamblin   , and is now living.

Mrs Nina Hamblin

WITNESSES TO MARK:
{

Subscribed and sworn to before me this   22"   day of   June, 1903   , 190......

Joseph P Smith
NOTARY PUBLIC.

AFFIDAVIT OF ATTENDING PHYSICIAN OR MID-WIFE.

UNITED STATES OF AMERICA, }
  INDIAN TERRITORY,
  Southern   District.

I,   G.M. Tralle   , a   Physician   , on oath state that I attended on Mrs.   Nina Hamblin   , wife of   C.M. Hamblin   on the   4"   day of October, 1902   , 1.........; that there was born to her on said date a   female   child; that said child is now living and is said to have been named   Mary Ruth Hamblin

G.M. Tralle

Applications for Enrollment of Chickasaw Newborn
Act of 1905   Volume III

WITNESSES TO MARK:

{

Subscribed and sworn to before me this 22" day of   June, 1903 , 190......

Joseph P Smith
NOTARY PUBLIC.

My commission expires
Nov. 6/1903

BIRTH AFFIDAVIT.

DEPARTMENT OF THE INTERIOR.
COMMISSION TO THE FIVE CIVILIZED TRIBES.

IN RE APPLICATION FOR ENROLLMENT, as a citizen of the   Chickasaw   Nation, of   Mary Ruth Hamblin   , born on the 4th day of   October , 1902

Name of Father: Charley M. Hamblin   a citizen of the   Chickasaw   Nation.
Name of Mother: Nina Hamblin   a citizen of the United States Nation.

Postoffice   Purcell, I.T.

AFFIDAVIT OF MOTHER.

UNITED STATES OF AMERICA, Indian Territory, ⎫
    Southern   DISTRICT. ⎬

I,   Nina Hamblin   , on oath state that I am   21   years of age and a citizen by   Blood   , of the   United States   Nation; that I am the lawful wife of   Charley M. Hamblin   , who is a citizen, by Blood   of the   Chickasaw   Nation; that a   Female   child was born to me on 4th day of   October   , 1902; that said child has been named   Mary Ruth Hamblin   , and was living March 4, 1905.

Signature
Nina Hamblin

Witnesses To ~~Mark~~:
{ C.M. McClain
  Nep Lawson

Subscribed and sworn to before me this 25th day of   March   , 1905

O.H. Loomis
Notary Public.

Applications for Enrollment of Chickasaw Newborn
Act of 1905 Volume III

AFFIDAVIT OF ATTENDING PHYSICIAN OR MID-WIFE.

UNITED STATES OF AMERICA, Indian Territory, }
Southern   DISTRICT.

I, Dr. G M Tralle, a Physician, on oath state that I attended on Mrs. Nina Hamblin, wife of Charley M Hamblin on the 4th day of October, 1902; that there was born to her on said date a Female child; that said child was living March 4, 1905, and is said to have been named Mary Ruth Hamblin

Signature   G.M. Tralle, M.D.
Witnesses To ~~Mark~~:
{ C M McClain
{ Nep Lawson

Subscribed and sworn to before me this 25th day of March, 1905

O.H. Loomis
Notary Public.

BIRTH AFFIDAVIT.
DEPARTMENT OF THE INTERIOR.
COMMISSION TO THE FIVE CIVILIZED TRIBES.

IN RE APPLICATION FOR ENROLLMENT, as a citizen of the Chickasaw Nation, of Lela Mildred Beatrice Hamblin, born on the 7th day of May, 1904.

Name of Father: Charley M. Hamblin   a citizen of the Chickasaw Nation.
Name of Mother: Nina Hamblin   a citizen of the United States Nation.

Postoffice   Purcell, I.T.

AFFIDAVIT OF MOTHER.

UNITED STATES OF AMERICA, Indian Territory, }
Southern   DISTRICT.

I, Nina Hamblin, on oath state that I am 21 years of age and a citizen by Blood, of the United States Nation; that I am the lawful wife of Charley M. Hamblin, who is a citizen, by Blood of the Chickasaw Nation; that a Female child was born to me on 7th day of May, 1904; that said child has been named Lela Mildred Beatrice Hamblin, and was living March 4, 1905.

Nina Hamblin

217

Applications for Enrollment of Chickasaw Newborn
Act of 1905   Volume III

Witnesses To ~~Mark~~ *Signature*:
{ C.M. McClain
  Nep Lawson

Subscribed and sworn to before me this 25th day of March, 1905

O.H. Loomis
Notary Public.

AFFIDAVIT OF ATTENDING PHYSICIAN OR MID-WIFE.

UNITED STATES OF AMERICA, Indian Territory,
Southern DISTRICT.

I, Dr. G M Tralle, a Physician, on oath state that I attended on Mrs. Nina Hamblin, wife of Charley M Hamblin on the 7th day of May, 1904; that there was born to her on said date a Female child; that said child was living March 4, 1905, and is said to have been named Lela Mildred Beatrice Hamblin

G.M. Tralle, M.D.

Witnesses To ~~Mark~~ *Signature*:
{ C M McClain
  Nep Lawson

Subscribed and sworn to before me this 25th day of March, 1905

O.H. Loomis
Notary Public.

BIRTH AFFIDAVIT.   *#151*

IN RE-APPLICATION FOR ENROLLMENT, as a citizen of the Chickasaw Nation, of Lela Mildred Beatrice Hamblin, born on the 7 day of May, 1904

Name of Father: Charley M Hamblin   a citizen of the Chickasaw Nation.
Name of Mother: Nina Hamblin   *application* a citizen of the Intermarried Nation.
made but not heard from

Postoffice   Purcell I T.

Applications for Enrollment of Chickasaw Newborn
Act of 1905 Volume III

AFFIDAVIT OF MOTHER.

UNITED STATES OF AMERICA, INDIAN TERRITORY,
Southern District.

I, Nina Hamblin, on oath state that I am 21 years of age and a citizen by *intermarriage* of Chickasaw *application* Nation *made but not heard from* that I am the lawful wife of Charley M Hamblin, who is a citizen, by Blood of the Chickasaw Nation; that a female child was born to me on 7 day of May, 1904, that said child has been named Lela Mildred Beatrice Hamblin, and is now living.

Signature
Witnesses To ~~Mark~~:
{ O.H. Loomis
{ Nep Lawson

Mrs Nina Hamblin

Subscribed and sworn to before me this 27th day of February, 1905.

O.H. Loomis
Notary Public.

AFFIDAVIT OF ATTENDING PHYSICIAN OR MID-WIFE.

UNITED STATES OF AMERICA, INDIAN TERRITORY,
Southern District.

I, Dr. G M Tralle, a Physician, on oath state that I attended on Mrs. Nina Hamblin, wife of Charley M Hamblin on the 7 day of May, 190 4; that there was born to her on said date a female child; that said child is now living and is said to have been named Lela Mildred Beatrice Hamblin

G.M. Tralle, M.D.

Signature
Witnesses To ~~Mark~~:
{ O.H. Loomis
{ Nep Lawson

Subscribed and sworn to before me this 27th day of February, 1905.

O.H. Loomis
Notary Public.

Applications for Enrollment of Chickasaw Newborn
Act of 1905   Volume III

BIRTH AFFIDAVIT.

DEPARTMENT OF THE INTERIOR,
COMMISSION TO THE FIVE CIVILIZED TRIBES.

In Re Application for Enrollment, as a citizen of the Chickasaw Nation, of Lela Mildred Beatrice Hamblin, born on the 7th day of May, 1904

Name of Father: Charles M. Hamblin   a citizen of the Chickasaw Nation.
Name of Mother: Nina Hamblin   a citizen of the United States Nation.

Post-office   Purcell, Indian Territory

AFFIDAVIT OF MOTHER.

UNITED STATES OF AMERICA,
INDIAN TERRITORY,
  Southern   District.

I, Nina Hamblin, on oath state that I am twenty years of age and a citizen by marriage, of the Chickasaw Nation; that I am the lawful wife of Charles M. Hamblin, who is a citizen, by blood of the Chickasaw Nation; that a female child was born to me on 7th day of May, 1904, that said child has been named Lela Mildred Beatrice Hamblin, and is now living.

Mrs Nina Hamblin

WITNESSES TO MARK:

Subscribed and sworn to before me this 28th day of October, 1904

Mattie Straight
NOTARY PUBLIC.

AFFIDAVIT OF ATTENDING PHYSICIAN OR MID-WIFE.

UNITED STATES OF AMERICA,
INDIAN TERRITORY,
................................District.

I, G.M. Tralle, a Physician, on oath state that I attended on Mrs. Nina Hamblin, wife of Charles M. Hamblin on the 7 day of May, 1904; that there was born to her on said date a Female child; that said child is now living and is said to have been named Lela Mildred Beatrice Hamblin

Applications for Enrollment of Chickasaw Newborn
Act of 1905   Volume III

WITNESSES TO MARK:

G.M. Tralle

{

Subscribed and sworn to before me this 27th day of October, 1904

Mattie Straight
NOTARY PUBLIC.

BIRTH AFFIDAVIT.   #150

IN RE-APPLICATION FOR ENROLLMENT, as a citizen of the Chickasaw Nation, of Mary Ruth Hamblin, born on the 4th day of October, 1902

Name of Father: Charley M Hamblin   a citizen of the Chickasaw Nation.

Name of Mother: Nina Hamblin   a citizen of the United States Nation. *Intermarried*

Postoffice   Purcell I T.

AFFIDAVIT OF MOTHER.

UNITED STATES OF AMERICA, INDIAN TERRITORY, }
Southern District.

I, Nina Hamblin, on oath state that I am 21 years of age and a citizen by *intermarriage* of Chickasaw *but not approved* Nation *application made not heard from* that I am the lawful wife of Charley M Hamblin, who is a citizen, by Blood of the Chickasaw Nation; that a female child was born to me on 4th day of October, 1902, that said child has been named Mary Ruth Hamblin, and is now living.

Signature   Mrs Nina Hamblin
Witnesses To ~~Mark~~:
{ O.H. Loomis
  Nep Lawson

Subscribed and sworn to before me this 27th day of February, 1905.

O.H. Loomis
Notary Public.

Applications for Enrollment of Chickasaw Newborn
Act of 1905 Volume III

AFFIDAVIT OF ATTENDING PHYSICIAN OR MID-WIFE.

UNITED STATES OF AMERICA, INDIAN TERRITORY,
Southern District.

I, Dr. G M Tralle, a Physician, on oath state that I attended on Mrs. Nina Hamblin, wife of Charley M Hamblin on the 4th day of October, 190 2; that there was born to her on said date a female child; that said child is now living and is said to have been named Mary Ruth Hamblin

G.M. Tralle, M.D.

Signature
Witnesses To ~~Mark~~:
  O.H. Loomis
  Nep Lawson

Subscribed and sworn to before me this 27 day of February, 1905.

O.H. Loomis
Notary Public.

(The letter below does not belong with the current applicant.)

Muskogee, Indian Territory, August 7, 1900.

Mr. Siloman Foster,
    Goodland, Indian Territory,

Dear Sir:

    The Commission is in receipt of the application for enrollment as a citizen of the Choctaw Nation of Thomas Harkin, the infant son of Hannah Austin and Siloman Foster; on June 8th, 1900, the Commission wrote you returning the inclosed application for the reason that the witnesses to Hannah Austin's signature signed their names by mark, and it was not stated whether Hannah Austin signed by mark. At that time there was sent you a new application to be filled out with this correction, and instead you return the same application with the errors uncorrected. The Commission cannot accept the birth certificate in its present form. Signatures by mark must be attested by witnesses who can write their own names. If Hannah Austin does not sign her name by mark, it is not necessary to have any witnesses to her signature. There is sent you herewith a new blank birth certificate to be filled out instead of the one returned you today. Upon receipt of this new application in proper form, the application for enrollment of Thomas Harkin will receive consideration.

                Yours truly,

7-4231
B.C.   Acting Chairman.
3-7

Applications for Enrollment of Chickasaw Newborn
Act of 1905   Volume III

(The letter below does not belong with the current applicant.)

Muskogee, Indian Territory, October 29, 1900

Hannah Austin,
    Goodland, Indian Territory.

Dear Madam:

    The Commission is in receipt of the application for enrollment as a citizen of the Choctaw Nation of Thomas Foster, the infant son of Solomon Foster and Hannah Austin, born March the 2nd, 1900, and the same being in proper form has been duly filed with the records of the Commission and the child listed for enrollment as a citizen of the Choctaw Nation.

                  Yours truly,

                              Acting Chairman.

7-4231

                              9-1593.

Muskogee, Indian Territory, July 16, 1903.

C. N[sic]. Hamblin,
    Purcell, Indian Territory.

Dear Sir:

    Receipt is hereby acknowledged of the affidavits of Nina Hamblin and G. M. Tralle, relative to the birth of Mary Ruth Hamblin, infant daughter of C. M. and Nina Hamblin, October 4, 1902.

    Your attention is invited to section 28 of the act of Congress approved July 1, 1902, and ratified by the citizens of the Choctaw and Chickasaw Nations, September 25, 1902, which is as follows:

    "The names of all persons living on the date of the final ratification of this agreement entitled to be enrolled as provided in section 27 hereof shall be placed upon the rolls made by said Commission; and no child born thereafter to a citizen or freedman and no person intermarried thereafter to a citizen shall be entitled to enrollment or to participate in the distribution of the tribal property of the Choctaws and Chickasaws."

Applications for Enrollment of Chickasaw Newborn
Act of 1905   Volume III

Under the above legislation the Commission is without authority to enroll children born to citizens of the Choctaw or Chickasaw Nations, subsequent to September 25, 1902, the date of the final ratification of the above act of Congress by the citizens of the Choctaw and Chickasaw Nations.

Respectfully,

Commissioner in Charge.

9-1593

Muskogee, Indian Territory, March 30, 1905.

Charley M. Hamblin,
    Purcell, Indian Territory.

Dear Sir:

Receipt is hereby acknowledged of your letter of March 25, 1905, enclosing the affidavits of Nina Hamblin and G. M. Tralle to the birth of Mary Ruth Hamblin and Lela Mildred Beatrice Hamblin, children of Charley M. and Nina Hamblin, October 4, 1902, and May 7, 1904, and the same have been filed with our records as an application for the enrollment of said children.

Respectfully,

Chairman.

---

9 N B 218

Muskogee, Indian Territory, April 15, 1905.

Charley M. Hamblin,
    Purcell, Indian Territory.

Dear Sir:

You are hereby advised that before the applications for the enrollment of your infant children, Mary Ruth Hamblin and Lela Mildred Beatrice Hamblin, can be finally disposed of, it will be necessary for you to furnish either the original or a certified copy of the license and certificate of your marriage to their mother, Nina Hamblin, forwarding same at the earliest practicable date.

Respectfully,

Chairman.

Applications for Enrollment of Chickasaw Newborn
Act of 1905 Volume III

9 N.B. 218.

Muskogee, Indian Territory, May 4, 1905.

Charlie M. Hamblin,
    Purcell, Indian Territory.

Dear Sir:

    Receipt is hereby acknowledged of your letter of April 8, enclosing a certified copy of the marriage license and certificate between C. M. Hamblin and Nina Lawson, which you offer in support of the application for the enrollment of Mary Ruth and Lela Mildred Beatrice Hamblin and the same has been filed with the records in this case.

        Respectfully,

        Chairman.

Chic. N.B. - 219
    (Thenia Vivian Burris
    Born November 19, 1904)
    (Laura Leceta Burris
    Born October 12, 1903)

BIRTH AFFIDAVIT.   *No 34*

DEPARTMENT OF THE INTERIOR.
COMMISSION TO THE FIVE CIVILIZED TRIBES.

IN RE APPLICATION FOR ENROLLMENT, as a citizen of the Chickasaw Nation, of Laura Leceta Burris, born on the 12th day of October, 1903

Name of Father: George Washington Burris   a citizen of the Chickasaw Nation.
Name of Mother: Thenia Burris, formerly Jennings a citizen of the Chickasaw Nation.

        Postoffice   Tishomingo, I.T.

Applications for Enrollment of Chickasaw Newborn
Act of 1905   Volume III

AFFIDAVIT OF MOTHER.

UNITED STATES OF AMERICA, Indian Territory, }
Southern Jucucial[sic]   DISTRICT.

    I, Thenia Burris, formerly Jennings   , on oath state that I am twenty four years of age and a citizen by   blood   , of the   Chickasaw   Nation; that I am the lawful wife of George Washington Burris   , who is a citizen, by   blood   of the   Chickasaw   Nation; that a   female   child was born to me on   12th   day of   October   , 1903, that said child has been named   Laura Leceta Burris   , and is now living.

                                                Thenia Burris

Witnesses To Mark:
{

    Subscribed and sworn to before me this 31st day of   January , 1905.

                                            J.B. O'Bryan
                                                Notary Public.

AFFIDAVIT OF ATTENDING PHYSICIAN OR MID-WIFE.

UNITED STATES OF AMERICA, Indian Territory, }
Southern Judicial   DISTRICT.

    I,   W.W. Vannoy   , a   physician   , on oath state that I attended on Mrs. Thenia Burris, formerly Jennings   , wife of   George Washington Burris   on the   12th   day of October , 1903; that there was born to her on said date a   female   child; that said child is now living and is said to have been named   Laura Leceta Burris

                                         W.W. Vannoy, M.D.

Witnesses To Mark:
{

    Subscribed and sworn to before me this 31st day of   January , 1905.

                                            J.B. O'Bryan
                                              Notary Public.

Applications for Enrollment of Chickasaw Newborn
Act of 1905 Volume III

BIRTH AFFIDAVIT.

DEPARTMENT OF THE INTERIOR.
COMMISSION TO THE FIVE CIVILIZED TRIBES.

IN RE APPLICATION FOR ENROLLMENT, as a citizen of the Chickasaw Nation, of Laura Leceta Burris, born on the 12th day of October, 1903

Name of Father: George Washington Burris   a citizen of the Chickasaw Nation.
Name of Mother: Thenia Burris, nee Jennings   a citizen of the Chickasaw Nation.

Postoffice   Tishomingo, Ind. Ter.

AFFIDAVIT OF MOTHER.

UNITED STATES OF AMERICA, Indian Territory,
Soutnern[sic] Judicial   DISTRICT.

I, Thenia Burris, nee Jennings, on oath state that I am 24 years of age and a citizen by blood, of the Chickasaw Nation; that I am the lawful wife of George Washington Burris, who is a citizen, by blood of the Chickasaw Nation; that a female child was born to me on 12th day of October, 1903; that said child has been named Laura Leceta Burris, and was living March 4, 1905.

Thenia Burris

Witnesses To Mark:
{

Subscribed and sworn to before me this 27th day of March, 1905

J.B. O'Bryan
Notary Public.

AFFIDAVIT OF ATTENDING PHYSICIAN OR MID-WIFE.

UNITED STATES OF AMERICA, Indian Territory,
Southern Judicial   DISTRICT.

I, W.W. Vannoy, a Physician, on oath state that I attended on Mrs. Thenia Burris, nee Jennings, wife of George Washington Burris on the 12th day of October, 1903; that there was born to her on said date a female child; that said child was living March 4, 1905, and is said to have been named Laura Leceta Burris

W.W. Vannoy M.D.

Witnesses To Mark:
{

Applications for Enrollment of Chickasaw Newborn
Act of 1905 Volume III

Subscribed and sworn to before me this 27th day of   March   , 1905

                        J.B. O'Bryan
                        Notary Public.

BIRTH AFFIDAVIT.   *No 30*

DEPARTMENT OF THE INTERIOR.
COMMISSION TO THE FIVE CIVILIZED TRIBES.

IN RE APPLICATION FOR ENROLLMENT, as a citizen of the   Chickasaw   Nation, of   Thenia Vivian Burris   , born on the   19th   day of   November   , 1904

Name of Father: George Washington Burris   a citizen of the   Chickasaw   Nation.
Name of Mother: Thenia Burris, formerly Jennings a citizen of the   Chickasaw   Nation.

              Postoffice   Tishomingo, I.T.

AFFIDAVIT OF MOTHER.

UNITED STATES OF AMERICA, Indian Territory, }
   Southern Judicial   DISTRICT.

    I,   Thenia Burris, formerly Jennings   , on oath state that I am   twenty four   years of age and a citizen by   blood   , of the   Chickasaw   Nation; that I am the lawful wife of   George Washington Burris   , who is a citizen, by   blood   of the   Chickasaw   Nation; that a   female   child was born to me on   19th   day of   November   , 1904, that said child has been named   Thenia Vivian Burris   , and is now living.

                        Thenia Burris

Witnesses To Mark:
{

Subscribed and sworn to before me this 31st day of   January , 1905.

                        J.B. O'Bryan
                        Notary Public.

Applications for Enrollment of Chickasaw Newborn
Act of 1905   Volume III

AFFIDAVIT OF ATTENDING PHYSICIAN OR MID-WIFE.

UNITED STATES OF AMERICA, Indian Territory, }
   Southern Judicial   DISTRICT.

I, Henrietta L. Jennings, a mid-wife, on oath state that I attended on Mrs. Thenia Burris, formerly Jennings, wife of George Washington Burris on the 19th day of November, 1904; that there was born to her on said date a female child; that said child is now living and is said to have been named Thenia Vivian Burris

Henrietta L Jennings

Witnesses To Mark:
{

Subscribed and sworn to before me this 6th day of February, 1905.

J.B. O'Bryan
Notary Public.

BIRTH AFFIDAVIT.

DEPARTMENT OF THE INTERIOR.
COMMISSION TO THE FIVE CIVILIZED TRIBES.

IN RE APPLICATION FOR ENROLLMENT, as a citizen of the Chickasaw Nation, of Thenia Vivian Burris, born on the 19th day of November, 1904

Name of Father: George Washington Burris   a citizen of the Chickasaw Nation.
Name of Mother: Thenia Burris, nee Jennings   a citizen of the Chickasaw Nation.

Postoffice   Tishomingo, I.T.

AFFIDAVIT OF MOTHER.

UNITED STATES OF AMERICA, Indian Territory, }
   Southern Judicial   DISTRICT.

I, Thenia Burris, nee Jennings, on oath state that I am 24 years of age and a citizen by blood, of the Chickasaw Nation; that I am the lawful wife of George Washington Burris, who is a citizen, by blood of the Chickasaw Nation; that a female child was born to me on 19th day of November, 1904; that said child has been named Thenia Vivian Burris, and was living March 4, 1905.

Thenia Burris

Witnesses To Mark:
{

Applications for Enrollment of Chickasaw Newborn
Act of 1905   Volume III

Subscribed and sworn to before me this 27th day of   March , 1905

J.B. O'Bryan
Notary Public.

AFFIDAVIT OF ATTENDING PHYSICIAN OR MID-WIFE.

UNITED STATES OF AMERICA, Indian Territory,
Southern Judicial   DISTRICT.

I, H.L. Jennings , a midwife , on oath state that I attended on Mrs. Thenia Burris, nee Jennings , wife of George Washington Burris   on the 19th day of November , 1904; that there was born to her on said date a   female child; that said child was living March 4, 1905, and is said to have been named Thenia Vivian Burris

H.L. Jennings

Witnesses To Mark:

Subscribed and sworn to before me this 27th day of   March , 1905

J.B. O'Bryan
Notary Public.

Chickasaw 1595.

Muskogee, Indian Territory, March 31, 1905.

George W. Burris,
    Attorney at Law,
        Tishomingo, Indian Territory.

Dear Sir:

Receipt is hereby acknowledged of your letter of March 27th, enclosing the affidavits of Thenia Burris (Jennings) and W. W. Vannoy to the birth of Laura Leseta[sic] Burris, daughter of George Washington Burris and Thenia Burris, October 12, 1903; also affidavits of Thenia Burris and H. L. Jennings to the birth of Thenia Vivian Burris, daughter of George Washington Burris and Thenia Burris, November 19, 1904. The same have been filed with our records as applications for the enrollment of the above named children.

Respectfully,

Chairman.

Applications for Enrollment of Chickasaw Newborn
Act of 1905   Volume III

Chic. N.B. - 20
    (Folsom Hume Colbert
    Born March 28, 1904)

BIRTH AFFIDAVIT.

DEPARTMENT OF THE INTERIOR.
COMMISSION TO THE FIVE CIVILIZED TRIBES.

IN RE APPLICATION FOR ENROLLMENT, as a citizen of the   Chickasaw   Nation, of   Folsom Hume Colbert   , born on the   28th day of   March   , 1904

Name of Father: Walter Colbert   a citizen of the   Chickasaw   Nation.
Name of Mother: Henrietta C Colbert   a citizen of the   Chickasaw   Nation.

Postoffice   Ardmore, I.T.

AFFIDAVIT OF MOTHER.

UNITED STATES OF AMERICA, Indian Territory, }
   Southern   DISTRICT.

    I,   Henrietta C Colbert   , on oath state that I am   42   years of age and a citizen by   Intermarriage   , of the   Chickasaw   Nation; that I am the lawful wife of   Walter Colbert   , who is a citizen, by blood   of the   Chickasaw   Nation; that a   male   child was born to me on   28th day of   March   , 1904; that said child has been named   Folsom Hume Colbert   , and was living March 4, 1905.

                                Henrietta C. Colbert

Witnesses To Mark:
{

    Subscribed and sworn to before me this   15th day of   March   , 1905

                           WH Wimberly
                              Notary Public.

AFFIDAVIT OF ATTENDING PHYSICIAN OR MID-WIFE.

UNITED STATES OF AMERICA, Indian Territory, }
   Southern   DISTRICT.

    I,   I W Folsom   , a   physician   , on oath state that I attended on Mrs.   Henrietta C Colbert   , wife of   Walter Colbert   on the   28th day of

Applications for Enrollment of Chickasaw Newborn
Act of 1905   Volume III

March   , 1904; that there was born to her on said date a   male   child; that said child was living March 4, 1905, and is said to have been named Folsom Hume Colbert

I.W. Folsom M.D.

Witnesses To Mark:
{

   Subscribed and sworn to before me this 15   day of   March   , 1905

WH Wimberly
Notary Public.

9-1599

Muskogee, Indian Territory, March 21, 1905.

Walter Colbert,
   Ardmore, Indian Territory.

Dear Sir:

   Receipt is hereby acknowledged of the affidavits of Henrietta C. Colbert and II[sic]. W. Folsom to the birth of Folsom Hume Colbert, son of Walter and Henrietta C. Colbert, March 28, 1904, and the same have been filed with our records as an application for the enrollment of said child.

Respectfully,

Chairman.

Chic. N.B. - 221
   (Alvin Bradley
   Born February 26, 1905)
   (Eula Bradley
   Born September 29, 1902)

Applications for Enrollment of Chickasaw Newborn
Act of 1905 Volume III

Certificate of Record of Marriage

UNITED STATES OF AMERICA,
    INDIAN TERRITORY, } sct.
    Southern District.

DEPARTMENT OF THE INTERIOR,
COMMISSION TO THE FIVE CIVILIZED TRIBES.
FILED
APR 26 1905
Tams Bixby CHAIRMAN.

I, C. M. CAMPBELL, Clerk of the United States Court, in the Territory and District aforesaid, DO HEREBY CERTIFY, that the License for and Certificate of Marriage of

Mr   Bruce Bradley   and
M   Ida Underwood

were filed in my office in said Territory and District the 28th day of Nov. A.D., 1900 and duly recorded in Book E of Marriage Record, Page 133

WITNESS my hand and seal of said Court, at Ardmore, this C. M. CAMPBELL, Clerk 1st day of Dec A.D. 1900

C. M. Campbell
CLERK.

Marriage License

No 1323

United States of America,
    INDIAN TERRITORY, } ss:
    SOUTHERN DISTRICT.

To Any Person Authorized by Law to Solemnize Marriage, Greeting:

You Are Hereby Commanded To solemnize the Rite and publish the Banns of Matrimony between Mr.   Bruce Bradley of   Hickory   in the Indian Territory, aged   23   years, and M   Ida Underwood   of   Hickory in the Indian Territory, aged   17   years, according to law; and do you officially sign and return this License to the parties therein named.

Applications for Enrollment of Chickasaw Newborn
Act of 1905   Volume III

𝔚𝔦𝔱𝔫𝔢𝔰𝔰 My hand and official Seal, this   24   day of   Nov.   A. D. 190 0

C.M. Campbell
Clerk of the United States Court.

Certificate of Marriage.

United States of America,   I,   R. W. Smith
  INDIAN TERRITORY,   ss: a   Minister
  SOUTHERN DISTRICT.

do hereby certify that on the   25   day of   Nov.   A. D. 190 0 , I did duly and according to law, as commanded in the foregoing License, solemnize the Rite and publish the Banns of Matrimony between the parties therein named.

WITNESS my hand, this   25   day of   Nov   A. D. 190 0

My credentials are recorded in the office of the Clerk of the United States Court, Indian Territory, Southern District, at Ardmore, Book   A , Page 72 & 73

(NOTE.--The person officiating should fill in the spaces   R.W. Smith
for book and page and sign here.) ☞   a   Minister

NOTE. (a) - This License and Certificate of Marriages must be returned to the office of the Clerk of the United States Court in the Indian Territory, at Ardmore, within sixty days from the date thereof, or the party to whom the License was issued will be liable in the amount of ONE HUNDRED DOLLARS ($100).

NOTE. (b) - No person is authorized to perform the Marriage Ceremony in the Southern District unless the proper credentials have first been recorded in the Clerk's office.

BIRTH AFFIDAVIT.

DEPARTMENT OF THE INTERIOR.
COMMISSION TO THE FIVE CIVILIZED TRIBES.

IN RE APPLICATION FOR ENROLLMENT, as a citizen of the   Chickasaw   Nation, of   Alvin Bradley , born on the 26 day of Feb , 1905

Name of Father: Bruce Bradley   a citizen of the   Chickasaw Nation.
Name of Mother: Ida E Bradley   a citizen of the .... Nation.

Postoffice ....

Applications for Enrollment of Chickasaw Newborn
Act of 1905   Volume III

AFFIDAVIT OF MOTHER.

UNITED STATES OF AMERICA, Indian Territory, }
Southern   DISTRICT.

I, Ida E Bradley, on oath state that I am 20 years of age and a citizen by .... of the .... Nation; that I am the lawful wife of Bruce Bradley, who is a citizen, by blood of the Chickasaw Nation; that a male child was born to me on 26" day of February, 1905; that said child has been named Alvin Bradley, and was living March 4, 1905.

                                        Ida E Bradley

Witnesses To Mark:
{

Subscribed and sworn to before me this 28 day of March, 1905

                                        J L Mentzer
                                        Notary Public.

AFFIDAVIT OF ATTENDING PHYSICIAN OR MID-WIFE.

UNITED STATES OF AMERICA, Indian Territory, }
Southern   DISTRICT.

I, N.D. Meredith, a phisian[sic], on oath state that I attended on Mrs. Ida E Bradley, wife of Bruce Bradley on the 26 day of February, 1905; that there was born to her on said date a male child; that said child was living March 4, 1905, and is said to have been named Alvin Bradley

                                        N.D. Meredith

Witnesses To Mark:
{

Subscribed and sworn to before me this 28 day of March, 1905

                                        J L Mentzer
                                        Notary Public.

Applications for Enrollment of Chickasaw Newborn
Act of 1905   Volume III

BIRTH AFFIDAVIT.

DEPARTMENT OF THE INTERIOR.
COMMISSION TO THE FIVE CIVILIZED TRIBES.

IN RE APPLICATION FOR ENROLLMENT, as a citizen of the Chickasaw Nation, of   Eula Bradley   , born on the 29 day of September , 1902

Name of Father: Bruce Bradley   a citizen of the   Chickasaw   Nation.
Name of Mother: Ida E Bradley   a citizen of the .... Nation.

Postoffice   Hickory I.T.

AFFIDAVIT OF MOTHER.

UNITED STATES OF AMERICA, Indian Territory, }
   Southern   DISTRICT.

I,   Ida E Bradley   , on oath state that I am 20   years of age and a citizen by .... of the .... Nation; that I am the lawful wife of   Bruce Bradley   , who is a citizen, by blood   of the   Chickasaw   Nation; that a female   child was born to me on   29th day of   September   , 1902; that said child has been named   Eula Bradley   , and was living March 4, 1905.

Ida E Bradley

Witnesses To Mark:
{

Subscribed and sworn to before me this   28 day of   March   , 1905

J L Mentzer
Notary Public.

AFFIDAVIT OF ATTENDING PHYSICIAN OR MID-WIFE.

UNITED STATES OF AMERICA, Indian Territory, }
.... DISTRICT.

I,   T. B. Laumann   , a   phisian[sic]   , on oath state that I attended on Mrs.   Ida E Bradley   , wife of   Bruce Bradley   on the   29 day of   September , 1902; that there was born to her on said date a   female   child; that said child was living March 4, 1905, and is said to have been named Eula Bradley

T.B. Laumann, M.D.

Witnesses To Mark:
{

Applications for Enrollment of Chickasaw Newborn
Act of 1905 Volume III

Subscribed and sworn to before me this 28 day of March , 1905

J L Mentzer
Notary Public.

Substitute   Chickasaw 1604

Muskogee, Indian Territory, October 16, 1902.

Bruce Bradley,
    Hickory, Indian Territory.

Dear Sir:

    Receipt is hereby acknowledged of the application for enrollment as a citizen of the Chickasaw Nation of Eula Bradley, the infant daughter of Bruce and Ida E. Bradley, born September 29, 1902.

    The same is returned to you herewith with the information that the Commission cannot receive or consider the application for the enrollment of this child as a citizen of the Chickasaw Nation, it appearing that the said child was born September 29, 1902, subsequent to the ratification of September 25, 1902, by the citizens of the Choctaw and Chickasaw Nations of an agreement recently entered into between the United States and the citizens of these two tribes.

    Section twenty-eight of the agreement above referred to provides as follows:

    "The names of all persons living on the date of the final ratification of this agreement entitled to be enrolled as provided in section 27 hereof shall be placed upon the rolls made by said Commission; and no child born thereafter to a citizen or freedman and no person intermarried thereafter to a citizen shall be entitled to enrollment or to participate in the distribution of the tribal property of the Choctaws and Chickasaws."

                                Respectfully,

                                              Acting Chairman.

Enc B. I. 97

Applications for Enrollment of Chickasaw Newborn
Act of 1905 Volume III

Chickasaw 1604.

Muskogee, Indian Territory, April 3, 1905.

Bruce Bradley,
    Hickory, Indian Territory.

Dear Sir:

    Receipt is hereby acknowledged of the affidavits of Ida E. Bradley and T. B. Laumann to the birth of Eula Bradley, daughter of Bruce and Ida E. Bradley, September 29, 1902; also affidavits of Ida E. Bradley and H. D. Meredith to the birth of Alvin Bradley, son of Bruce and Ida E. Bradley, February 26, 1905, and the Same[sic] have been filed with our records as applications for the enrollment of said children.

Respectfully,

Chairman.

---

9 N B 221

Muskogee, Indian Territory, April 15, 1905.

Bruce Bradley,
    Hickory, Indian Territory.

Dear Sir:

    You are hereby advised that before the applications for the enrollment of your infant children, Eula Bradley and Alvin Bradley, can be finally disposed of, it will be necessary for you to furnish the Commission with either the original or a certified copy of the license and certificate of your marriage to their mother Ida E. Bradley.

    Please give this matter your immediate attention.

Respectfully,

Chairman.

Applications for Enrollment of Chickasaw Newborn
Act of 1905   Volume III

221

9 NB ~~361~~

Muskogee, Indian Territory, April 27, 1905.

Bruce Bradley,
Hickory, Indian Territory.

Dear Sir:

Receipt is hereby acknowledged of your letter of April 21, 1905, enclosing marriage license and certificate between yourself and Ida Underwood which you offer in support of the application for the enrollment of your children Eula and Alvin Bradley and the same have been filed with the record in this case.

Respectfully,

Chairman.

Chic. N.B. - 222
 (Raymond Edington Perry
 Born October 4, 1903)

(COPY)

MARRIAGE LICENSE.
No. 777/

UNITED STATES OF AMERICA,	)	To Any Person Authorized By Law
INDIAN TERRITORY	)ss.	To Solemnize Marriage- Greeting:
SOUTHERN DISTRICT.	)	

YOU ARE HEREBY COMMANDED to solemnize the Rite and publish the Banns of Matrimony between Mr. Charles E. Perry, of Naples, in the Indian Territory, aged 27 years, and Miss Lucy Ratliff, of Dibble, in the Indian Territory, aged 20 years, according to law, and do you officially sign and return this License to the parties therein named.

Witness my hand and official seal, this 2nd day of October, A. D. 1902.

C. M. Campbell,
Clerk of the United States Court.

By J. W. Speake, Deputy.

Applications for Enrollment of Chickasaw Newborn
Act of 1905   Volume III

CERTIFICATE OF MARRIAGE.

UNITED STATES OF AMERICA,   )
INDIAN TERRITORY,   )ss.
SOUTHERN DISTRICT.   )   I, W. T. Cantrell, a minister of the Gospel, do hereby certify that on the 23rd day of Oct., A. D. 1902, I did duly and according to law, as commanded in the foregoing license, solemnize the Rite and publish the Banns of matrimony between the parties therein named.
   Witness my hand this 24 day of Oct. 1902.
   My credentials are recorded in the office of the Clerk of the United States Court, Indian Territory, Central District, at S. McAlester, Book B, Page 227.

(Signed) W. T. Cantrell.
a minister of the Gospel.

The foregoing is endorsed as follows: CERTIFICATE OF RECORD OF MARRIAGE. United States of America, Indian Territory, Southern District, sct. I, C. M. Campbell, Clerk of the United States Court, in the Territory and District aforesaid, do hereby certify that the License for and certificate of marriage of Mr. C. E. Perry and Miss Lucy Ratliff were filed in my office in said Territory and District the 24" day of October, A. D. 1902, and duly recorded in book F of Marriage Record, Page 542. Witness my hand and seal of said court at Ardmore, Indian Territory this 24" day of October, A. D. 1902, C. M. Campbell, Clerk. FILED Oct. 24, 1902 2 P M, C. M. Campbell, Clerk Southern Dist. Ind. Ter.

--------------------oOo--------------------

   I, J. E. Williams, a Notary Public within and for the Southern District of the Indian Territory, do hereby certify that the above and foregoing is a true and correct copy of the Marriage License and Certificate of Marriage of Charles E. Perry and Miss Lucy Ratliff, offered in evidence in the matter of the application for the enrollment as a citizen of the Chickasaw Nation of Raymon[sic] Edington Perry.

JE Williams
Notary Public.

BIRTH AFFIDAVIT.

   IN RE-APPLICATION FOR ENROLLMENT, as a citizen of the   Chickasaw   Nation, of   Raymond Edington Perry   , born on the 4th day of Oct. , 190 3

Name of Father: Charley Perry   a citizen of the   Chickasaw   Nation.
Name of Mother: Lucy Perry   a citizen of the   U.S.   Nation.

Postoffice   Naples, I. T.

Applications for Enrollment of Chickasaw Newborn
Act of 1905 Volume III

AFFIDAVIT OF MOTHER.

UNITED STATES OF AMERICA, INDIAN TERRITORY,
Southern District.

I, Lucy Perry, on oath state that I am 23 years of age and a citizen by Blood, of the United States Nation; that I am the lawful wife of Charley Perry, who is a citizen, by Blood of the Chickasaw Nation; that a male child was born to me on 4th day of Oct, 1903, that said child has been named Raymond Edington Perry, and is now living.

Lucy Perry

Witnesses To Mark:

Subscribed and sworn to before me this 6 day of April, 1905.

James B. Pilgrim
Notary Public.

AFFIDAVIT OF ATTENDING PHYSICIAN OR MID-WIFE.

UNITED STATES OF AMERICA, INDIAN TERRITORY,
Southern District.

I, M J Clark, a Midwife, on oath state that I attended on Mrs. Lucy Perry, wife of Charley Perry on the 4th day of Oct, 190 3; that there was born to her on said date a male child; that said child is now living and is said to have been named Raymond Edington Perry

M J Clark

Witnesses To Mark:

Subscribed and sworn to before me this 6 day of April, 1905.

James B. Pilgrim
Notary Public.

My commission expires on the 18 March 1909

Applications for Enrollment of Chickasaw Newborn
Act of 1905 Volume III

BIRTH AFFIDAVIT.

DEPARTMENT OF THE INTERIOR,
COMMISSION TO THE FIVE CIVILIZED TRIBES.

In Re Application for Enrollment, as a citizen of the Chickasaw Nation, of Raymond Edington Perry , born on the 4 day of October , 1903

Name of Father: Charles Perry a citizen of the Chickasaw Nation.
Name of Mother: Lucy Perry a citizen of the .... Nation.

Post-office Naples I.T.

AFFIDAVIT OF MOTHER.

UNITED STATES OF AMERICA,
   INDIAN TERRITORY,
.... District.

I, Lucy Perry , on oath state that I am Twenty one years of age and a citizen by Intermarriage , of the Chickasaw Nation; that I am the lawful wife of Charles Perry , who is a citizen, by Blood of the Chickasaw Nation; that a male child was born to me on 4th day of October , 1903 , that said child has been named Raymond Edington , and is now living.

                          Lucy Perry

WITNESSES TO MARK:
  Martha Clark
  R.E. Albright

Subscribed and sworn to before me this ~~April~~ 9 day of April , 1904

                    B Ward
                      NOTARY PUBLIC.

AFFIDAVIT OF ATTENDING PHYSICIAN OR MID-WIFE.

UNITED STATES OF AMERICA,
   INDIAN TERRITORY,
.... District.

I, J B*(illegible)* McBride , a Physician , on oath state that I attended on Mrs. Lucy Perry , wife of Charles Perry on the 4 day of October , 1903 ; that there was born to her on said date a boy child; that said child is now living and is said to have been named Raymond Edington Perry

Applications for Enrollment of Chickasaw Newborn
Act of 1905   Volume III

J B *(illegible)* McBride

WITNESSES TO MARK:
{ Martha Clark
R.E. Albright

Subscribed and sworn to before me this   9   day of   April   , 1904

B Ward

NOTARY PUBLIC.

---

9 N B 222

Muskogee, Indian Territory, April 14, 1905.

J. E. Williams,
    Tishomingo, Indian Territory.

Dear Sir:

    There is inclosed you herewith a copy of the license and certificate of marriage of Charles E. Perry and Miss Lucy Ratliff. Please certify to the same in your official capacity as a Notary Public for the Southern District of Indian Territory, and after attaching your seal thereto, forward to the Commission at the earliest practicable date.

                Respectfully,

LM 14-125   Commissioner in Charge.

Chic. N.B. - 223
    (Vaughon Cochran
    Born February 10, 1903)

Applications for Enrollment of Chickasaw Newborn
Act of 1905 Volume III

BIRTH AFFIDAVIT.

DEPARTMENT OF THE INTERIOR.
COMMISSION TO THE FIVE CIVILIZED TRIBES.

IN RE APPLICATION FOR ENROLLMENT, as a citizen of the Chickasaw Nation, of Vaughon Cochran, born on the 10 day of Feby, 1903

Name of Father: W H Cochran   a citizen of the Chickasaw Nation.
Name of Mother: Corrie[sic] Cochran   a citizen of the Chickasaw Nation.

Postoffice Marietta I T

AFFIDAVIT OF MOTHER.

UNITED STATES OF AMERICA, Indian Territory, }
Southern   DISTRICT.

I, Corrie Cochran, on oath state that I am 27 years of age and a citizen by Intermarriage, of the Chickasaw Nation; that I am the lawful wife of W H Cochran, who is a citizen, by Blood of the Chickasaw Nation; that a Male child was born to me on 10 day of Feby, 1903; that said child has been named Vaughon Cochran, and was living March 4, 1905.

           Carrie Cochran

Witnesses To Mark:
{

Subscribed and sworn to before me this 20 day of Mch, 1905

           D G Bartlett
           Notary Public.

AFFIDAVIT OF ATTENDING PHYSICIAN OR MID-WIFE.

UNITED STATES OF AMERICA, Indian Territory, }
Southern   DISTRICT.

I, A E Martin, a Physician, on oath state that I attended on Mrs. Carrie Cochran, wife of W H Cochran on the 10 day of Feby, 1903; that there was born to her on said date a Male child; that said child was living March 4, 1905, and is said to have been named Vaughon Cochran

           AE Martin M.D.

Witnesses To Mark:
{

Applications for Enrollment of Chickasaw Newborn
Act of 1905   Volume III

Subscribed and sworn to before me this 20 day of   Mch   , 1905

                                           D G Bartlett
                                           Notary Public.

Chic. N.B. - 224
    (Leslie Connelly
    Born January 23, 1903)

BIRTH AFFIDAVIT.   No 70
DEPARTMENT OF THE INTERIOR.
COMMISSION TO THE FIVE CIVILIZED TRIBES.

    IN RE APPLICATION FOR ENROLLMENT, as a citizen of the   Chickasaw   Nation, of   Leslie Connelly   , born on the   23   day of   January , 1903

Name of Father: John William Connelly   a citizen of the   Chickasaw   Nation.
Name of Mother: Hannah Connelly   a citizen of the   Chickasaw   Nation.

                  Postoffice   Yarnaby

AFFIDAVIT OF MOTHER.

UNITED STATES OF AMERICA, Indian Territory, }
    Central   DISTRICT.

    I,   Hannah Connelly   , on oath state that I am 42   years of age and a citizen by   intermarriage   , of the   Chickasaw   Nation; that I am the lawful wife of   John William Connelly   , who is a citizen, by   blood   of the   Chickasaw   Nation; that a   male   child was born to me on   23   day of   January   , 1903, that said child has been named   Lesley[sic]   , and is now living.

                                  Hannah Connelly

Witnesses To Mark:
  { Lizzie Bedwell
    D.L. Bedwell

Applications for Enrollment of Chickasaw Newborn
Act of 1905 Volume III

Subscribed and sworn to before me this 19 day of January , 1905.

S M Mead
Notary Public.

AFFIDAVIT OF ATTENDING PHYSICIAN OR MID-WIFE.

UNITED STATES OF AMERICA, Indian Territory, }
Central DISTRICT.

I, M. M. Pantsky , a Midwife , on oath state that I attended on Mrs. Hannah Connelly , wife of John W Connelly on the 23rd day of Jan , 1903; that there was born to her on said date a male child; that said child is now living and is said to have been named Leslie Connelly

her
M M x Pantsky
mark

Witnesses To Mark:
{ (Name Illegible)
{ L.E. Temple

Subscribed and sworn to before me this 4th day of Jan , 1905.

W.J. O'Donby
Notary Public.

BIRTH AFFIDAVIT.

DEPARTMENT OF THE INTERIOR.
COMMISSION TO THE FIVE CIVILIZED TRIBES.

IN RE APPLICATION FOR ENROLLMENT, as a citizen of the Chickasaw Nation, of Leslie Connelly , born on the 23 day of January , 1903

Name of Father: John Wm Connelly a citizen of the Chickasaw Nation.
Name of Mother: Hannah Connelly a citizen of the Chickasaw Nation.

Postoffice Yarnaby I.T.

AFFIDAVIT OF MOTHER.

UNITED STATES OF AMERICA, Indian Territory, }
Central DISTRICT.

I, Hannah Connelly , on oath state that I am 42 years of age and a citizen by Intermarriage , of the Chickasaw Nation; that I am the lawful wife

Applications for Enrollment of Chickasaw Newborn
Act of 1905 Volume III

of John Wm Connelly , who is a citizen, by Blood of the Chickasaw Nation; that a male child was born to me on 23 day of January , 1903; that said child has been named Leslie Connelly , and was living March 4, 1905.

                                            her
Witnesses To Mark: Hannah x Connelly
  { Lida Thaxton   mark
    Rosa Thaxton

Subscribed and sworn to before me this 29 day of March , 1905

                          W.T. Thaxton
                          Notary Public.

AFFIDAVIT OF ATTENDING PHYSICIAN OR MID-WIFE.

UNITED STATES OF AMERICA, Indian Territory,
    Central   DISTRICT.

I, Mary Mildon Pantsky , a mid-wife , on oath state that I attended on Mrs. Hannah Connelly , wife of John Wm Connelly on the 23 day of January , 1903; that there was born to her on said date a male child; that said child was living March 4, 1905, and is said to have been named Leslie Connelly

                                     her
                            Mary Mildon x Pantsky
Witnesses To Mark: mark
  { Lida Thaxton
    Rosa Thaxton

Subscribed and sworn to before me this 29 day of March , 1905

                          W.T. Thaxton
                          Notary Public.

Chic. N.B. - 225
    (John Taylor Moore
    Born February 19, 1905)

Applications for Enrollment of Chickasaw Newborn
Act of 1905 Volume III

BIRTH AFFIDAVIT.

DEPARTMENT OF THE INTERIOR.
COMMISSION TO THE FIVE CIVILIZED TRIBES.

IN RE APPLICATION FOR ENROLLMENT, as a citizen of the Chickasaw Nation, of John Taylor Moore, born on the 19" day of Feby, 1905

Name of Father: John C. Moore   a citizen of the Chickasaw Nation.
Name of Mother: Mary Ellen Moore   a citizen of the Chickasaw Nation.

Postoffice   Aylesworth I.T.

AFFIDAVIT OF MOTHER.

UNITED STATES OF AMERICA, Indian Territory,
Southern   DISTRICT.

I, Mary Ellen Moore, on oath state that I am ....years of age and a citizen by blood, of the Chickasaw Nation; that I am the lawful wife of John C. Moore, who is a citizen, by intermarriage of the Chickasaw Nation; that a male child was born to me on 19" day of Feb, 1905; that said child has been named John Taylor Moore, and was living March 4, 1905.

Mary Ellen Moore

Witnesses To Mark:
{

Subscribed and sworn to before me this 25" day of March, 1905

Frank Adams
Notary Public.

AFFIDAVIT OF ATTENDING PHYSICIAN OR MID-WIFE.

UNITED STATES OF AMERICA, Indian Territory,
Southern   DISTRICT.

I, W. N. Dean, a Physician, on oath state that I attended on Mrs. Mary Ellen Moore, wife of John C. Moore on the 19" day of Feb, 1905; that there was born to her on said date a male child; that said child was living March 4, 1905, and is said to have been named John Taylor Moore

W.N. Dean, MD

Witnesses To Mark:
{

Applications for Enrollment of Chickasaw Newborn
Act of 1905 Volume III

Subscribed and sworn to before me this 25" day of March , 1905

                                              Frank Adams
                                              Notary Public.

<u>Chic. N.B. - 226</u>
    (Donald Speairs Marshall
    Born October 29, 1904)

BIRTH AFFIDAVIT.

DEPARTMENT OF THE INTERIOR.
COMMISSION TO THE FIVE CIVILIZED TRIBES.

IN RE APPLICATION FOR ENROLLMENT, as a citizen of the Chickasaw Nation, of Donald Speairs Moore , born on the 29th day of October , 1904

Name of Father: J. Horace Marshall   a citizen of the Chickasaw Nation.
Name of Mother: Lillie Marshall   a citizen of the Chickasaw Nation.

                              Postoffice   Durant I.T.

AFFIDAVIT OF MOTHER.

UNITED STATES OF AMERICA, Indian Territory,
    Central   DISTRICT.

    I, Lillie Marshall , on oath state that I am 26 years of age and a citizen by blood , of the Chickasaw Nation; that I am the lawful wife of J. Horace Marshall , who is a citizen, by intermarriage of the Chickasaw Nation; that a male child was born to me on 29th day of October , 1904, that said child has been named Donald Speairs Moore , and is now living.

                                      Lillie Marshall

Witnesses To Mark:

Applications for Enrollment of Chickasaw Newborn
Act of 1905 Volume III

Subscribed and sworn to before me this 20th day of March , 1905.

                                              BS Johnson
                                              Notary Public.

AFFIDAVIT OF ATTENDING PHYSICIAN OR MID-WIFE.

UNITED STATES OF AMERICA, Indian Territory, }
    Central   DISTRICT. }

I, Y. M. Rushing , a M.D. , on oath state that I attended on Mrs. Lillie Marshall , wife of J. Horace Marshall on the 29th day of October , 1904; that there was born to her on said date a male child; that said child is now living and is said to have been named Donald Speairs Moore

                                    Y. M. Rushing M.D.

Witnesses To Mark:
{

Subscribed and sworn to before me this 20 day of March , 1905.

                                        BS Johnson
                                        Notary Public.

Chic. N.B. - 227
      (Cicel Perry Powell
      Born September 13, 1903)

BIRTH AFFIDAVIT.
DEPARTMENT OF THE INTERIOR.
COMMISSION TO THE FIVE CIVILIZED TRIBES.

IN RE APPLICATION FOR ENROLLMENT, as a citizen of the Chickasaw Nation, of Cicel Perry Powell , born on the 13 day of September , 1903

Name of Father: Thomas Porter Powell   a citizen of the Chickasaw Nation.
Name of Mother: Ellen Jane Powell   a citizen of the Chickasaw Nation.

                              Postoffice   Kemp Ind Ter

Applications for Enrollment of Chickasaw Newborn
Act of 1905   Volume III

AFFIDAVIT OF MOTHER.

UNITED STATES OF AMERICA, Indian Territory, }
   Central   DISTRICT.

    I,   Ellen Jane Powell   , on oath state that I am   37   years of age and a citizen by   Birth   , of the   Chickasaw   Nation; that I am the lawful wife of Thomas Porter Powell   , who is a citizen, by Marriage   of the   Chickasaw Nation; that a   male   child was born to me on   13 day of September   , 1903; that said child has been named   Cicel Perry Powell   , and was living March 4, 1905.

                                 Ellen Jane Powell

Witnesses To Mark:
{

    Subscribed and sworn to before me this   27 day of   March   , 1905

                                 S T Johns
                                    Notary Public.

AFFIDAVIT OF ATTENDING PHYSICIAN OR MID-WIFE.

UNITED STATES OF AMERICA, Indian Territory, }
   Central   DISTRICT.

    I,   J.N. Taylor   , a Physician   , on oath state that I attended on Mrs. Ellen J Powell   , wife of   T P Powell   on the 13 day of September   , 1903; that there was born to her on said date a   male   child; that said child was living March 4, 1905, and is said to have been named ....

                                 J.N. Taylor M.D.

Witnesses To Mark:
{

    Subscribed and sworn to before me this   27 day of   March   , 1905

                                 S T Johns
                                    Notary Public.

Applications for Enrollment of Chickasaw Newborn
Act of 1905   Volume III

Chic. N.B. - 228
(Joseph Maytubby Seifried
Born March 15, 1903)

It appearing from the within affidavits that Joe Maytubbie[sic] Seifried, born March 15, 1903, for whose enrollment as a citizen by blood of the Chickasaw Nation application was made under the provisions of the Act of Congress approved March 3, 1905, (33 Stat., 1071) died September 8, 1904, it is hereby ordered that the application for the enrollment of said Joseph Maytubby Seifried as a citizen by blood of the Chickasaw Nation be dismissed.

Tams Bixby
Commissioner.

Muskogee, Indian Territory.
AUG 23 1905

DEPARTMENT OF THE INTERIOR.
COMMISSION TO THE FIVE CIVILIZED TRIBES.

In the matter of the death of   Joseph Maytubby Seifried a citizen of the   Chickasaw   Nation, who formerly resided at or near   Purcell   , Ind. Ter., and died on the   8th day of   September   , 1904

AFFIDAVIT OF RELATIVE.

UNITED STATES OF AMERICA, Indian Territory,
Southern   DISTRICT.

I,   Wm F. Seifried   , on oath state that I am   28   years of age and a citizen by blood   , of the   Chickasaw   Nation; that my postoffice address is   Purcell   , Ind. Ter.; that I am   the father   of   Joseph Maytubby Seifried   who was a citizen, by blood   , of the   Chickasaw   Nation and that said   Joseph Maytubby Seifried   died on the   8th day of   September   , 1904

W^m F Seifried

Witnesses To Mark:

Subscribed and sworn to before me this   14th day of   July   , 1905.

Dorset Carter
Notary Public.

Applications for Enrollment of Chickasaw Newborn
Act of 1905   Volume III

AFFIDAVIT OF ACQUAINTANCE.

UNITED STATES OF AMERICA, Indian Territory,
Southern   DISTRICT.

I, Mary F. Seifried, on oath state that I am .... years of age, and a citizen by blood of the Chickasaw Nation; that my postoffice address is Purcell, Ind. Ter.; that I was personally acquainted with Joseph Maytubby Seifried who was a citizen, by blood, of the Chickasaw Nation; and that said Joseph Maytubby Seifried died on the 8th day of September, 1904

Mary Seifried

Witnesses To Mark:
{

Subscribed and sworn to before me this 14th day of July, 1905.

Dorset Carter
Notary Public.

BIRTH AFFIDAVIT.

DEPARTMENT OF THE INTERIOR,
COMMISSION TO THE FIVE CIVILIZED TRIBES.

In Re Application for Enrollment, as a citizen of the Chickasaw Nation, of Joe Maytubbie Seifried, born on the 15th day of March, 1903

Name of Father: William F Seifried   a citizen of the Chickasaw Nation.
Name of Mother: Mary Florence Seifried   a citizen of the Chickasaw Nation.
by enrolment[sic]

Post-office   Purcell I.T.

AFFIDAVIT OF MOTHER.

UNITED STATES OF AMERICA,
INDIAN TERRITORY,
Southern   District.

I, Mary Florence Seifried, on oath state that I am 22 years of age and a citizen by Marriage, of the Chickasaw Nation; that I am the lawful wife of William F Seifried, who is a citizen, by blood of the Chickasaw Nation; that a male child was born to me on the 15th day of March, 1903, that said child has been named Joe Maytubbie Seifried, and is now living.

Mary Florence Seifried

WITNESSES TO MARK:
{ C.B. Gold
  Geo W Miller

Applications for Enrollment of Chickasaw Newborn
Act of 1905   Volume III

Subscribed and sworn to before me this 20th day of July , 1903

Geo W Miller
NOTARY PUBLIC.

AFFIDAVIT OF ATTENDING PHYSICIAN OR MID-WIFE.

UNITED STATES OF AMERICA, }
INDIAN TERRITORY,
.... District.

I, Joseph S Childs , a Physician , on oath state that I attended on Mrs. Mary Florence Seifried , wife of W^m F Seifried on the 15 day of March , 1903 ; that there was born to her on said date a male child; that said child is now living and is said to have been named Joe Maytubby Seifried

J.S. Childs

WITNESSES TO MARK:
{ C.B. Gold
{ Geo W Miller

Subscribed and sworn to before me this 20th day of July , 1903

Geo W Miller
NOTARY PUBLIC.

---

9 N B 228

Muskogee, Indian Territory, April 17, 1905.

William F. Seifried,
    Purcell, Indian Territory.

Dear Sir:

    There is inclosed you herewith for execution application for the enrollment of your infant child, Joe Maytubbie Seifried, born March 15, 1903.

    The affidavits heretofore filed with the Commission show the child was living on July 20, 1903. It is necessary, for the child to be enrolled, that he was living on March 4, 1905.

    In having these affidavits executed care should be exercised to see that all names are written in full, as they appear in the body of the affidavit, and in the event that either of the persons signing the affidavit are unable to write, signatures by mark must be

Applications for Enrollment of Chickasaw Newborn
Act of 1905   Volume III

attested by two witnesses. Each affidavit must be executed before a Notary Public and the notarial seal and signature of the officer must be attached to each separate affidavit.

Respectfully,

LM 17-135 Chairman.

9-NB-228.

Muskogee, Indian Territory, June 29, 1905.

William Seifried,
    Purcell, Indian Territory.

Dear Sir:

    There is enclosed herewith for execution application for the enrollment of your infant child, Joe Maytubbie Seifried, born March 15, 1903. Your attention is called to the Commission's letter of April 17, 1905, in which there was enclosed an affidavit similar to the one above mentioned, to which you have failed to reply.

    The affidavits heretofore filed with the Commission show that the child was living on July 20, 1903. It is necessary for the child to be enrolled, that he was living on March 4, 1905.

    In having these affidavits executed care should be used to see that all names are written in full as they appear in the body of the affidavits, and if either of the persons signing the affidavits is unable to write, signature by mark must be attested by two witnesses. Each affidavit must be executed before a Notary Public and the notarial seal and signature of the officer must be attached to each separate affidavit.

    You are requested to give this matter your immediate attention as no further action can be taken until these affidavits are filed with the Commission.

Respectfully,

Chairman.

Deb--4/29.

Applications for Enrollment of Chickasaw Newborn
Act of 1905 Volume III

9-NB-228

Muskogee, Indian Territory, July 11, 1905.

William F. Seifried,
    Purcell, Indian Territory.

Dear Sir:

    Receipt is hereby acknowledged of your letter of July 6, 1905, stating that your child Joe Maytubby Seifried died before March 4, 1905.

    For the purpose of making his death a matter of record there is inclosed herewith blank form for proof of death which please have executed and returned to this office as early as practicable in the enclosed envelope.

                      Respectfully,

D. C.   Commissioner.
Env.

Substitute

Muskogee, Indian Territory, July 22, 1905.

William F. Seifried,
    Purcell, Indian Territory.

Dear Sir:

    Receipt is hereby acknowledged of your affidavit of Mary Seifried to the death of Joseph Maytubby Seifried, which occurred September 8, 1904, and the same have been filed as evidence of the death of said child.

                      Respectfully,

                                      Commissioner.

Applications for Enrollment of Chickasaw Newborn
Act of 1905   Volume III

9-NB 228

COPY

Muskogee, Indian Territory, August 23, 1905.

William Seifried,
    Purcell, Indian Territory.

Dear Sir:

    You are hereby advised that it appearing from the records of this office that your child, Joe Maytubbie Seifried died prior to March 4, 1905, the Commission to the Five Civilized Tribes on August 23, 1905, dismissed the application for the enrollment of said child as a citizen by blood of the Chickasaw Nation.

                              Respectfully,
                                  SIGNED

                               Tams Bixby
                               Commissioner.

9-NB-228

COPY

Muskogee, Indian Territory, August 23, 1905.

Mansfield, McMurray & Cornish,
    Attorneys for Choctaw and Chickasaw Nations,
        South McAlester, Indian Territory.

Gentlemen:

    You are hereby advised that it appearing from the records of this office that Joe Maytubbie Seifried died prior to March 4, 1905, the Commission to the Five Civilized Tribes on August 23, 1905, dismissed the application for the enrollment of said child as a citizen by blood of the Chickasaw Nation.

                              Respectfully,
                                  SIGNED

                               Tams Bixby
                               Commissioner.

Applications for Enrollment of Chickasaw Newborn
Act of 1905   Volume III

Chic. N.B. - 229
(Jessie A. Seifried
Born April 10, 1903)

BIRTH AFFIDAVIT.

DEPARTMENT OF THE INTERIOR,
COMMISSION TO THE FIVE CIVILIZED TRIBES.

IN RE *Application for Enrollment,* as a citizen of the   Chickasaw   Nation, of   Jessie A. Seifried   , born on the   10th day of   April   , 1903

Name of Father: Henry D. Seifried   a citizen of the Chickasaw   Nation.
Name of Mother: Emma Seifried   a citizen of the Chickasaw   Nation.
by Marriage

Post-Office: Wayne Indian Territory

AFFIDAVIT OF MOTHER.

UNITED STATES OF AMERICA,
INDIAN TERRITORY.
Southern   District.

I,   Emma Seifried   , on oath state that I am   24   years of age and a citizen by   Marriage   , of the   Chickasaw   Nation; that I am the lawful wife of   Henry D. Seifried   , who is a citizen, by   birth   of the Chickasaw Nation; that a   Female   child was born to me on   10th day of   April   , 1903 , that said child has been named   Jessie A. Seifried   , and is now living.

Emma Seifried

WITNESSES TO MARK:

Subscribed and sworn to before me this   27th day of   July   , 1903

M.S. Clemens
NOTARY PUBLIC.

My term expires July 22, 1907

Applications for Enrollment of Chickasaw Newborn
Act of 1905   Volume III

AFFIDAVIT OF ATTENDING PHYSICIAN OR MID-WIFE.

UNITED STATES OF AMERICA,
    INDIAN TERRITORY.
    Southern   District.

I,   G.A. Barger M.D.   , a   Physician   , on oath state that I attended on Mrs.   Emma   , wife of   Henry D. Seifried   on the   10th day of   April   , 190 3; that there was born to her on said date a   female   child; that said child is now living and is said to have been named   Jessie A Seifried

G.A. Barger M.D.

WITNESSES TO MARK:

{

Subscribed and sworn to before me this   27th day of   July   , 1903

M.S. Clemens
NOTARY PUBLIC.

My term expires July 22, 1907

BIRTH AFFIDAVIT.

DEPARTMENT OF THE INTERIOR.
COMMISSION TO THE FIVE CIVILIZED TRIBES.

IN RE APPLICATION FOR ENROLLMENT, as a citizen of the   Chickasaw   Nation, of   Indian Territory   , born on the   10th day of   April   , 1903

Name of Father: Henry D. Seifried   a citizen of the   Chickasaw   Nation.
Name of Mother: Emma Seifried   a citizen of the   Chickasaw   Nation.

Postoffice   Wayne Chickasaw Nation I.T.

AFFIDAVIT OF MOTHER.

UNITED STATES OF AMERICA, Indian Territory,
    Southern   DISTRICT.

I,   Emma Seifried   , on oath state that I am   26   years of age and a ~~citizen~~ ~~by~~   Non citizen   , of the   Chickasaw   Nation; that I am the lawful wife of Henry D. Seifried   , who is a citizen, by   birth   of the   Chickasaw   Nation; that a   Female   child was born to me on the 10th day of   April   , 1903; that said child has been named   Jessie A. Seifried   , and was living March 4, 1905.

Emma Seifried

Applications for Enrollment of Chickasaw Newborn
Act of 1905 Volume III

Witnesses To Mark:

{

Subscribed and sworn to before me this 18th day of March , 1905

M.S. Clemens
Notary Public.

AFFIDAVIT OF ATTENDING PHYSICIAN OR MID-WIFE.

UNITED STATES OF AMERICA, Indian Territory, }
Southern DISTRICT. }

I, GS Barger , a Physician , on oath state that I attended on Mrs. Emma Seifried , wife of Henry D. Seifried on the 10 day of April , 1903; that there was born to her on said date a Female child; that said child was living March 4, 1905, and is said to have been named Jessie A. Seifried

GS Barger M.D.

Witnesses To Mark:

{

Subscribed and sworn to before me this 18th day of March , 1905

M.S. Clemens
Notary Public.

My term expires July 22, 1907

(The letter below does not belong with the current applicant.)

REFER IN REPLY TO THE FOLLOWING:

DEPARTMENT OF THE INTERIOR,
COMMISSIONER TO THE FIVE CIVILIZED TRIBES.

Muskogee, Indian Territory, January 11, 1907.

Clerk in Charge,
Choctaw-Chickasaw Enrollment Division.

Dear Sir:-

You are advised that Willie Black, May Black and Effie Black, minor children of George Black and Martha Black, have been enrolled as citizens of the Cherokee Nation,

Applications for Enrollment of Chickasaw Newborn
Act of 1905   Volume III

their names appearing on Roll Card No. 7495 opposite Roll Numbers 32784, 32785 and 32786, respectively, their enrollment having been finally approved by the Department of the Interior on January 13, 1906.

No allotments of land have been made to any of the above named citizens.

Respectfully,
Tams Bixby
Commissioner.

GAL

Chic. N.B. - 230
    (Vera Rowe
    Born May 26, 1903)

BIRTH AFFIDAVIT.

DEPARTMENT OF THE INTERIOR.
COMMISSION TO THE FIVE CIVILIZED TRIBES.

IN RE APPLICATION FOR ENROLLMENT, as a citizen of the   Chickasaw   Nation, of   Vera Rowe   , born on the 26 day of May , 1903

Name of Father: Clyde Rowe   a citizen of the   U. S.   ~~Nation~~.
Name of Mother: Letitia Rowe   a citizen of the   Chickasaw   Nation.

Postoffice   Mill Creek, Ind. Ter.

AFFIDAVIT OF MOTHER.

UNITED STATES OF AMERICA, Indian Territory, }
   Southern   DISTRICT. }

I, Letitia Rowe , on oath state that I am   28 years of age and a citizen by blood , of the   Chickasaw   Nation; that I am the lawful wife of Clyde Rowe , who is a citizen, ~~by~~   of the United States ---------------   Nation; that a female   child was born to me on   26 day of May , 1903; that said child has been named   Vera Rowe , and was living March 4, 1905.

Letitia Rowe

Witnesses To Mark:
{

Applications for Enrollment of Chickasaw Newborn
Act of 1905   Volume III

Subscribed and sworn to before me this 22 day of   March   , 1905

James T. Walter
Notary Public.

AFFIDAVIT OF ATTENDING PHYSICIAN OR MID-WIFE.

UNITED STATES OF AMERICA, Indian Territory,
Southern   DISTRICT.

I,   J. F. Sturdivant   , a   P. Physician , on oath state that I attended on Mrs. Letitia Rowe   , wife of   Clyde Rowe   on the 26 day of   May , 1903; that there was born to her on said date a   female   child; that said child was living March 4, 1905, and is said to have been named   Vera Rowe

John F Sturdivant

Witnesses To Mark:

Subscribed and sworn to before me this 23 day of   March   , 1905

James T. Walter
Notary Public.

Chic. N.B. - 231
   (Joseph Morris
   Born December 4, 1904)

BIRTH AFFIDAVIT.   No 57

DEPARTMENT OF THE INTERIOR.
COMMISSION TO THE FIVE CIVILIZED TRIBES.

IN RE APPLICATION FOR ENROLLMENT, as a citizen of the   Chickasaw   Nation, of   Joseph Morris   , born on the 4 day of December , 1904

Name of Father: Joseph D. Morris   a citizen of the Chickasaw Nation.
Name of Mother: Maggie Morris   a citizen of the   U.S.   ~~Nation~~.

Postoffice   Roff, I.T.

Applications for Enrollment of Chickasaw Newborn
Act of 1905   Volume III

AFFIDAVIT OF MOTHER.

UNITED STATES OF AMERICA, Indian Territory, }
   Southern   DISTRICT.

I, Maggie Morris , on oath state that I am nineteen   years of age and a citizen by — — — , of the United States; that I am the lawful wife of Joseph D. Morris , who is a citizen, by Blood of the Chickasaw Nation; that a male   child was born to me on the 4 day of December , 1904, that said child has been named Joseph Morris , and is now living.

Maggie Morris

Witnesses To Mark:
{

Subscribed and sworn to before me this 30 day of Dec , 1904

Joseph Anderson
Notary Public.

AFFIDAVIT OF ATTENDING PHYSICIAN OR MID-WIFE.

UNITED STATES OF AMERICA, Indian Territory, }
   Southern   DISTRICT.

I, J.L. Jeffries[sic]   , a   Physician   , on oath state that I attended on Mrs. Maggie Morris , wife of Joseph D. Morris   on the 4 day of Dec. , 1904; that there was born to her on said date a   male   child; that said child is now living and is said to have been named Joseph Morris

J.L. Jeffress

Witnesses To Mark:
{

Subscribed and sworn to before me this 30 day of Dec , 1904

Joseph Anderson
Notary Public.

Applications for Enrollment of Chickasaw Newborn
Act of 1905   Volume III

BIRTH AFFIDAVIT.

DEPARTMENT OF THE INTERIOR.
COMMISSION TO THE FIVE CIVILIZED TRIBES.

    IN RE APPLICATION FOR ENROLLMENT, as a citizen of the   Chickasaw   Nation, of   Joe Morris   , born on the   4   day of   December   , 1904

Name of Father: Joseph Daniel Morris   a citizen of the   Chickasaw   Nation.
Name of Mother: Maggie Morris   a citizen of the   Chickasaw   Nation.

    Postoffice   Roff, I.T.

AFFIDAVIT OF MOTHER.

UNITED STATES OF AMERICA, Indian Territory,
    Southern   DISTRICT.

    I,   Maggie Morris   , on oath state that I am   19   years of age and a citizen ~~by~~ of the   United States   Nation; that I am the lawful wife of   Joseph Daniel Morris   , who is a citizen, by   blood   of the   Chickasaw   Nation; that a   male   child was born to me on   4   day of   December   , 1904; that said child has been named   Joe Morris   , and was living March 4, 1905.

                          Maggie Morris

Witnesses To Mark:

    Subscribed and sworn to before me this   29   day of   March   , 1905

                          J.C. Little
                              Notary Public.

AFFIDAVIT OF ATTENDING PHYSICIAN OR MID-WIFE.

UNITED STATES OF AMERICA, Indian Territory,
    Southern   DISTRICT.

    I,   J.L. Jeffress   , a   Physician   , on oath state that I attended on Mrs.   Maggie Morris   , wife of   Joseph Daniel Morris   on the   4   day of   December   , 1904; that there was born to her on said date a .... child; that said child was living March 4, 1905, and is said to have been named   Joe Morris

                          J.L. Jeffress M.D.

Witnesses To Mark:

Applications for Enrollment of Chickasaw Newborn
Act of 1905 Volume III

Subscribed and sworn to before me this 29 day of March, 1905

J.C. Little
Notary Public.

BIRTH AFFIDAVIT.

9 NB 231

DEPARTMENT OF THE INTERIOR.
COMMISSION TO THE FIVE CIVILIZED TRIBES.

IN RE APPLICATION FOR ENROLLMENT, as a citizen of the Chickasaw Nation, of Joe Morris, born on the 4th day of December, 1904

Name of Father: Joseph D Morris   a citizen of the Chickasaw Nation.
Name of Mother: Maggie Morris   a citizen of the U.S. ~~Nation~~.

Postoffice   Roff Ind. Ter

AFFIDAVIT OF MOTHER.

UNITED STATES OF AMERICA, Indian Territory,
Southern DISTRICT.

I, Maggie Morris, on oath state that I am 19 years of age and a citizen ~~by~~ ——— of the United States ~~Nation~~; that I am the lawful wife of Joseph Daniel Morris, who is a citizen, by blood of the Chickasaw Nation; that a male child was born to me on 4th day of December, 1904; that said child has been named Joe Morris, and was living March 4, 1905.

Maggie Morris

Witnesses To Mark:

Subscribed and sworn to before me this 31 day of July, 1905

My Comm expires July 2, 1906   Jno. G. James
Notary Public. *in & for Southern Dist, I.T.*

Applications for Enrollment of Chickasaw Newborn
Act of 1905   Volume III

AFFIDAVIT OF ATTENDING PHYSICIAN OR MID-WIFE.

UNITED STATES OF AMERICA, Indian Territory,
Southern   DISTRICT.

I, J L Jeffress, a physician, on oath state that I attended on Mrs. Maggie Morris, wife of Joseph D Morris on the 4th day of December, 1904; that there was born to her on said date a male child; that said child was living March 4, 1905, and is said to have been named Joe Morris

J.L. Jeffress M.D.

Witnesses To Mark:

Subscribed and sworn to before me this 31 day of July, 1905

My Comm expires July 2, 1906   Jno. G. James
                                      Notary Public. *in & for*
                                      Southern Dist, I.T.

Marriage License

No 4

United States of America,   To Any Person Authorized by Law
INDIAN TERRITORY,   ss: to Solemnize Marriage, Greeting:
SOUTHERN DISTRICT.

You Are Hereby Commanded To solemnize the Rite and publish the Banns of Matrimony between Mr.   J.D. Morris of   Dolberg   in the Indian Territory, aged   28   years, and M iss Maggie L Dumas   of   Dolberg in the Indian Territory, aged   25   years, according to law; and do you officially sign and return this License to the parties therein named.

Witness My hand and official Seal, this   27th day of   February   A. D. 190 1

CHAS. M. CAMPBELL
Clerk of the United States Court.

Applications for Enrollment of Chickasaw Newborn
Act of 1905   Volume III

Certificate of Marriage.

United States of America, } I, S.B. Robinson
    INDIAN TERRITORY, } ss: a minister of the gospel
    SOUTHERN DISTRICT. }

do hereby certify that on the 27 day of February A. D. 190 1 ,
I did duly and according to law, as commanded in the foregoing License, solemnize the Rite and publish the Banns of Matrimony between the parties therein named.

    WITNESS my hand, this 27 day of February A. D. 190 1

    My credentials are recorded in the office of the Clerk of the United States Court, Indian Territory, Southern District, at Ardmore, Book D , Page 91

(NOTE.--The person officiating should fill in the spaces S.B. Robinson
    for book and page and sign here.) ☞ a minister of the gospel

NOTE. (a) - This License and Certificate of Marriages must be returned to the office of the Clerk of the United States Court in the Indian Territory, at Ardmore, within sixty days from the date thereof, or the party to whom the License was issued will be liable in the amount of ONE HUNDRED DOLLARS ($100).

NOTE. (b) - No person is authorized to perform the Marriage Ceremony in the Southern District unless the proper credentials have first been recorded in the Clerk's office.

Certificate of Record of Marriage

UNITED STATES OF AMERICA, }
    INDIAN TERRITORY, } sct.
    Southern District. }

    I, C. M. CAMPBELL, Clerk of the United States Court, in the Territory and District aforesaid, Do HEREBY CERTIFY, that the License for and Certificate of Marriage of

DEPARTMENT OF THE INTERIOR,
COMMISSION TO THE FIVE CIVILIZED TRIBES.

FILED
MAY 23 1905
Tams Bixby CHAIRMAN.

Mr J. D. Morris and
M Maggie L Dumas

were filed in my office in said Territory and District the 8th day of Mar A.D., 190 1 and duly recorded in Book E of Marriage Record, Page 357

    WITNESS my hand and Seal of said Court, at Ardmore, this 8th day of March A.D. 190 1

FILED
MAR 8 1905 AM
C. M. CAMPBELL, Clerk

    C. M. Campbell
        CLERK.

Applications for Enrollment of Chickasaw Newborn
Act of 1905 Volume III

9-NB-231.

Muskogee, Indian Territory, May 13, 1905.

Joseph D. Morris,
    Roff, Indian Territory.

Dear Sir:

    Referring to the application for the enrollment of your infant child, Joe Morris, born December 4, 1904, it is noted that he claims through you.

    Before this application can be finally disposed of it will be necessary for you to file with the Commission either the original or a certified copy of the license and certificate of your marriage to the applicant's mother, Maggie Morris.

Respectfully,

Chairman.

9-N.B. 231.

Muskogee, Indian Territory, May 24, 1905.

J. C. Little,
    Attorney at Law,
        Roff, Indian Territory.

Dear Sir:

    Receipt is hereby acknowledged of your letter of May 18, enclosing the marriage license and certificate between J. D. Morris and Maggie L. Dumas, which you offer in support of the application of Joe Morris, infant child of Joseph D. and Maggie L. Morris, for enrollment as a citizen of the Chickasaw Nation, and the same have been filed with the records in this case.

Respectfully,

Chairman.

Applications for Enrollment of Chickasaw Newborn
Act of 1905 Volume III

9 N.B. 231.

Muskogee, Indian Territory, June 2, 1905.

J. C. Little,
    Attorney at Law,
        Roff, Indian Territory.

Dear Sir:

    Receipt is hereby acknowledged of your letter of May 27, replying to our recent letter relative to the enrollment of Joe Morris, in which you state that you forwarded the license and certificate of marriage between J. D. Morris and Maggie L. Dumas on May 18, and that receipt thereof was acknowledged to you on May 24, 1905.

    In reply to your letter you are advised that the marriage license and certificate between J. D. Morris and Maggie L. Dumas were filed with our records on May 24, 1903, in support of the application for the enrollment of Joe Morris as a citizen by blood of the Chickasaw Nation.

        Respectfully,

                Commissioner in Charge.

9-NB-231

Muskogee, Indian Territory, July 29, 1905.

Joseph D. Morris,
    Roff, Indian Territory.

Dear Sir:

    There is inclosed you herewith for execution application for the enrollment of your infant child, born December 4, 1904.

    In the affidavits of December 30, 1904, heretofore filed in this office, the name of the applicant is given as Joseph Morris while in the affidavits of March 29, 1905, the name is given as Joe Morris.

    In the inclosed application the name of the child is left blank, please insert correct name and return to this office when the affidavits have been properly executed.

    This matter should receive your immediate attention as no further action can be taken relative to the enrollment of your said child until the evidence is supplied.

        Respectfully,

LM 5/29
                Commissioner.

Applications for Enrollment of Chickasaw Newborn
Act of 1905   Volume III

9-NB-231

Muskogee, Indian Territory, August 4, 1905.

Joseph D. Morris,
    Roff, Indian Territory.

Dear Sir:

    Receipt is hereby acknowledged of the affidavits of Maggie Morris and J. L. Jeffress to the birth of Joe Morris, son of Joseph D. and Maggie Morris, December 4, 1904, and the same have been filed with the records of this office in the matter of the enrollment of said child.

                      Respectfully,

                                    Commissioner.

Chic. N.B. - 232
    (Girtha Lindsey
    Born December 11, 1904)

BIRTH AFFIDAVIT.

DEPARTMENT OF THE INTERIOR.
COMMISSION TO THE FIVE CIVILIZED TRIBES.

    IN RE APPLICATION FOR ENROLLMENT, as a citizen of the   Chickasaw   Nation, of   Girtha Lindsey   , born on the   11th day of December   , 1904

Name of Father: B. H. H. Lindsey   a citizen of the   U.S.   Nation.
Name of Mother: Ethel Lindsey   a citizen of the   Chickasaw   Nation.

                      Postoffice   Ardmore Ind Ter

Applications for Enrollment of Chickasaw Newborn
Act of 1905 Volume III

AFFIDAVIT OF MOTHER.

UNITED STATES OF AMERICA, Indian Territory,
Southern DISTRICT.

I, Ethel Lindsey, on oath state that I am 20 years of age and a citizen by blood, of the Chickasaw Nation; that I am the lawful wife of B. H. H. Lindsey, who is a citizen, by .... of the U.S. Nation; that a female child was born to me on 11th day of December, 1904; that said child has been named Girtha Lindsey, and was living March 4, 1905.

Ethel Lindsey

Witnesses To Mark:
{

Subscribed and sworn to before me this 25th day of March, 1905

H.C. Potter
Notary Public.
Southern Dist. Ind Ter

AFFIDAVIT OF ATTENDING PHYSICIAN OR MID-WIFE.

UNITED STATES OF AMERICA, Indian Territory,
Southern DISTRICT.

I, Elizabeth J. Lindsey, a Mid-wife, on oath state that I attended on Mrs. Ethel Lindsay[sic], wife of B. H. H. Lindsey on the 11th day of December, 1904; that there was born to her on said date a female child; that said child was living March 4, 1905, and is said to have been named Girtha Lindsey

Elizabeth J Lindsey

Witnesses To Mark:
{

Subscribed and sworn to before me this 25th day of March, 1905

H.C. Potter
Notary Public.
Southern District
Ind Ter

Applications for Enrollment of Chickasaw Newborn
Act of 1905   Volume III

Chic. N.B. - 233
(Claud Franklin Elmore
Born January 26, 1904)

BIRTH AFFIDAVIT.

DEPARTMENT OF THE INTERIOR.
COMMISSION TO THE FIVE CIVILIZED TRIBES.

IN RE APPLICATION FOR ENROLLMENT, as a citizen of the   Chickasaw   Nation, of   Claud Franklin Elmore   , born on the 26 day of January , 1904

Name of Father: George Elmore   a citizen of the U.S. citizen ~~Nation~~.
Name of Mother: Lorena Elmore   a citizen of the   Chickasaw Nation.

Postoffice   Ardmore Ind. Ter.

AFFIDAVIT OF MOTHER.

UNITED STATES OF AMERICA, Indian Territory,
Southern   DISTRICT.

I, Lorena Elmore , on oath state that I am 20 years of age and a citizen by   blood , of the   Chickasaw   Nation; that I am the lawful wife of   George Elmore   , who is a citizen, ~~by~~ .... of the   United States ~~Nation~~; that a male   child was born to me on 26th day of   January , 1904; that said child has been named   Claud Franklin Elmore   , and was living March 4, 1905.

                                    her
                          Lorena x Elmore
Witnesses To Mark: mark
 { *(Name Illegible)*
 { B.F. Turner

Subscribed and sworn to before me this 21st day of   March   , 1905

                       (Name Illegible)
                             Notary Public.

Applications for Enrollment of Chickasaw Newborn
Act of 1905 Volume III

AFFIDAVIT OF ATTENDING PHYSICIAN OR MID-WIFE.

UNITED STATES OF AMERICA, Indian Territory,
Southern DISTRICT.

I, Mrs. L. F. Elmore , a Mid-wife , on oath state that I attended on Mrs. Lorena Elmore , wife of George Elmore on the 26th day of January , 1904; that there was born to her on said date a male child; that said child was living March 4, 1905, and is said to have been named Claud Franklin Elmore

L F Elmore

Witnesses To Mark:
{

Subscribed and sworn to before me this 21st day of March , 1905

(Name Illegible)
Notary Public.

Chic. N.B. - 234
(Edgar Warren Welch
Born December 16, 1902)

BIRTH AFFIDAVIT.

Department of the Interior,
COMMISSION TO THE FIVE CIVILIZED TRIBES.

IN RE APPLICATION FOR ENROLLMENT, as a citizen of the Chickasaw Nation, of Edgar Warren , born on the 16 day of December , 1902

Name of Father: Chas A Welch   a citizen of the Chickasaw Nation.
Name of Mother: Adelia Welch   a citizen of the Chickasaw Nation.

Post-Office: Poteau I T

Applications for Enrollment of Chickasaw Newborn
Act of 1905   Volume III

AFFIDAVIT OF MOTHER.

UNITED STATES OF AMERICA,
INDIAN TERRITORY,
Central   District.

I,   Adelia Welch   , on oath state that I am   32   years of age and a citizen by   Marriage , of the   Chickasaw   Nation; that I am the lawful wife of Chas A Welch   , who is a citizen, by Blood   of the   Chickasaw   Nation; that a   Male   child was born to me on   16 day of   December   , 190 2, that said child has been named   Edgar Warren   , and is now living.

Adelia Welch

WITNESSES TO MARK:

{

Subscribed and sworn to before me this   27   day of   Jan   , 1903

RD *(Illegible)*
Notary Public.
My Commission exp Mch 12-06

AFFIDAVIT OF ATTENDING PHYSICIAN OR MID-WIFE.

UNITED STATES OF AMERICA,
INDIAN TERRITORY,
Central   District.

I,   S B Ragon   , a   Physician   , on oath state that I attended on Mrs.   Adelia Welch   , wife of   Chas A Welch   on the   16   day of December , 190 2; that there was born to her on said date a   Male   child; that said child is now living and is said to have been named   Edgar Warren

S.B. Ragon

WITNESSES TO MARK:

{

Subscribed and sworn to before me this 21st day of January   , 190 3

P.C. Bolger
Notary Public.

My Com. Ex. Nov. 1, 1903

Applications for Enrollment of Chickasaw Newborn
Act of 1905   Volume III

BIRTH AFFIDAVIT.

DEPARTMENT OF THE INTERIOR.
COMMISSION TO THE FIVE CIVILIZED TRIBES.

IN RE APPLICATION FOR ENROLLMENT, as a citizen of the   Chickasaw   Nation, of   Edgar Warren Welch   , born on the   16th   day of   December   , 1902

Name of Father: Charles A. Welch   a citizen of the   Chickasaw Nation.
Name of Mother: Adelia Welch   a citizen of the   Chickasaw Nation.

Postoffice   Talihina, Indian Territory.

AFFIDAVIT OF MOTHER.

UNITED STATES OF AMERICA, Indian Territory,
Central   DISTRICT.

I,   Adelia Welch   , on oath state that I am   35   years of age and a citizen by inter-marriage   , of the   Chickasaw   Nation; that I am the lawful wife of   Charles A. Welch   , who is a citizen, by blood   of the   Chickasaw   Nation; that a male   child was born to me on   16th   day of   December   , 1902; that said child has been named   Edgar Warren   , and was living March 4, 1905.

Adelia Welch

Witnesses To Mark:
{

Subscribed and sworn to before me this   5th   day of   April   , 1905

W A Welch
Notary Public.

AFFIDAVIT OF ATTENDING PHYSICIAN OR MID-WIFE.

UNITED STATES OF AMERICA, Indian Territory,
Central   DISTRICT.

I,   S.B. Ragon   , a physician   , on oath state that I attended on Mrs.   Adelia Welch   , wife of   Chas A Welch   on the   16th   day of   December   , 1902; that there was born to her on said date a   male   child; that said child was living March 4, 1905, and is said to have been named   Edgar Warren

S.B. Ragon

Witnesses To Mark:
{

Applications for Enrollment of Chickasaw Newborn
Act of 1905   Volume III

Subscribed and sworn to before me this 6th day of April , 1905

My Comm expires
Dec 11, 1906

Malcolm E Rosser
Notary Public.

Chickasaw 1667.

Muskogee, Indian Territory, April 12, 1905.

Charles A. Welch,
    Talihina, Indian Territory.

Dear Sir:

    Receipt is hereby acknowledged of your letter of April 7th, enclosing affidavits of Adelia Welch and S. B. Ragon to the birth of Edgar Warren Welch, son of Charles A. and Adelia Welch, December 16th, 1903, and the same have been filed with our records as an application for the enrollment of said child.

Respectfully,

Commissioner in Charge.

Chic. N.B. - 235
    (Myrtle Jauneta Neighbors
    Born December 2, 1902)

BIRTH AFFIDAVIT.

DEPARTMENT OF THE INTERIOR.
COMMISSION TO THE FIVE CIVILIZED TRIBES.

IN RE APPLICATION FOR ENROLLMENT, as a citizen of the Chickasaw Nation, of Myrtle Jauneta Neighbors , born on the Second day of December , 1902

Name of Father: William Neighbors   a citizen of the Chickasaw Nation.
Name of Mother: Lillian Ethel Neighbors   a citizen of the Chickasaw Nation.

Postoffice   Sulphur Indian Territory

Applications for Enrollment of Chickasaw Newborn
Act of 1905   Volume III

AFFIDAVIT OF MOTHER.

UNITED STATES OF AMERICA, Indian Territory, }
Southern   DISTRICT.

I, Lillian Ethel Neighbors   , on oath state that I am   27   years of age and a citizen by   Marriage   , of the   Chickasaw   Nation; that I am the lawful wife of William Neighbors   , who is a citizen, by   blood   of the   Chickasaw Nation; that a   female   child was born to me on Second   day of December   , 1902; that said child has been named   Myrtle Jauneta   , and was living March 4, 1905.

Lillian Ethel Neighbors

Witnesses To Mark:
{

Subscribed and sworn to before me this 20 day of   March   , 1905

H B Webster
Notary Public.

My commission expires January 25, 1909

AFFIDAVIT OF ATTENDING PHYSICIAN OR MID-WIFE.

UNITED STATES OF AMERICA, Indian Territory, }
Southern   DISTRICT.

I,   A. V. Williams   , a   mid-wife   , on oath state that I attended on Mrs.   Lillian Ethel Neighbors   , wife of   William Neighbors   on the 2 day of December   , 1902; that there was born to her on said date a   female   child; that said child was living March 4, 1905, and is said to have been named   Myrtle Jauneta

A. V. Williams

Witnesses To Mark:
{

Subscribed and sworn to before me this 20 day of   March   , 1905

H B Webster
Notary Public.

My commission expires January 25, 1909

Applications for Enrollment of Chickasaw Newborn
Act of 1905   Volume III

Chic. N.B. - 236
(Cherokee Rose Lynch
Born May 16. 1903)

BIRTH AFFIDAVIT.

DEPARTMENT OF THE INTERIOR,
COMMISSION TO THE FIVE CIVILIZED TRIBES.

In Re Application for Enrollment, as a citizen of the Chickasaw Nation, of   Cherokee Rose Lynch   , born on the   16   day of   May   , 1903

Name of Father: J. J. Lynch   a citizen of the   Cherokee   Nation.
Name of Mother: Georgia Vann Lynch   a citizen of the   Chickasaw Nation.

Post-office   Webbers Falls, Ind. Ter.

AFFIDAVIT OF MOTHER.

UNITED STATES OF AMERICA,
INDIAN TERRITORY,
Southern   District.

I,   Georgia Vann Lynch   , on oath state that I am   25   years of age and a citizen by   blood   , of the   Chickasaw   Nation; that I am the lawful wife of   J J Lynch   , who is a citizen, by blood of the   Cherokee   Nation; that a   female   child was born to me on   16   day of   May   , 1903 , that said child has been named   Cherokee Rose Lynch   , and is now living.

Georgia Vann Lynch

WITNESSES TO MARK:

Subscribed and sworn to before me this   12th day of   May   , 1903

Robert S. Bell
NOTARY PUBLIC.

Applications for Enrollment of Chickasaw Newborn
Act of 1905 Volume III

AFFIDAVIT OF ATTENDING PHYSICIAN OR MID-WIFE.

UNITED STATES OF AMERICA,
   INDIAN TERRITORY,
  Southern   District.

I, E A Jones , a physician , on oath state that I attended on Mrs. Georgia Vann Lynch , wife of J J Lynch on the 16 day of May , 1903 ; that there was born to her on said date a female child; that said child is now living and is said to have been named Cherokee Rose Lynch

                             E.A. Jones M.D.

WITNESSES TO MARK:

Subscribed and sworn to before me this 12th day of May , 1903

                             Robert S Bell
                                NOTARY PUBLIC.

BIRTH AFFIDAVIT.

DEPARTMENT OF THE INTERIOR.
COMMISSION TO THE FIVE CIVILIZED TRIBES.

IN RE APPLICATION FOR ENROLLMENT, as a citizen of the Chickasaw Nation, of Cherokee Rose Lynch , born on the 16th day of May , 1902[sic]

Name of Father: Joseph J Lynch   a citizen of the Cherokee Nation.
Name of Mother: Georgia V Lynch   a citizen of the Chickasaw Nation.

                    Postoffice   Webbers Falls, I.T.

AFFIDAVIT OF MOTHER.

UNITED STATES OF AMERICA, Indian Territory,
  Southern   DISTRICT.

I, Georgia V Lynch , on oath state that I am 28 years of age and a citizen by blood , of the Chickasaw Nation; that I am the lawful wife of Joseph J Lynch , who is a citizen, by blood of the Cherokee Nation; that a female child was born to me on the 16th day of May , 1903, that said child has been named Cherokee Rose Lynch , and is now living.

                               Georgia V Lynch

Applications for Enrollment of Chickasaw Newborn
Act of 1905   Volume III

Witnesses To Mark:

{

Subscribed and sworn to before me this   12ᵗʰ day of   April , 1905.

JE Williams
Notary Public.

AFFIDAVIT OF ATTENDING PHYSICIAN OR MID-WIFE.

UNITED STATES OF AMERICA, Indian Territory, ⎫
  Southern   DISTRICT. ⎭

I,   EA Jones   , a physician   , on oath state that I attended on Mrs.   Georgia V Lynch   , wife of   Joseph J Lynch   on the   16ᵗʰ   day of May , 1903; that there was born to her on said date a   female   child; that said child is now living and is said to have been named   Cherokee Rose Lynch

E.A. Jones M.D.

Witnesses To Mark:

{

Subscribed and sworn to before me this   27th day of   April , 1905.

Robert S. Bell
Notary Public.

---

9 N B 236

Muskogee, Indian Territory, April 15, 1905.

J. J. Lynch,
  Webbers Falls, Indian Territory.

Dear Sir:

There is inclosed you herewith for execution application for the enrollment of your infant child, Cherokee Rose Lynch, born May 16, 1903.

The affidavits heretofore filed with the Commission show the child was living in May 1903. It is necessary, for the child to be enrolled, that she was living on March 4, 1905. Please insert the mother's age in space for the purpose.

In having these affidavits executed care should be exercised to see that all names are written in full, as they appear in the body of the affidavit, and in the event that either

Applications for Enrollment of Chickasaw Newborn
Act of 1905   Volume III

of the persons signing the affidavit are unable to write, signatures by mark must be attested by two witnesses. Each affidavit must be executed before a Notary Public and the notarial seal and signature of the officer must be attached to each separate affidavit.

Respectfully,

LM 15-160   Chairman.

¶ NB 236

Muskogee, Indian Territory, April 21, 1905.

Joseph J. Lynch,
    Webbers Falls, Indian Territory.

Dear Sir:

    Receipt is hereby acknowledged of the affidavits of Georgia V. Lynch and E. A. Jones to the birth of Cherokee Rose, daughter of Joseph an[sic] and Georgia V. Lynch, May 16, 1902[sic].

    It appears that the Notary Public failed to affix his name and seal to the affidavit of the physician and for the purpose of correcting this omission there is inclosed herewith another blank on which kindly have executed the affidavit of the physician to the birth of Cherokee Rose Lynch.

Respectfully,

B. C.   Chairman.

(The above letter given again except with the date of April 24, 1905.)

Chickasaw N.B. 236.

Muskogee, Indian Territory, May 1, 1905.

J. Ernest Williams,
    Chickasaw Land Office,
        Tishomingo, Indian Territory.

Dear Sir:

    There is enclosed herewith application for the enrollment of Cherokee Rose Lynch in order that you may attach your seal to the affidavit of the mother.

Applications for Enrollment of Chickasaw Newborn
Act of 1905   Volume III

Kindly give this matter immediate attention and return the application to this office without delay.

Respectfully,

Chairman.

DeB--1/1

Chic. N.B. - 237
    (Leona McKinney
    Born September 7, 1903)

T.W.L.
G.D.A.   DEPARTMENT OF THE INTERIOR,
                COMMISSION TO THE FIVE CIVILIZED TRIBES.

In the matter of the application of Harris McKinney, et al., for enrollment as citizensxby[sic] blood of the Chickasaw Nation, consolidating the applications of --

Harris McKinney, et al.,	9 D 176
Oyd McKinney,	9 D 339
Fannie Garsides, et al.,	9 D 292

COPY

--- D E C I S I O N ---

It appears from the census cards in the possession of the Commission and the other records in this case that at Colbert, Indian Territory, on October 14, 1898, application was made for the enrollment of Harris McKinney and his minor child, Laura Etta McKinney, as citizens by blood of the Chickasaw Nation, since which time birth affidavits have been filed in the matter of the application for the enrollment of his infant children, Cecial Berthal and Maude Lee McKinney, as citizens by blood of the Chickasaw Nation; that at the same place and on the same date application was made for the enrollment of Charley Hayes as a citizen by intermarriage of the Chickasaw Nation, and for the enrollment of his minor children, Daniel, Minnie, Maggie and Edward Hayes, as citizens by blood of the Chickasaw Nation, that also at the same place and on the same date application was made for the enrollment of Martha McKinney as a citizen by intermarriage of the Chickasaw Nation; that at Ardmore, Indian Territory, on November 25, 1898, application was made for the enrollment of Oyd McKinney as a citizen by blood of the Chickasaw Nation; that at Atoka, Indian Territory, on December 5, 1899,

Applications for Enrollment of Chickasaw Newborn
Act of 1905   Volume III

application was made for the enrollment of Joseph Garsides as a citizen by intermarriage of the Chickasaw Nation, and for the enrollment of his seven minor children, Fannie, Ben, Alex, Jim, Nellie, Mattie and Joe Garsides Jr., as citizens by blood of the Chickasaw Nation.

Further proceedings in the matter of said applications were had at Durant, Indian Territory, at the session of the Commission commencing August 14, and ending August 18, 1899, and at Atoka, Indian Territory, on December 3, and December 8, 1900.

The applicants, Martha McKinney, Charley Hayes and his minor children, Daniel, Minnie, Maggie and Edward Hayes, and Joseph Garsides, are differently classified and are not embraced in this decision.

It appears from the evidence submitted and the records in the possession of the Commission that the applicants, Harris McKinney, and his three minor children, Laura Etta, Cecial Berthal and Maude Lee McKinney, and Oyd McKinney, Fannie Garsides, Ben Garsides, Alex Garsides, Jim Garsides, Nellie Garsides, Mattie Garsides and Joe Garsides Jr., claim rights to enrollment as citizens by blood of the Chickasaw Nation, by reason of being descendants of Polly McKinney (or McKinnie), who obtained a patent to land in Mississippi under the treaty of 1834 between the United States and the Chickasaw Nation, in which patent the said Polly McKinney (or McKinnie) was characterized as "a Chickasaw Indian;" that the principal applicants herein are, and have been for may[sic] years past, actual and bona fide residents of the Chickasaw country in Indian Territory, and are duly recognized as citizens of the Chickasaw Nation; that Harris McKinney's name is identified on the 1893 Chickasaw pay roll, book 2, page 8, No. 226; that Oyd McKinney's name is identified on the 1893 Chickasaw pay roll, No. 1, at page 140; that the applicants, Fannie Garsides, Ben Garsides, Ale Garsides, Jim Garsides, Nellie Garsides, Mattie Garsides and Joe Garsides Jr., are identified on the Maytubby 1893 Chickasaw pay roll, No. 2, duly enrolled with their father, Joseph Garsides; that Laura Etta McKinney, Cecial Berthal McKinney and Maude Lee McKinney, the minor children of the principal applicant, Harris McKinney, having been born subsequent to the tribal enrollment of their father, are identified from proper birth affidavits filed herein and made a part of the record in this case.

It is the contention of counsel for the Choctaw and Chickasaw Nations that the said Polly McKinney (or McKinnie) was a Cherokee Indian by blood, and that notwithstanding the recognition given the principal applicants herein as citizens of the Chickasaw Nation, they are not entitled to said citizenship as they are Cherokee Indians by blood and are not citizens by adoption of the Chickasaw Nation by an act of the Chickasaw legislature.

The contention that the said Polly McKinney (or McKinnie) was a Cherokee Indian and had no Chickasaw blood is not established by the evidence. She was recognized by the government of the United States as a Chickasaw Indian when the patent referred to was given to her, and was also recognized by the Chickasaws themselves, both in Mississippi and Indian Territory, as a member of said tribe of Indians; and it further appears from the testimony submitted, and the records in the possession of the Commission, that her descendants have been recognized and enrolled as citizens of the Chickasaw tribe of Indians.

The records in the possession of the Commission further show that none of the applicants herein has ever been recognized or enrolled by the Cherokee tribal authorities

Applications for Enrollment of Chickasaw Newborn
Act of 1905 Volume III

as a citizen of said Nation, nor has any of them ever been listed for enrollment as a citizen of the Cherokee Nation by the Commission to the Five Civilized Tribes.

It further appears that all of the applicants considered herein, except Cecial Berthal McKinney, who was born February 17, 1901, were residents in good faith of Indian Territory on June 28, 1898.

It is therefore the opinion of the Commission that the applications for the enrollment of Harris McKinney, Laura Etta McKinney, Cecial Berthal McKinney, Maude Lee McKinney, Oyd McKinney, Fannie Garsides, Ben Garsides, Alex Garsides, Jim Garsides, Nellie Garsides, Mattie Garsides and Joe Garsides Jr., as citizens by blood of the Chickasaw Nation should be granted under the provisions of section twenty-one of the Act of Congress approved June 28, 1898 (30 Stats., 495), and it is so ordered.

COMMISSION TO THE FIVE CIVILIZED TRIBES,

SIGNED *Tams Bixby*
Chairman.

SIGNED *T. B. Needles.*
Commissioner.

SIGNED *C.R. Breckinridge.*
Commissioner.

Muskogee, Indian Territory.
FEB 2 1 1903

W.J.

9-NB-237.

DEPARTMENT OF THE INTERIOR,
COMMISSIONER TO THE FIVE CIVILIZED TRIBES.

In the matter of the application for the enrollment of Leona McKinney as a citizen of the Chickasaw Nation.

--: D E C I S I O N :--

It appears from the record herein that on April 7, 1905 there was filed with the Commission application for the enrollment of Leona McKinney as a citizen by blood of the Chickasaw Nation.

It further appears from the record herein and the records of the Commission that the applicant was born on September 7, 1903 and is a daughter of Oyd McKinney, a recognized and enrolled citizen of the Chickasaw Nation whose name appears as number 4647 upon the final roll of citizens of the Chickasaw Nation, approved by the Secretary of the Interior April 11, 1903, and Fannie McKinney, a noncitizen.

From a copy of a letter of the Commission to the Honorable Secretary of the Interior dated March 23, 1903 transmitting partial roll of citizens of the Chickasaw

Applications for Enrollment of Chickasaw Newborn
Act of 1905 Volume III

Nation, numbers 4564 to 4659, inclusive, upon which partial roll the name of the said Oyd McKinney is found, it appears that it was stated in said letter that the rights of the said Oyd McKinney, and other specifically mentioned therein, to enrollment as citizens of the Chickasaw Nation "are established by tribal recognition and by their descent from Polly McKinney, who was adopted by the Chickasaw tribe of Indians in the State of Mississippi prior to the year 1834, and who obtained a patent to land in that state under the treaty of 1834, between the United States and the Chickasaw Nation, in which patent the said Polly McKinney was characterized as 'a Chickasaw Indian'." However, on February 21, 1903 the Commission rendered a decision enrolling the said Oyd McKinney, and others, as citizens by blood of the Chickasaw Nation, thereby establishing the status of the said Oyd McKinney as a citizen by blood of said nation. A copy of said decision is filed herewith and made a part of the record in this case.

It further appears from the record herein that the applicant was living on March 4, 1905.

The Act of Congress approved March 3, 1905 (Public No. 212) among other things provides:

"That the Commission to the Five Civilized Tribes is authorized for sixty days after the date of the approval of this act to receive and consider applications for enrollment of children born subsequent to September twenty-fifth, nineteen hundred and two, and prior to March fourth, nineteen hundred and five, and who were living on said latter date, to citizens by blood of the Choctaw and Chickasaw tribes of Indians whose enrollment has been approved by the Secretary of the Interior prior to the date of the approval of this act; and to enroll and make allotments to such children."

It is the opinion of this Commission that Leona McKinney is a child of a citizen by blood of the Chickasaw tribe of Indians within the meaning of the provision of the law above quoted and that, therefore, the application for her enrollment as a citizen by blood of the Chickasaw Nation should be granted and it is so ordered.

COMMISSION TO THE FIVE CIVILIZED TRIBES,

<u> Tams Bixby </u>
Chairman.

<u> T. B. Needles </u>
Commissioner.

<u> C.R. Breckinridge </u>
Commissioner.

Muskogee, Indian Territory.
JUN 22 1905

Applications for Enrollment of Chickasaw Newborn
Act of 1905   Volume III

BIRTH AFFIDAVIT.   No 6

DEPARTMENT OF THE INTERIOR.
COMMISSION TO THE FIVE CIVILIZED TRIBES.

IN RE APPLICATION FOR ENROLLMENT, as a citizen of the   Chickasaw   Nation, of Leona McKinney , born on the 7 day of Sept , 1903

Name of Father: Oyd McKinney   a citizen of the   Chickasaw   Nation.
Name of Mother: Fannie McKinney   a citizen of the   marriage   Nation.

Postoffice   Olney I.T.

AFFIDAVIT OF MOTHER.

UNITED STATES OF AMERICA, Indian Territory,
   Central   DISTRICT.

I, Fannie McKinney , on oath state that I am 23 years of age and a citizen by marriage , of the Chickasaw Nation; that I am the lawful wife of Oyd McKinney , who is a citizen, by blood of the Chickasaw Nation; that a Female child was born to me on 7 day of Sept , 1903, that said child has been named Leona McKinney , and is now living.

                                her
                        Fannie x McKinney
Witnesses To Mark: mark
  { J J Hunter
    N. T. Brashears

Subscribed and sworn to before me this 19 day of Jan , 1905.

                        W.A. Austin
                          Notary Public.

AFFIDAVIT OF ATTENDING PHYSICIAN OR MID-WIFE.

UNITED STATES OF AMERICA, Indian Territory,
   Central   DISTRICT.

I, J E Payte , a physician , on oath state that I attended on Mrs. Fannie McKiney[sic] , wife of Oyd McKinney on the 7 day of Sept , 1903; that there was born to her on said date a female child; that said child is now living and is said to have been named Leona McKinney

                        JE Payte MD

Applications for Enrollment of Chickasaw Newborn
Act of 1905   Volume III

Witnesses To Mark:
{ W.W. Grist
{ O.B. Fox

    Subscribed and sworn to before me this   17   day of   Jan   , 1905.

                            D A Spears
                                    Notary Public.

BIRTH AFFIDAVIT. *Copy*

DEPARTMENT OF THE INTERIOR.
COMMISSION TO THE FIVE CIVILIZED TRIBES.

    IN RE APPLICATION FOR ENROLLMENT, as a citizen of the   Chickasaw   Nation, of   Leona McKinney   , born on the   7   day of   Sept   , 1903

Name of Father: Oyd McKinney   a citizen of the   Chickasaw   Nation.
Name of Mother: Fannie McKinney   a citizen of the   marriage   Nation.

                  Postoffice   Olney I.T.

AFFIDAVIT OF MOTHER.

UNITED STATES OF AMERICA, Indian Territory, }
    Central   DISTRICT. }

    I,   Fannie McKinney   , on oath state that I am   23   years of age and a citizen by   marriage   , of the   Chickasaw   Nation; that I am the lawful wife of   Oyd McKinney   , who is a citizen, by blood   of the   Chickasaw   Nation; that a   Female   child was born to me on   7   day of   Sept   , 1903; that said child has been named   Leona McKinney   , and was living March 4, 1905.

                                 her   *(Seal)*
                            Fannie x McKinney
Witnesses To Mark: mark
{ J.J. Hunter
{ N.B. Brashears

    Subscribed and sworn to before me this   16   day of   Jan   , 1905

                      (signed)   W. A. Austin
                                  Notary Public.

Applications for Enrollment of Chickasaw Newborn
Act of 1905   Volume III

AFFIDAVIT OF ATTENDING PHYSICIAN OR MID-WIFE.

UNITED STATES OF AMERICA, Indian Territory, }
Central   DISTRICT.

I,   J.E. Payte   , a physician   , on oath state that I attended on Mrs. Fannie McKinney   , wife of   Oyd McKinney   on the 7 day of Sept   , 1903; that there was born to her on said date a   female   child; that said child was living March 4, 1905, and is said to have been named Leona McKinney

(*signed*)   J.E. Payte - M.D.

Witnesses To Mark:
{ W.W. Grist
{ O.B. Fox
(*Seal*)

Subscribed and sworn to before me this   17   day of   Jan   , 1905.

(*signed*)   D A Spears
Notary Public.

BIRTH AFFIDAVIT.   *Copy*

DEPARTMENT OF THE INTERIOR.
COMMISSION TO THE FIVE CIVILIZED TRIBES.

IN RE APPLICATION FOR ENROLLMENT, as a citizen of the   Chickasaw   Nation, of   Leona McKinney   , born on the   7   day of   Sept   , 1903

Name of Father: Oyd McKinney   a citizen of the   Chickasaw Nation.
Name of Mother: Fannie McKinney   a citizen of the   marriage   Nation.

Postoffice   Olney I.T.

AFFIDAVIT OF MOTHER.

UNITED STATES OF AMERICA, Indian Territory, }
Central   DISTRICT.

I,   Fannie McKinney   , on oath state that I am   24   years of age and a citizen by   marriage   , of the   Chickasaw   Nation; that I am the lawful wife of Oyd McKinney   , who is a citizen, by Blood   of the   Chickasaw   Nation; that a   Female   child was born to me on   7th   day of   September   , 1903; that said child has been named Leona McKinney   , and was living March 4, 1905.

(*signed*)
Fannie McKinney

Applications for Enrollment of Chickasaw Newborn
Act of 1905 Volume III

Witnesses To Mark:
{ L.H. Riggs
{ Mrs. J.D. Baldwin

(Seal)

Subscribed and sworn to before me this 31st day of March , 1905

commission   (signed) Jno.D. Baldwin
expires 4/ /08   Notary Public.

AFFIDAVIT OF ATTENDING PHYSICIAN OR MID-WIFE.

UNITED STATES OF AMERICA, Indian Territory, }
    Central   DISTRICT. }

I, J.E. Payte , a physician , on oath state that I attended on Mrs. Fannie McKinney , wife of Oyd McKinney on the 7 day of Sept , 1903; that there was born to her on said date a Female child; that said child was living March 4, 1905, and is said to have been named Leona McKinney

(Seal)   (signed) J.E. Payte - M.D.
Witnesses To Mark:
{ J.D. Baldwin
{ Arthur Payte

Subscribed and sworn to before me this 29 day of Mch , 1905.
         (signed)
         D A Spears
         Notary Public.

BIRTH AFFIDAVIT.

DEPARTMENT OF THE INTERIOR.
COMMISSION TO THE FIVE CIVILIZED TRIBES.

IN RE APPLICATION FOR ENROLLMENT, as a citizen of the Chickasaw Nation, of Leona McKinney , born on the 7 day of Sept , 1903

Name of Father: Oyd McKinney   a citizen of the Chickasaw Nation.
Name of Mother: Fannie McKinney   a citizen of the Chickasaw Nation.

         Postoffice   Olney I.T.

Applications for Enrollment of Chickasaw Newborn
Act of 1905 Volume III

AFFIDAVIT OF MOTHER.

UNITED STATES OF AMERICA, Indian Territory, }
    Central   DISTRICT.

    I, Fannie McKinney, on oath state that I am 24 years of age and a citizen by marriage, of the Chickasaw Nation; that I am the lawful wife of Oyd McKinney, who is a citizen, by Blood of the Chickasaw Nation; that a Female child was born to me on 7th day of September, 1903; that said child has been named Leona McKinney, and was living March 4, 1905.

                            Fannie McKinney

Witnesses To Mark:
{ L.H. Riggs
{ Mrs. J.D. Baldwin

    Subscribed and sworn to before me this 31st day of March, 1905

commission   Jno.D. Baldwin
expires 4/ /08   Notary Public.

AFFIDAVIT OF ATTENDING PHYSICIAN OR MID-WIFE.

UNITED STATES OF AMERICA, Indian Territory, }
    Central   DISTRICT.

    I, J.E. Payte, a physician, on oath state that I attended on Mrs. Fannie McKinney, wife of Oyd McKinney on the 7 day of Sept, 1903; that there was born to her on said date a Female child; that said child was living March 4, 1905, and is said to have been named Leona McKinney

                            J.E. Payte M.D.

Witnesses To Mark:
{ J.D. Baldwin
{ Arthur Payte

    Subscribed and sworn to before me this 29 day of Mch, 1905.

                            D. A. Spears
                            Notary Public.

Applications for Enrollment of Chickasaw Newborn
Act of 1905 Volume III

9-
NB 237

No. 1154

Certificate of Record of Marriages.

United States of America, }
The Indian Territory, } sct.
Central   District. }

I,   E. J. Fannin   Clerk
of the United States Court, in the Indian Territory and District aforesaid, do hereby CERTIFY, that the License for and Certificate of the Marriage of

Mr.   Oid[sic] McKinney   and

M   Fannie Brashears   was

filed in my office in said Territory and District the 3rd day of Aug A.D., 190 1, and duly recorded in Book "I" of Marriage Record, Page   577

DEPARTMENT OF THE INTERIOR,
COMMISSION TO THE FIVE CIVILIZED TRIBES.
FILED
APR 17 1905
Tams Bixby CHAIRMAN.

WITNESS my hand and Seal of said Court, at
Atoka
this   3rd   day of   Aug
A.D. 190 1

E.J. Fannin
Clerk.
By   W^m H Reynolds   Deputy.

P. O. ─────────────

UNITED STATES OF AMERICA:
INDIAN TERRITORY:
CENTRAL DISTRICT:

I, E. J. Fannin, Clerk of the United States Court, for the Central District of the Indian Territory, do hereby certify that the within and foregoing is a true and correct copy of the Marriage License granted to Oid McKinney and Fannie Brashears, on the 29th day of July, A.D., 1901, and the certificate of marriage attached to same, as the same appears of record in this office.

Applications for Enrollment of Chickasaw Newborn
Act of 1905 Volume III

IN TESTIMONY WHEREOF I have hereunto set my hand and affixed the official seal of said Court, at my office in Atoka, Indian Territory on this the 6th day of April, A. D., 1905.

                E. J. Fannin, Clerk.
                By" *(Name Illegible)* Deput.y[sic]

No. 1154

MARRIAGE LICENSE

United States of America,   The Indian Territory,
                                           Central   DISTRICT, SS.

To any Person Authorized by Law to Solemnize Marriage, Greeting:

You are hereby commanded to Solemnize the Rite and publish the Banns of Matrimony between Mr.   Oid McKinney
of   Oconee   *in the Indian Territory, aged*   23   *years,*
and M   Fannie Brashears   *of*   Oconee
in the Indian Territory., aged   20   *years, according to law, and do you officially sign and return this License to the parties therein named.*

               WITNESS my hand and official seal, this   29   *day*
               of   July   *A. D. 190* 1

   Seal   E.J. Fannin
                            Clerk of the United States Court.

             W^m H Reynolds   *Deputy*

Certificate of Marriage.

United States of America,
  The Indian Territory, } ss.
    Central   District.   *I,*   J H Johnson

a Minister of the Gospel   , *do hereby certify, that on the*   1   *day of*   Aug   *A. D. 190* 1 , *I did, duly and according to law, as commanded in the foregoing License, solemnize the Rite and publish the Banns of Matrimony between the parties therein named.*

Applications for Enrollment of Chickasaw Newborn
Act of 1905   Volume III

Witness my hand, this   1ˢᵗ   *day of*   Aug   *A. D. 190* 1

My credentials are recorded in the office of the Clerk of
the United States Court in the Indian Territory,   J.H. Johnson
Central District, Book   A   , Page   104   a   M.G.

Note—This License and Certificate of Marriage must be returned to the Office of the Clerk of the United States Court of the Indian Territory, from whence it was issued, within sixty days from the date thereof, or the party to whom the License was issued will be liable in the amount of the One Hundred Dollars ($100.00)

9-NB-237
9-1675

Muskogee, Indian Territory, July 21, 1905.

Oid McKinney,
    Coalgate, Indian Territory.

Dear Sir:

    Receipt is hereby acknowledged of your letter of July 16, 1905, asking when you will be notified that you can file for your infant children Georgie and Leona McKinney.

    In reply to your letter you are advised that the name of your child Georgie McKinney has been placed upon a schedule of citizens by blood of the Chickasaw Nation prepared for forwarding to the Secretary of the Interior and you will be notified when her enrollment is approved by the Department.

    You are further advised that the name of your child Leona McKinney will probably be placed upon the next schedule of new born citizens of the Chickasaw Nation prepared for forwarding to the Secretary of the Interior, and when her enrollment is approved you will be notified.

                              Respectfully,

                                              Commissioner.

Applications for Enrollment of Chickasaw Newborn
Act of 1905   Volume III

9-NB-237

Muskogee, Indian Territory, November 23, 1905.

Oyd McKinney,
    Olney, Indian Territory.

Dear Sir:

    Replying to that portion of your letter of November 19, 1905, in which you ask the status of the enrollment of your child Leona McKinney you are advised that the name of your child Leona McKinney has been placed upon a schedule of new born citizens of the Chickasaw Nation which has been forwarded the Secretary of the Interior, but this office has not yet been notified of Departmental action thereon.

        Respectfully,

        Acting Commissioner.

REFER IN REPLY TO THE FOLLOWING:
9 NB 237

DEPARTMENT OF THE INTERIOR,
COMMISSIONER TO THE FIVE CIVILIZED TRIBES.

Muskogee, Indian Territory, December 2, 1905.

Oyd McKinney,
    Coalgate, Indian Territory.

Dear Sir:

    You are hereby advised that on November 24, 1905, the Secretary of the Interior approved the enrollment of your minor child, Leona McKinney, as a citizen of the Chickasaw Nation, and that the name of said child appears upon the roll of new born citizens of the Chickasaw Nation as number 551.

    The child is now entitled to an allotment, and application therefor should be made without delay at the Land Office for the Nation in which the prospective allotment is located.

    An entire allotment for said child must be selected at the time of the original application.

        Respectfully,
        W^m. O. Beall
        Acting Commissioner.

Applications for Enrollment of Chickasaw Newborn
Act of 1905   Volume III

D 318-1909

Muskogee, Oklahoma, April 12, 1909.

Subject:

Report on Departmental
letter of March 12, 1909,
as to degree of Indian
blood of Harris McKinney
and the Garside family.

The Honorable,
 The Secretary of the Interior.

Sir:

    Receipt is hereby acknowledged of Departmental letter of March 12, 1909, inclosing copy of a communication addressed by the Department to Honorable Charles D. Carter, relative to his request to be advised whether it would be possible to have designated on the approved rolls of the Chickasaw Nation the degree of Indian blood possessed by Harris McKinney and his family and other Chickasaw citizens by the name of Garsides.

    It is observed that the printed rolls of citizens by blood of the Chickasaw Nation do not show the degree of Indian blood possessed by said persons and the Department states this may be due to an oversight in the preparation of the roll or it may be that the original enrollment records do not furnish thy information on the point.

    The office is, therefore, requested to cause an examination to be made of the original enrollment records in the cases of these persons and to report to the Department as to the information contained therein relative to the degree of Indian blood of each, including therein such information as is found on the census cards bearing their names

    Reporting in this matter I have the honor to advise that it appears from the records of this office that Harris McKinney and Oyd McKinney, Charles Hayes and Joseph Garsides and their respective families were applicants for enrollment as citizens by blood of the Chickasaw Nation, claiming descent from one Polly McKinney, to whom a patent for land was issued November 16, 1840 by President Martin Van Buren, under the fifth article of the treaty made May 24, 1834 between the United States and the Chickasaw Indians, under which, the patent recites, Polly McKinney (as Polly McKinnie) became entitled out of the lands ceded to the United States by the treaty with the Chickasaw Nation entered into October 20, 1832, to three sections and a half of land, which was conveyed by said patent, and which was entered as number 1202 in the abstract of reservations under the fifth article of the aforesaid treaty of May 24, 1834.

Applications for Enrollment of Chickasaw Newborn
Act of 1905 Volume III

Harris and Oyd McKinney are brothers, the children of William McKinney, son of Polly McKinney. Charley Hayes and Joseph Garsides claim the right to enrollment as intermarried citizens by reason of their marriage to Mattie McKinney and Mary Louise McKinney, both deceased sisters of Harris and Oyd McKinney, and made application for the enrollment of their children, Daniel Hayes, Minnie Hayes, Maggie Hayes and Edward Hayes and Fannie Garsides, Ben Garsides, Alex Garsides, Jim Garsides, Nellie Garsides, Mattie Garsides and Joe Garsides Jr., by reason of their descent from the said Mattie McKinney and Mary Louise McKinney, their names appearing on the roll of citizens by blood of the Chickasaw Nation at Numbers 4652 to 4658 inclusive, respectively.

The said Joseph Garsides and Charley Hayes appear upon the roll of citizens by marriage of the Chickasaw Nation at Numbers 535 and 619 respectively.

Harris McKinney made application for the enrollment of himself and his three children, Laura Etta McKinney, Cecial Berthal McKinney and Maude Lee McKinney, as citizens of the Chickasaw Nation under the Act of Congress approved June 28, 1898 and the Act of Congress approved July 1, 1902, and also made application for the enrollment of his child, Emma May McKinney, under the Act of Congress approved March 3, 1905. The names of Harris McKinney and his children enrolled under the Act of Congress approved July 1, 1902, appear at Numbers 4668[sic] to 4651 inclusive upon the roll of citizens by blood of the Chickasaw Nation while the name of Emma Ma[sic] McKinney appears upon the roll of new born citizens of said nation, enrolled under the Act of March 3, 1905, at number 558.

Oyd McKinney made application for the enrollment of himself and his child, Georgie McKinney, as citizens of the Chickasaw Nation under the Act of Congress approved June 28, 1898 and the Act of Congress approved July 1, 1902, their names appearing at Numbers 4647 and 4980 respectively upon the approved roll of citizens by blood of the Chickasaw Nation. He also made application for the enrollment of Leona McKinney under the Act of Congress approved March 3, 1905, and her name appears upon said roll at Number 551. Under the Act of Congress approved April 26, 1906, he made application for the enrollment of his child, Williams McKinney, whose name appears upon the roll of minor citizens enrolled under said act of Number 299.

Daniel Hayes made application for the enrollment of his child, Henry Charles Preston Hayes, as a citizen of the Chickasaw Nation under the Act of Congress approved April 26, 1906, and his name appears upon the roll of minor citizens of the Chickasaw Nation enrolled under said act at Number 317.

Fannie Garsides married James Self, who is enrolled at Number 346 upon the roll of Citizens by Marriage of the Chickasaw Nation, and they made application for the enrollment of their children, Sarah Arinda Self and Joseph W. Self under the Act of Congress approved March 3, 1905, their names appearing upon said roll at Numbers 552 and 553 respectively. They also made application under the Act of Congress approved April 26, 1906, for the enrollment of their child, Cecil Newton Self, and his name appears at Number 183 on the roll of minor citizens of the Chickasaw nation enrolled under said act.

Applications for Enrollment of Chickasaw Newborn
Act of 1905   Volume III

None of the persons above named who appear upon the roll of citizens by blood of the Chickasaw Nation appear to be possessed of Chickasaw Indian blood except Emma May McKinney, who appears upon the roll of newborn citizens of the Chickasaw Nation under the Act of Congress approved March 3, 1905, at Number 558 as a one-eighth blood Chickasaw, Cecil Newton Self, who appears upon the roll of Minor Chickasaws under the Act of Congress approved April 26, 1905, at Number 183 as possessed of one-sixteenth Indian blood, Williams McKinney, who appears upon said roll at Number 299 as possessed of one-sixty-fourth Indian blood and Henry Charles Preston Hayes, who appears upon the same roll at Number 317 as possessed of one-eighth Chickasaw blood.

It appears that the persons above referred to have, prior to the time they were enrolled upon the roll of citizens by blood of the Chickasaw Nation, claimed that they were possessed of Chickasaw Indian blood but that they did not know the degree of Indian blood possessed by Polly McKinney, the Indian ancestor from whom they claimed descent. They were accordingly enrolled upon the roll of citizens by blood of the Chickasaw Nation, no degree of Indian blood being given; they were not enrolled as adopted whites for the reason that they claimed to be possessed of some degree of Chickasaw Indian blood.

July 17, 1905, this office transmitted a schedule of citizens by blood of the Chickasaw Nation, Numbers 4968 to 4981 inclusive, containing the name of Georgie McKinney at Number 4980 thereon. August 18, 1905 (Land 59356-1905) the Commissioner of Indian Affairs recommended that the schedule be approved except as to Georgia McKinney, Number 4980, but that her name be eliminated from the roll and that the roll be changed as to her father, Oyd McKinney, to show that he is an adopted citizen of the Chickasaw Nation.

August 23, 1905, the report of the Commissioner of Indian Affairs was referred to the Assistant Attorney General for an opinion as to whether Georgie McKinney was entitled to enrollment under the Act of Congress approved March 3, 1905. September 1, 1905, he held that Georgie McKinney was entitled to enrollment within the meaning of the Act of Congress of March 3, 1905, even though she were the descendant of an adopted citizen. A copy of this opinion was transmitted with Departmental letter of September 7, 1905 (I. T D 10622,11176-1905) and the scheduled[sic] of Chickasaws by blood above referred to was approved by the secretary of on the date last named.

February 28, 1907 further opinion was rendered by the Assistant Attorney General on a motion for review of the case of Georgie McKinney, filed by counsel for the Chickasaw Nation recommending that the applicant be enrolled and the motion denied. This opinion was transmitted with Departmental letter of March 1, 1907 (I. T. D. 5754-1907).

May 28, 1906 (I. T. D. 9586-1906) the Department returned a schedule of newborn citizens of the Chickasaw Nation enrolled under the Act of Congress approved March 3, 1905, Numbers 558 to 567 inclusive, containing the name of Emma May McKinney at Number 558 thereon, for the reason that the quantum of Indian blood

Applications for Enrollment of Chickasaw Newborn
Act of 1905   Volume III

possessed by this child did not appear on said schedule, and, in view of the provision of the Act of April 26, 1906, providing that for all purposes the quantum of Indian blood possessed by any number of said tribes shall be determined by the rolls of citizens of said tribes approved by the Secretary of the Interior, this office was directed to endeavor to secure the necessary information as to the blood of Emma May McKinney.

June 14, 1906, in response to a request from this office, there was filed an affidavit of Harris McKinney to the effect that he was a one quarter blood Chickasaw and that his children, Laura Etta, Cecil Berthal and Maude Lee and Emma May McKinney were possessed of one-eighth Chickasaw blood.

Similar requests were also addressed to the other members of this family who had made application for the enrollment of their minor children under the Act of Congress approved April 26, 1906, and affidavits were received as follows:

December 7, 1906, affidavit was filed by Oyd McKinney stating that his son, Williams McKinney, Minor Chickasaw Roll Number 299 was a one-sixtyfourth[sic] blood Chickasaw Indian. November 9, 1906, however, joint affidavit of Oyd and Fannie McKinney was filed stating that they do not know the exact amount of Chickasaw Indian blood contained by the said Oyd McKinney or his children.

July 5, 1906, the affidavit of Fannie Self was filed, giving the degree of Chickasaw blood of her child, Cecil Newton Self, Minor Chickasaw Roll Number 183, as one-sixteenth.

January 28, 1907, there was referred to this office by the Department letter from Daniel Hayes of January 18, 1907, in which he states that he does not know the degree of Indian blood possessed by him and his family but that the nearest he can get to it is between one-fourth and one-sixteenth, and the degree of Chickasaw blood placed opposite the name of his child, Henry Charles Preston Hayes, Minor Chickasaw roll Number 317, was estimated at one-eighth and it so appears upon the approved roll of Minor Chickasaws.

There are inclosed you herewith copies of Chickasaw cards Number 1675, Oyd McKinney, et al. Number 1826, Charley Hayes, et al., Number 1677, Harris McKinney, et al., Number 1678, Joseph Garsides, et al.; copies of Chickasaw New Born cards, (Act of March 3, 1905) Number 237, Leona McKinney, Number 238, Emma May McKinney, Number 233, Sarah Arinda Self, et al. and copes[sic] of Minor Chickasaw card, (Act of Congress approved April 26, 1906), Numbers 296, Williams McKinney, 258, Henry Charles Preston Hayes and 100, Cecil Newton Self.

There are also inclosed copies of the affidavits of Fannie Self, Oyd McKinney, joint affidavit of Oyd and Fannie McKinney, affidavit of Harris McKinney and communication of Daniel Hayes of January 18, 1907.

**Applications for Enrollment of Chickasaw Newborn
Act of 1905 Volume III**

Respectfully,

AB

Chickasaw 1677.   (Signed) J. G. Wright,

Through the Commissioner   Commissioner.
of Indian Affairs.

DEPARTMENT OF THE INTERIOR
OFFICE OF
SUPERINTENDENT FOR THE FIVE CIVILIZED TRIBES
MUSKOGEE, OKLAHOMA
THIS IS TO CERTIFY THAT I AM THE OFFICER HAVING CUSTODY OF THE RECORDS PERTAINING TO THE ENROLLMENT OF THE MEMBERS OF THE CHOCTAW, CHICKASAW, CHEROKEE, CREEK AND SEMINOLE TRIBES OF INDIANS AND THE DISPOSITION OF THE LAND OF SAID TRIBES, AND THAT THE ABOVE AND FOREGOING IS A TRUE AND CORRECT COPY OF Report dated April 12, 1909

from J. G. Wright, Commissioner to The Secretary of the Interior.

A. M. LANDMAN, SUPERINTENDENT,

A. M. LANDMAN, SUPERINTENDENT,
By..Clerk
In charge   Chickasaw   Records
Date   June 26, 1935.

Chic. N.B. - 238
    *(Emma May McKinney
    Born August 1, 1904)*

Applications for Enrollment of Chickasaw Newborn
Act of 1905   Volume III

T.W.L.
G.D.A.   DEPARTMENT OF THE INTERIOR,
                    COMMISSION TO THE FIVE CIVILIZED TRIBES.

In the matter of the application of Harris McKinney, et al., for enrollment as citizensxby[sic] blood of the Chickasaw Nation, consolidating the applications of --

Harris McKinney, et al.,	9 D 176
Oyd McKinney,	9 D 339
Fannie Garsides, et al.,	9 D 292

COPY

--- D E C I S I O N ---

It appears from the census cards in the possession of the Commission and the other records in this case that at Colbert, Indian Territory, on October 14, 1898, application was made for the enrollment of Harris McKinney and his minor child, Laura Etta McKinney, as citizens by blood of the Chickasaw Nation, since which time birth affidavits have been filed in the matter of the application for the enrollment of his infant children, Cecial Berthal and Maude Lee McKinney, as citizens by blood of the Chickasaw Nation; that at the same place and on the same date application was made for the enrollment of Charley Hayes as a citizen by intermarriage of the Chickasaw Nation, and for the enrollment of his minor children, Daniel, Minnie, Maggie and Edward Hayes, as citizens by blood of the Chickasaw Nation, that also at the same place and on the same date application was made for the enrollment of Martha McKinney as a citizen by intermarriage of the Chickasaw Nation; that at Ardmore, Indian Territory, on November 25, 1898, application was made for the enrollment of Oyd McKinney as a citizen by blood of the Chickasaw Nation; that at Atoka, Indian Territory, on December 5, 1899, application was made for the enrollment of Joseph Garsides as a citizen by intermarriage of the Chickasaw Nation, and for the enrollment of his seven minor children, Fannie, Ben, Alex, Jim, Nellie, Mattie and Joe Garsides Jr., as citizens by blood of the Chickasaw Nation.

Further proceedings in the matter of said applications were had at Durant, Indian Territory, at the session of the Commission commencing August 14, and ending August 18, 1899, and at Atoka, Indian Territory, on December 3, and December 8, 1900.

The applicants, Martha McKinney, Charley Hayes and his minor children, Daniel, Minnie, Maggie and Edward Hayes, and Joseph Garsides, are differently classified and are not embraced in this decision.

It appears from the evidence submitted and the records in the possession of the Commission that the applicants, Harris McKinney, and his three minor children, Laura Etta, Cecial Berthal and Maude Lee McKinney, and Oyd McKinney, Fannie Garsides, Ben Garsides, Alex Garsides, Jim Garsides, Nellie Garsides, Mattie Garsides and Joe Garsides Jr., claim rights to enrollment as citizens by blood of the Chickasaw Nation, by reason of being descendants of Polly McKinney (or McKinnie), who obtained a patent to

Applications for Enrollment of Chickasaw Newborn
Act of 1905   Volume III

land in Mississippi under the treaty of 1834 between the United States and the Chickasaw Nation, in which patent the said Polly McKinney (or McKinnie) was characterized as "a Chickasaw Indian;" that the principal applicants herein are, and have been for may[sic] years past, actual and bona fide residents of the Chickasaw country in Indian Territory, and are duly recognized as citizens of the Chickasaw Nation; that Harris McKinney's name is identified on the 1893 Chickasaw pay roll, book 2, page 8, No. 226; that Oyd McKinney's name is identified on the 1893 Chickasaw pay roll, No. 1, at page 140; that the applicants, Fannie Garsides, Ben Garsides, Ale Garsides, Jim Garsides, Nellie Garsides, Mattie Garsides and Joe Garsides Jr., are identified on the Maytubby 1893 Chickasaw pay roll, No. 2, duly enrolled with their father, Joseph Garsides; that Laura Etta McKinney, Cecial Berthal McKinney and Maude Lee McKinney, the minor children of the principal applicant, Harris McKinney, having been born subsequent to the tribal enrollment of their father, are identified from proper birth affidavits filed herein and made a part of the record in this case.

It is the contention of counsel for the Choctaw and Chickasaw Nations that the said Polly McKinney (or McKinnie) was a Cherokee Indian by blood, and that notwithstanding the recognition given the principal applicants herein as citizens of the Chickasaw Nation, they are not entitled to said citizenship as they are Cherokee Indians by blood and are not citizens by adoption of the Chickasaw Nation by an act of the Chickasaw legislature.

The contention that the said Polly McKinney (or McKinnie) was a Cherokee Indian and had no Chickasaw blood is not established by the evidence. She was recognized by the government of the United States as a Chickasaw Indian when the patent referred to was given to her, and was also recognized by the Chickasaws themselves, both in Mississippi and Indian Territory, as a member of said tribe of Indians; and it further appears from the testimony submitted, and the records in the possession of the Commission, that her descendants have been recognized and enrolled as citizens of the Chickasaw tribe of Indians.

The records in the possession of the Commission further show that none of the applicants herein has ever been recognized or enrolled by the Cherokee tribal authorities as a citizen of said Nation, nor has any of them ever been listed for enrollment as a citizen of the Cherokee Nation by the Commission to the Five Civilized Tribes.

It further appears that all of the applicants considered herein, except Cecial Berthal McKinney, who was born February 17, 1901, were residents in good faith of Indian Territory on June 28, 1898.

It is therefore the opinion of the Commission that the applications for the enrollment of Harris McKinney, Laura Etta McKinney, Cecial Berthal McKinney, Maude Lee McKinney, Oyd McKinney, Fannie Garsides, Ben Garsides, Alex Garsides, Jim Garsides, Nellie Garsides, Mattie Garsides and Joe Garsides Jr., as citizens by blood of the Chickasaw Nation should be granted under the provisions of section twenty-one of the Act of Congress approved June 28, 1898 (30 Stats., 495), and it is so ordered.

COMMISSION TO THE FIVE CIVILIZED TRIBES,

Applications for Enrollment of Chickasaw Newborn
Act of 1905 Volume III

SIGNED   *Tams Bixby*
Chairman.

SIGNED   *T. B. Needles.*
Commissioner.

SIGNED   *C.R. Breckinridge.*
Commissioner.

Muskogee, Indian Territory.
FEB 2 1 1903

W.J.
9-NB-238.

DEPARTMENT OF THE INTERIOR,
COMMISSIONER TO THE FIVE CIVILIZED TRIBES.

In the matter of the application for the enrollment of Emma May McKinney as a citizen of the Chickasaw Nation.

--: D E C I S I O N :--

It appears from the record herein that on April 3, 1905 there was filed with the Commission to the Five Civilized Tribes an application for the enrollment of Emma May McKinney as a citizen by blood of the Chickasaw Nation.
It further appears from the record in this case and the records of this office that the applicant was born August 1, 1904 and is a daughter of Harris McKinney, a recognized and enrolled citizen of the Chickasaw Nation whose name appears opposite number 4648 upon the final roll of citizens of the Chickasaw Nation, approved by the Secretary of the Interior April 11, 1903, and Mollie McKinney, a citizen of the United States.
From a copy of a letter of the Commission to the Five Civilized Tribes to the Honorable Secretary of the Interior, dated March 23, 1903, transmitting partial roll of citizens of the Chickasaw Nation, numbers 4564 to 4659, inclusive, upon which partial roll the name of of[sic] the said Harris McKinney is found, it appears that it was stated in said letter that the rights of said Harris McKinney, and others specifically mentioned therein, to enrollment as citizens of the Chickasaw Nation "are established by tribal recognition and by their descent from Polly McKinney, who was adopted by the Chickasaw tribe of Indians in the state of Mississippi prior to the year 1834, and who obtained as patent to land in that state under the treaty of 1834, between the United States and Chickasaw Nation, in which patent the said Polly McKinney was characterized as 'a Chickasaw Indian'." However, on Feburary[sic] 21, 1903, the Commission to the Five Civilized Tribes rendered a decision enrolling the said Harris McKinney, and others, as citizens by blood of the Chickasaw Nation, thereby establishing the status of said Harris McKinney as a citizen by blood of said nation. A copy of said decision is filed herewith and made a part of the record in this case.

Applications for Enrollment of Chickasaw Newborn
Act of 1905 Volume III

It further appears from the record herein that the applicant was living March 4, 1905.

The Act of Congress approved March 3, 1905 (Public No. 212) among other things provides:

"That the Commission to the Five Civilized Tribes is authorized for sixty days after the date of the approval of this act to receive and consider applications for enrollment of children born subsequent to September twenty-fifth, nineteen hundred and two, and prior to March fourth, nineteen hundred and five, and who were living on said latter date, to citizens by blood of the Choctaw and Chickasaw tribes of Indians whose enrollment has been approved by the Secretary of the Interior prior to the date of the approval of this act; and to enroll and make allotments to such children."

I am of the opinion that Emma May McKinney is a child of a citizen by blood of the Chickasaw tribe of Indians, within the meaning of the provision of law above quoted and that, therefore, the application for her enrollment as a citizen by blood of the Chickasaw Nation should be granted and it is so ordered.

Tams Bixby   Commissioner.

Muskogee, Indian Territory,
OCT 4- 1905

BIRTH AFFIDAVIT.

DEPARTMENT OF THE INTERIOR.
COMMISSION TO THE FIVE CIVILIZED TRIBES.

IN RE APPLICATION FOR ENROLLMENT, as a citizen of the   Chickasaw   Nation, of   Emma May McKinney   , born on the   1st day of   August   , 1904

Name of Father: Harris McKinney   a citizen of the   Chickasaw Nation.
Name of Mother: Mollie McKinnie[sic]   a citizen of the   United States Nation.

Postoffice   Platter Ind Ter

AFFIDAVIT OF MOTHER.

UNITED STATES OF AMERICA, Indian Territory,
        Central   DISTRICT.

I,   Mollie McKinney   , on oath state that I am   23   years of age and a citizen by   Birth   , of the   United States   Nation; that I am the lawful wife of   Harris McKinney   , who is a citizen, by Blood   of the   Chickasaw Nation; that a   Female   child was born to me on   first   day of   August   , 1904; that said child has been named   Emma May McKinney   , and was living March 4, 1905.

Applications for Enrollment of Chickasaw Newborn
Act of 1905   Volume III

                                                    her
                                        Mollie x McKinney
Witnesses To Mark: mark
{ *(Name Illegible)*
  J W Gist

Subscribed and sworn to before me this .... day of ...., 1905.

                                                Notary Public.

AFFIDAVIT OF ATTENDING PHYSICIAN OR MID-WIFE.

UNITED STATES OF AMERICA, Indian Territory, }
    Central   DISTRICT.

    I,   M E Scott   , a........................., on oath state that I attended on Mrs.   Mollie McKinney , wife of   Harris McKinney   on the first   day of   Aug   , 1904; that there was born to her on said date a   female   child; that said child was living March 4, 1905, and is said to have been named Emma May McKinney

                                            M E Scott
Witnesses To Mark:

{

Subscribed and sworn to before me this 29 day of March   , 1905

                                            G.O. Reves
                                            Notary Public.

BIRTH AFFIDAVIT.
                            DEPARTMENT OF THE INTERIOR.
                      COMMISSION TO THE FIVE CIVILIZED TRIBES.

    IN RE APPLICATION FOR ENROLLMENT, as a citizen of the   Chickasoaw   Nation, of   Emma May McKinney   , born on the   1st   day of   August   , 1904

Name of Father: Harris McKinney   a citizen of the   Chickasaw   Nation.
Name of Mother: Mollie McKinney   a citizen of the   United States Nation.

                              Postoffice   Platter Ind Ter

Applications for Enrollment of Chickasaw Newborn
Act of 1905   Volume III

AFFIDAVIT OF MOTHER.

UNITED STATES OF AMERICA, Indian Territory, }
....DISTRICT. }

I,   Mollie McKinney   , on oath state that I am   23   years of age and a citizen by   ———   , of the   United States   Nation; that I am the lawful wife of   Harris McKinney   , who is a citizen, by   blood   of the   Chickasaw Nation; that a   female   child was born to me on   1st day of   August   , 1904; that said child has been named   Emma May McKinney   , and was living March 4, 1905.

                                      her
                                Mollie x McKinney
Witnesses To Mark: mark
{ Joseph M Franklin
{ *(Name Illegible)*

Subscribed and sworn to before me this   6   day of   July   , 1905

                                Geo. O. Reves
                                Notary Public.

AFFIDAVIT OF ATTENDING PHYSICIAN OR MID-WIFE.

UNITED STATES OF AMERICA, Indian Territory, }
    Central   DISTRICT. }

I,   M E Scott   , a..................................., on oath state that I attended on Mrs.   Mollie McKinney   , wife of   Harris McKinney   on the   1st day of   August   , 1904; that there was born to her on said date a   female   child; that said child was living March 4, 1905, and is said to have been named Emma May McKinney

                                M. E. Scott

Witnesses To Mark:

{

Subscribed and sworn to before me this   6"   day of   July   , 1905

                                Geo. O. Reves
                                Notary Public.

Applications for Enrollment of Chickasaw Newborn
Act of 1905   Volume III

Chickasaw 1677.

Muskogee, Indian Territory, April 3, 1905.

Harris McKinney,
    Platter, Indian Territory.

Dear Sir:

    Receipt is hereby acknowledged of the affidavits of Mollie McKinney and M. E. Scott to the birth of Emma May McKinney, daughter of Harris and Mollie McKinney, August 1, 1904, and the same have been filed with our records as an application for the enrollment of said child.

                  Respectfully,

                                    Chairman.

---

9 N B 238

Muskogee, Indian Territory, April 17, 1905.

Harris McKinney,
    Platter, Indian Territory.

Dear Sir:

    There is inclosed you herewith for execution application for the enrollment of your infant child, Emma May McKinney, born August 1, 1904.

    The affidavit of the mother heretofore filed with the Commission was not acknowledged before a Notary Public. It is, therefore, necessary the application be re-executed.

    The affidavit also shows that the child claims through you. It will be necessary, for the child to be enrolled, that you furnish the Commission with either the original or a certified copy of the license and certificate of your marriage to her mother, Mollie McKinney.

    In having these affidavits executed care should be exercised to see that all names are written in full, as they appear in the body of the affidavit, and in the event that either of the persons signing the affidavit are unable to write, signatures by mark must be attested by two witnesses. Each affidavit must be executed before a Notary Public and the notarial seal and signature of the officer must be attached to each separate affidavit.

                  Respectfully,

LM 17-130   Chairman.

Applications for Enrollment of Chickasaw Newborn
Act of 1905   Volume III

9-NB-238.

Muskogee, Indian Territory June 10, 1905.

Harris McKinney,
    Platter, Indian Territory.

Dear Sir:

    On April 17, 1905 the Commission addressed a letter to you advising you that it would be necessary for you to furnish the Commission with proper proof of the birth of your daughter Emma May McKinney before the rights of said child as a citizen of the Chickasaw Nation could be determined, stating in said letter that the affidavit of the mother of said child heretofore filed with the Commission was not acknowledged before a notary public. No response has been received to said letter. You are therefore again requested to furnish such proof of birth and are advised that until the same is supplied the rights of your said daughter as a citizen of the Chickasaw Nation can not be determined.

Respectfully,

Chairman.

COPY.

9-NB-238

Muskogee, Indian Territory, October 4, 1905.

Harris McKinney,
    Platter, Indian Territory.

Dear Sir:

    Inclosed herewith you will find a copy of the decision of the Commissioner to the Five Civilized Tribes, rendered October 4, 1905, granting the application for the enrollment of your minor daughter, Emma May McKinney, as a citizen by blood of the Chickasaw Nation.

    The attorneys for the Choctaw and Chickasaw Nations have been furnished a copy of this decision and have been allowed fifteen days from the date of this notice within which to file protest against the enrollment of your said daughter. If at the expiration of that time no protest has been filed her name will be placed upon the final roll of citizens by blood of the Chickasaw Nation to be submitted to the Secretary of the Interior for his approval.

Applications for Enrollment of Chickasaw Newborn
Act of 1905   Volume III

Respectfully,
SIGNED
Tams Bixby
Commissioner.

Register
9-NB-238.

9-NB-238

COPY.

Muskogee, Indian Territory, October 4, 1905.

Mansfield, McMurray & Cornish,
    Attorneys for Choctaw and Chickasaw Nations,
        South McAlester, Indian Territory.

Gentlemen:

    Inclosed herewith you will find a copy of the decision of the Commissioner to the Five Civilized Tribes, rendered October 4, 1905, granting the application for the enrollment of Emma May McKinney as a citizen by blood of the Chickasaw Nation.

    You are hereby advised that you will be allowed fifteen days from the date of this notice within which to file protest against the enrollment of said applicant. If at the expiration of that time no protest has been filed her name will be placed upon the final roll of citizens by blood of the Chickasaw Nation to be submitted to the Secretary of the Interior for his approval.

Respectfully,

SIGNED   *Tams Bixby*
Commissioner.

Register
9-NB-238.

Applications for Enrollment of Chickasaw Newborn
Act of 1905   Volume III

9-NB-238

Muskogee, Indian Territory, February 12, 1906.

Harris McKinney,
    Platter, Indian Territory.

Dear Sir:

    Receipt is hereby acknowledged of your letter of February 5, 1906, asking if you can file for your daughter Emma May McKinney.

    In reply to your letter you are advised that the name of your daughter Emma May McKinney will be placed upon the next schedule of new born citizens of the Chickasaw Nation prepare for forwarding the Secretary of the Interior.

    Respectfully,

    Acting Commissioner.

9-NB-238

Muskogee, Indian Territory, June 6, 1906.

Harris McKinney,
    Platter, Indian Territory.

Dear Sir:

    May 28, 1906, the Secretary of the Interior returned without approval a schedule of new born citizens of the Chickasaw Nation under the act of Congress approved March 3, 1905, for the reason that the degree of Chickasaw blood possessed b your daughter Emma May McKinney did not appear thereon.

    I have therefore to request that you advise this office at the earliest practicable date the degree of Chickasaw blood possessed by your child Emma May McKinney.

    Respectfully,

    Commissioner.

Applications for Enrollment of Chickasaw Newborn
Act of 1905   Volume III

9-NB-238

Muskogee, Indian Territory, June 20, 1906.

Chief Clerk,
    Chickasaw Land Office,
        Ardmore, Indian Territory.

Dear Sir:

    Referring to Chickasaw NB card No. 238, Emma May McKinney, you are advised that the degree of Chickasaw blood of this citizen has been made to appear as 1/8 and the following notation placed on said card:

    "As to Chickasaw blood of No. 1 see affidavit of Harris McKinney of June 12, 1906, filed in Chickasaw #1677 June 20, 1906."

    You are therefore directed to make duplicate card of this number in your possession conform to the information thereon.

Respectfully,

Commissioner.

9-NB-238

Muskogee, Indian Territory, June 20, 1906.

Chief Clerk,
    Choctaw Land Office,
        Atoka, Indian Territory.

Dear Sir:

    Referring to Chickasaw NB card No. 238, Emma May McKinney, you are advised that the degree of Chickasaw blood of this citizen has been made to appear as 1/8 and the following notation placed on said card:

    "As to Chickasaw blood of No. 1 see affidavit of Harris McKinney of June 12, 1906, filed in Chickasaw #1677 June 20, 1906."

    You are therefore directed to make duplicate card of this number in your possession conform to the information thereon.

Respectfully,

Commissioner.

Applications for Enrollment of Chickasaw Newborn
Act of 1905 Volume III

Muskogee, Indian Territory, June 22, 1906.

The Honorable,
    The Secretary of the Interior.

Sir:

    Receipt is hereby acknowledged of Departmental letter of May 28, 1906, (I.T.D. 9586-1906) returning a schedule of children of citizens by blood of the Chickasaw Nation of the Chickasaw Nation numbers 558 to 567 inclusive, which was forwarded May 3, 1906, for the reason that Emma May McKinney at No. 558 upon said schedule was admitted as a citizen by blood of the Chickasaw Nation but the quantum of Chickasaw blood possessed by her did not appear thereon.

    Inasmuch as Section 19 of the act of April 26, 1906, provides that " for all purposes the quantum of Indian blood possessed by any member of said tribes shall be determined by the rolls of citizens of said tribes approved by the Secretary of the Interior," the Department does not care to approve a schedule not bearing evidence of blood opposite one of the persons shown thereon. The schedule was therefore returned unapproved and this office was requested to endeavor to secure the necessary information as to the blood of Emma May McKinney.

    I have the honor to report in this matter that immediately upon receipt of Departmental instructions of May 28, 1906, a letter was addressed to Harris McKinney, father of Emma May McKinney, requesting him to advise this office the degree of Chickasaw blood possessed by his child Emma May McKinney. This office is now in receipt of an affidavit from Harris McKinney stating that he is possessed of one-fourth Chickasaw blood and that his children, among whom is Emma May McKinney, are possessed of one-eighth Chickasaw blood.

    The schedule of citizens by blood of the Chickasaw Nation numbers 558 to 567 inclusive has been corrected to show the Chickasaw blood of Emma May McKinney and the same is returned herewith.

                                  Respectfully,

Through the Commissioner   Commissioner.
    of Indian Affairs.

Applications for Enrollment of Chickasaw Newborn
Act of 1905   Volume III

Chic. N.B. - 239
  (Gussie Agnes Rider
  Born February 13, 1905)

BIRTH AFFIDAVIT.

DEPARTMENT OF THE INTERIOR.
COMMISSION TO THE FIVE CIVILIZED TRIBES.

  IN RE APPLICATION FOR ENROLLMENT, as a citizen of the   Chickasaw   Nation, of   Gussie Agnes Rider   , born on the 13th day of   Feb   , 1905

Name of Father: Thomas S. Rider   a citizen of the   Chickasaw   Nation.
Name of Mother: Nellie Rider   a citizen of the   Chickasaw   Nation.
by addoption[sic]

  Postoffice   Chelsea, Ind. Ty.

AFFIDAVIT OF MOTHER.

UNITED STATES OF AMERICA, Indian Territory,
  Northern   DISTRICT.

  I,   Nellie Rider   , on oath state that I am   27   years of age and a citizen by Adoption   , of the   Chickasaw   Nation; that I am the lawful wife of   Thomas S. Rider   , who is a citizen, by —— of the   Chickasaw   Nation; that a Female   child was born to me on   13th day of   Feb   , 1905; that said child has been named   Gussie Agnes Rider   , and was living March 4, 1905.

  Nellie Rider

Witnesses To Mark:
{

  Subscribed and sworn to before me this   1st day of   April   , 1905

  John G Scott
  Notary Public.

My term expires
May 26-1908

Applications for Enrollment of Chickasaw Newborn
Act of 1905 Volume III

AFFIDAVIT OF ATTENDING PHYSICIAN OR MID-WIFE.

UNITED STATES OF AMERICA, Indian Territory,
    Northern   DISTRICT.

I, J.W. Bone , a Physician , on oath state that I attended on Mrs. Mrs Nellie Rider , wife of Thomas S Rider on the 13th day of Feb., 1905; that there was born to her on said date a Female child; that said child was living March 4, 1905, and is said to have been named Gussie Agnes Rider

                        J.W. Bone M.D.

Witnesses To Mark:

Subscribed and sworn to before me this 1st day of April , 1905

                        John G Scott
                        Notary Public.

My term expires May 26-1908

                                      9-1681

           Muskogee, Indian Territory, April 6, 1905.

Thomas S. Rider,
    Chelsea, Indian Territory.

Dear Sir:

    Receipt is hereby acknowledged of the affidavits of Nellie Rider and J. W. Bone to the birth of Gussie Agnes Rider, daughter of Thomas S. and Nellie Rider February 13, 1905, and the same have been filed with our records as an application for the enrollment of said child.

                        Respectfully,

                                   Commissioner in Charge.

Applications for Enrollment of Chickasaw Newborn
Act of 1905   Volume III

9-NB-239

Muskogee, Indian Territory, February 15, 1907.

Mrs. Nellie Rider,
    Chelsea, Indian Territory.

Dear Madam:

Receipt is hereby acknowledged of your letter of February 4, 1907, asking relative to your right as an intermarried citizen of the Chickasaw Nation; you state your husband is enrolled as a citizen of the Chickasaw Nation.

In reply to your letter you are advised that it does not appear that any application has been made for your enrollment as a citizen by intermarriage of the Chickasaw Nation and there is no authority for the reception of an original application in your behalf.

The matter of the patents referred to in your letter will be made the subject of a separate communication.

Respectfully,

Commissioner.

Chic. N.B. - 240
    (Roscoe Hampton Turner
    Born December 6, 1902)

BIRTH AFFIDAVIT.

IN RE-APPLICATION FOR ENROLLMENT, as a citizen of the   Chickasaw   Nation, of   Roscoe Hampton Turner   , born on the   6"   day of   December , 190 2

Name of Father: Hiram G. Turner   a citizen of the   Chickasaw   Nation.
Name of Mother: Daisy Turner   a citizen of the   Chickasaw   Nation.

Postoffice   Purcell I.T.

Applications for Enrollment of Chickasaw Newborn
Act of 1905   Volume III

AFFIDAVIT OF MOTHER.

UNITED STATES OF AMERICA, INDIAN TERRITORY,
Southern District.

I, Daisy Turner, on oath state that I am 29 years of age and a citizen by blood, of the Chickasaw Nation; that I am the lawful wife of Hiram G. Turner, who is a citizen, by marriage of the Chickasaw Nation; that a male child was born to me on 6" day of December, 1902, that said child has been named Roscoe Hampton Turner, and is now living.

                                        Daisy Turner

Witnesses To Mark:

{

    Subscribed and sworn to before me this 14" day of March, 1905.

                                        Joseph P Smith
                                        Notary Public.

AFFIDAVIT OF ATTENDING PHYSICIAN OR MID-WIFE.

UNITED STATES OF AMERICA, INDIAN TERRITORY,
Southern District.

I, G. M. Tralle, a Physician, on oath state that I attended on Mrs. Daisy Turner, wife of Hiram G. Turner on the 6" day of Dec, 190 2; that there was born to her on said date a .... child; that said child is now living and is said to have been named Roscoe Hampton Turner

                                        G.M. Tralle, M.D.

Witnesses To Mark:

{

    Subscribed and sworn to before me this 14" day of March, 1905.

                                        Joseph P Smith
                                        Notary Public.

Applications for Enrollment of Chickasaw Newborn
Act of 1905   Volume III

9-1688

Muskogee, Indian Territory, March 25, 1905

Hiram G. Turner,
    Purcell, Indian Territory.

Dear Sir:

    Receipt is hereby acknowledged of the affidavits of Daisy Turner and G. M. Tralle to the birth of Roscoe Hampton Turner, son of Hiram G. and Daisy Turner, December 6, 1902, and the same have been filed with our records as an application for the enrollment of said child.

                        Respectfully,

                                    Chairman.

Chickasaw 1690.

Muskogee, Indian Territory, April 4, 1905.

William J. Norman,
    Kemp, Indian Territory.

Dear Sir:

    Receipt is hereby acknowledged of the affidavits of Sallie Norman and C. A. Kirby to the birth of Daniel Norman, son of William J. and Sallie Norman, January 21, 1903, and the same have been filed with our records as an application for the enrollment of said child.

                        Respectfully,

                                    Commissioner in Charge.

Applications for Enrollment of Chickasaw Newborn
Act of 1905   Volume III

Chic. N.B. - 241
*(Daniel Norman
Born January 21, 1903)*

BIRTH AFFIDAVIT.   #95

DEPARTMENT OF THE INTERIOR.
COMMISSION TO THE FIVE CIVILIZED TRIBES.

IN RE APPLICATION FOR ENROLLMENT, as a citizen of the   Chickasaw   Nation, of   Danniel[sic] Norman   , born on the 21   day of January   , 1903

Name of Father: William J. Norman   a citizen of the   Chickasaw   Nation.
Name of Mother: Sallie Norman   a citizen of the   Chickasaw   Nation.

Postoffice   Kemp

AFFIDAVIT OF MOTHER.

UNITED STATES OF AMERICA, Indian Territory,
   Central   DISTRICT.

I,   Sallie Norman   , on oath state that I am   21   years of age and a citizen by Intermarriage   , of the   Chickasaw   Nation; that I am the lawful wife of   W G Norman   , who is a citizen, by   blood   of the   Chickasaw   Nation; that a male   child was born to me on   21   day of   January   , 1903, that said child has been named   Danniel   , and is now living.

                                Sallie Norman

Witnesses To Mark:
   { C.A. Kerby
     D.S. Norman

Subscribed and sworn to before me this   11   day of   February   , 1905.

                                S M Mead
                                   Notary Public.

Applications for Enrollment of Chickasaw Newborn
Act of 1905   Volume III

AFFIDAVIT OF ATTENDING PHYSICIAN OR MID-WIFE.

UNITED STATES OF AMERICA, Indian Territory, ⎫
    Central   DISTRICT. ⎭

I, C A Kerby, a midwife, on oath state that I attended on Mrs. Sallie Norman, wife of W J Norman on the 21 day of January, 1903; that there was born to her on said date a male child; that said child is now living and is said to have been named Danniel

                        C A Kerby

Witnesses To Mark:
{ C A Kerby
  D S Norman

    Subscribed and sworn to before me this 11 day of February, 1905.

                        S M Mead
                        Notary Public.

BIRTH AFFIDAVIT.

DEPARTMENT OF THE INTERIOR.
COMMISSION TO THE FIVE CIVILIZED TRIBES.

IN RE APPLICATION FOR ENROLLMENT, as a citizen of the Chickasaw Nation, of Daniel Norman, born on the 21 day of January, 1903

Name of Father: William J. Norman   a citizen of the Chickasaw Nation.
Name of Mother: Sallie Norman   a citizen of the Chickasaw Nation.

                Postoffice   Kemp, Indian Territory.

AFFIDAVIT OF MOTHER.

UNITED STATES OF AMERICA, Indian Territory, ⎫
    Central   DISTRICT. ⎭

I, Sallie Norman, on oath state that I am 21 years of age and a citizen by marriage, of the Chickasaw Nation; that I am the lawful wife of William J. Norman, who is a citizen, by blood of the Chickasaw Nation; that a male child was born to me on 21 day of January, 1903; that said child has been named Daniel Norman, and was living March 4, 1905.

                        Sallie Norman

Witnesses To Mark:
{

Applications for Enrollment of Chickasaw Newborn
Act of 1905   Volume III

Subscribed and sworn to before me this 27 day of   March   , 1905

                            O.R. Fowler
                            Notary Public.

AFFIDAVIT OF ATTENDING PHYSICIAN OR MID-WIFE.

UNITED STATES OF AMERICA, Indian Territory, ⎫
    Central   DISTRICT. ⎬

    I,   Mrs. C. A. Kirby   , a   Mid-Wife   , on oath state that I attended on Mrs. Sallie Norman   , wife of   William J Norman   on the   21 day of   January   , 1903; that there was born to her on said date a   male   child; that said child was living March 4, 1905, and is said to have been named   Daniel Norman

                            her
                        C.A. x Kirby
Witnesses To Mark: mark
  ⎰ Alice A Lewallen
  ⎱ L. Pope

Subscribed and sworn to before me this 27 day of   March   , 1905

                            O.R. Fowler
                            Notary Public.

Chic. N.B. - 242
    (Aron Anita McBride
    Born July 20, 1904)

                                    Chickasaw *(Illegible)*

                Muskogee, Indian Territory, March 31, 1905.

Hiram Young McBride,
    Tuttle, Indian Territory.

Dear Sir:

    Receipt is hereby acknowledged of the affidavits of Lovica Colbert McBride and W. E. Brown to the birth of Aron Anita McBride, daughter of Hiram Young and Lovica

Applications for Enrollment of Chickasaw Newborn
Act of 1905   Volume III

Chic. N.B. - 244
    (Claud Leonard Moreland
    Born April 30, 1903)

(The Birth Affidavit below typed as given.)

Birth affidavit.

DEPARTMENT OF THE INTERIOR.

Commission to the Five Civilized Tribes.

IN RE APPLICATION for Enrollment, as a citizen of the **Chickasaw** Nation of **Claud Leonard Moreland** born on the **30th.** day of **April**, 190 **3**

Name of Father: **Claud Moreland** , a citizen of the **United States**
Name of Mother **Fannie Moreland** , a citizen of the **Chickasaw** Nation.

Post Office **Foyil, Ind. Ter.**

AFFIDAVIT OF MOTHER.

United States of America,)
Indian Territory,) SS.
Central District.)

I, **Fannie Moreland** , on oath state that I am **32** yaers of age and a citizen by **blood** of the **Chickasaw** Nation; that I am the lawful wife of **Claud Moreland** , who is a citizen of **United States** , that a **male** child was born to me on the **30** day of **April** , 190 **3**; that said child has been named **Claud Leonard Moreland** and is now living.

                                                Fannie Moreland

Witnesses to Mark:
 (must be two)
           Nellie Rider
           Lula Landrum

Subscribed and sworn to before me this the **22** day of **March** 1905.

                                        John T. Ezzard
                                        Notary Public.

My commission expires **November 1, 1908**

Applications for Enrollment of Chickasaw Newborn
Act of 1905 Volume III

AFFIDAVIT OF ATTENDING PHYSICIAN, OR MIDWIFE.

United States of America, }
Indian Territory, } SS.
Central District. }

I, **J.W. Bone**, a **Physician**, on oath state that I attended on Mrs. **Fannie Moreland**, wife of **Claud Moreland** on the **30** day of **April**, 190 **3**; that there was born to her on said date a **male** child; that said child was living March 4, 1905, and is said to have been named **Claud Leonard Moreland**

J.W. Bone M.D.

Witnesses to Mark:
(must be two)
  Nellie Rider
  Lula Landrum

Subscribed and sworn to before me this the **22** day of **March** 1905.

John T. Ezzard
Notary Public.

My commission expires **November 1, 1908**

BIRTH AFFIDAVIT.

DEPARTMENT OF THE INTERIOR,
COMMISSION TO THE FIVE CIVILIZED TRIBES.

In Re Application for Enrollment, as a citizen of the Chickasaw Nation, of Claud Linnad[sic] Morland, born on the 30 day of April, 1903

Name of Father: Claud Morland   a citizen of the U.S. ~~Nation~~.
Name of Mother: Fannie Morland   a citizen of the Chickasaw Nation.

Post-office   Chelsea IT

AFFIDAVIT OF MOTHER.

UNITED STATES OF AMERICA, }
 INDIAN TERRITORY, }
 Northern   District. }

I, Fannie Morland, on oath state that I am 32 years of age and a citizen by Blood, of the Chickasaw Nation; that I am the lawful wife of Claud Morland, who is a citizen, by............of the U.S. Nation; that a

Applications for Enrollment of Chickasaw Newborn
Act of 1905 Volume III

male   child was born to me on   30   day of   April   , 1903 , that said child has been named   Claud L. Morland   , and is now living.

Fannie Morlan[sic]

WITNESSES TO MARK:

{

Subscribed and sworn to before me this   14   day of   July   , 1903

David G Elliott
NOTARY PUBLIC.

AFFIDAVIT OF ATTENDING PHYSICIAN OR MID-WIFE.

UNITED STATES OF AMERICA,
INDIAN TERRITORY,
Northern   District.

I,   J W Bone MD   , a physician   , on oath state that I attended on Mrs.   Fannie Morland   , wife of   Claud Morland   on the   30   day of   April   , 1903 ; that there was born to her on said date a   male   child; that said child is now living and is said to have been named   Claud L Morland

J. W. Bone

WITNESSES TO MARK:

{

Subscribed and sworn to before me this   14   day of   July   , 1903

David G Elliott
NOTARY PUBLIC.

9-1701

Muskogee, Indian Territory, April 5, 1905.

Claud Moreland,
    Foyil, Indian Territory.

Dear Sir:

    Receipt is hereby acknowledged of the affidavits of Fannie Moreland and J. W. Bone to the birth of Claud Leonard Moreland, son of Claud and Fannie Moreland, April 30, 1903, and the same have been filed with our records as an application for the enrollment of said child.

Applications for Enrollment of Chickasaw Newborn
Act of 1905   Volume III

Respectfully,

Commissioner in Charge.

9-NB 244 244

Muskogee, Indian Territory, April 19, 1905.

C. M. Moreland,
    Berwyn, Indian Territory.

Dear Sir:

Receipt is hereby acknowledged of your letter without date asking if application has been received for the enrollment of your child Claud Leonard Moreland.

In reply to your letter you are informed that the affidavits heregofore[sic] forwarded to the birth of Claud Leonard Moreland, son of Claud and Fannie Moreland, April 30, 1903, have been filed with our records as an application for his enrollment.

Respectfully,

Chairman.

Chic. N.B. - 245
    (Wesley Spencer
    Born May 18, 1903)
    (Irene Spencer
    Born January 26, 1905)

BIRTH AFFIDAVIT.

DEPARTMENT OF THE INTERIOR.
COMMISSION TO THE FIVE CIVILIZED TRIBES.

IN RE APPLICATION FOR ENROLLMENT, as a citizen of the Chickasaw Nation, of Wesley Spencer, born on the 18th day of May, 1903

Name of Father: Walter S. Spencer   a citizen of the _____ Nation.
Name of Mother: Margaret E. Spencer   a citizen of the Chickasaw Nation.

Applications for Enrollment of Chickasaw Newborn
Act of 1905   Volume III

Postoffice   Bradley, Ind. Ter.

AFFIDAVIT OF MOTHER.

UNITED STATES OF AMERICA, Indian Territory, }
Southern   DISTRICT.

I, Margaret E. Spencer , on oath state that I am 24 years of age and a citizen by birth , of the Chickasaw Nation; that I am the lawful wife of Walter S. Spencer , who is a citizen, by .... of the .... Nation; that a male child was born to me on 18th day of May , 1903; that said child has been named Wesley Spencer , and was living March 4, 1905.

Margaret E. Spencer

Witnesses To Mark:
{

Subscribed and sworn to before me this 25th day of March , 1905

J.D. Armstrong
Notary Public.

AFFIDAVIT OF ATTENDING PHYSICIAN OR MID-WIFE.

UNITED STATES OF AMERICA, Indian Territory, }
Southern   DISTRICT.

I, W. H. Parks , a Physician , on oath state that I attended on Mrs. Margaret E Spencer , wife of Walter S. Spencer on the 18th day of May , 1903; that there was born to her on said date a male child; that said child was living March 4, 1905, and is said to have been named Wesley Spencer

W.H. Parks MD

Witnesses To Mark:
{

Subscribed and sworn to before me this 25th day of March , 1905

J.D. Armstrong
Notary Public.
My commission expires Feb 21 1909

Applications for Enrollment of Chickasaw Newborn
Act of 1905 Volume III

BIRTH AFFIDAVIT.

DEPARTMENT OF THE INTERIOR.
COMMISSION TO THE FIVE CIVILIZED TRIBES.

IN RE APPLICATION FOR ENROLLMENT, as a citizen of the Chickasaw Nation, of Irene Spencer, born on the 26th day of January, 1905

Name of Father: Walter S. Spencer a citizen of the _____ Nation.
Name of Mother: Margaret E. Spencer a citizen of the Chickasaw Nation.

Postoffice Bradley, Ind. Ter.

AFFIDAVIT OF MOTHER.

UNITED STATES OF AMERICA, Indian Territory,
Southern DISTRICT.

I, Margaret E. Spencer, on oath state that I am 24 years of age and a citizen by birth, of the Chickasaw Nation; that I am the lawful wife of Walter S. Spencer, who is a citizen, by _____ of the _____ Nation; that a female child was born to me on 26th day of January, 1905; that said child has been named Irene Spencer, and was living March 4, 1905.

Margaret E. Spencer

Witnesses To Mark:
{

Subscribed and sworn to before me this 25th day of March, 1905

J.D. Armstrong
Notary Public.

AFFIDAVIT OF ATTENDING PHYSICIAN OR MID-WIFE.

UNITED STATES OF AMERICA, Indian Territory,
Southern DISTRICT.

I, W. R. Barry, a Physician, on oath state that I attended on Mrs. Margaret E Spencer, wife of Walter S. Spencer on the 26th day of January, 1905; that there was born to her on said date a female child; that said child was living March 4, 1905, and is said to have been named Irene Spencer

Wm R. Barry MD

Witnesses To Mark:
{

Applications for Enrollment of Chickasaw Newborn
Act of 1905   Volume III

Subscribed and sworn to before me this   25th day of   March   , 1905

                                      J.D. Armstrong
                                            Notary Public.
My commission expires Feb 21 1909

Index

ABBOTT, W D 158
ADAMS
   Frank.................................248,249
   J Frank...............................100,101
ADLER, Ire 179
ALBRIGHT, R E 242,243
ALLEN
   Albert...................................107
   Albert, MD 107
ANDERSON, Joseph.......................263
ANGELL, W H 199,200,201
ARCHARD
   Charley 18
   Henry A 18
   X..18
ARCHERD
   Charley 11,13,14,15,16,17
   Henry......................................12
   Henry A 17
   Henry Adolphus........13,14,15,16,17
   Mary B.....................................14
   Mary Buckner............13,14,15,16,17
ARMSTRONG, J D....139,140,325,326
ARNOLD
   Dr J H 205,206,207
   J H 205,206
ARNOTE, A J 186,188
ASKEW
   Dorthey Hazell.............................24
   Minnie Holden.............................24
   Minnie Holder 24
   Thomas D 24
ATKINSON
   Clarence E 118,119
   Mattie 118
   Mrs Mattie 119
   Virginia..................................118
   Virginia Louise....................118,119
AUSTIN
   Hannah 222,223
   W A 286,287
AUTREY, D 24
BACON, Chas E..................66,67,68,77
BAILEY, David A...........................181
BAKER
   Frank Elmer..................................151
   Mary Emma........................151,152

Mary V 151
BALDWIN
   J D 289,290
   Jno D 289,290
   Mrs J D 289,290
BANNER, L L.................................192
BARGER
   G A, MD................................259
   G S..260
   G S, MD................................260
BARKSDALE, N N 196
BARNES
   S L...................................210,211
   T C...................................122,123
   T C, MD 122
BARRY
   W R 326
   Wm R, MD 326
BARTLETT, D G...........23,24,244,245
BATSON
   J D 23,24
   J D, MD......................................24
BATTS, W O............................148,149
BEALL, Wm O 161,294
BEDWELL
   D L..245
   Lizzie...245
BELCHER, A M 54
BELL, Robert S.................278,279,280
BESHIRS
   Aaron...................................104,106
   Aron C................................105,106
   Laura Bell 105,106
   Laura Belle 104
   Lee Ora......................104,105,106
   Leeora.......................104,105,106
   Mrs 106
   Mrs Laura Belle........................104
BIRD
   Jesse....................................168,169
   Jesse, MD 168,169
BIXBY, Tams.... 12,53,63,120,129,136,
156,159,160,162,171,173,174,175,176,
208,213,233,252,257,261,267,284,285,
291,302,303,308
BLACK
   Effie..260

Index

George 260
Martha 260
May 260
Willie 260
BOLGER, P C 274
BOND & MELTON 140
BONE
   J W 313,322,323
   J W, MD 313,322,323
BOWER, James 95
BRADLEY
   Alvin 232,234,235,238,239
   Bruce 233,234,235,236,237, 238,239
   Eula 232,236,237,238,239
   Ida E 234,235,236,237,238
   Mrs Ida E 236
BRASHEARS
   Fannie 291,292
   N B 287
   N T 286
BRECKINRIDGE, C R 284,285,302
BRISHER
   Miss Tennie 129
   Tennie 129
BRISHERS, Tennie 133
BROWN
   Bessie 34
   W E 319
BRYANT, Hughes 154
BURCH, L S 145,146
BURNEY
   Ada 134,135
   Alice Marzie 133,134
   Edward Sehon 134,135
BURRIS
   George W 230
   George Washington 225,226,227, 228,229,230
   Laura Leceta 225,226,227
   Laura Leseta 230
   Mrs Thenia 226,229,230
   Thenia 225,226,227,228,230
   Thenia Vivian 225,228,229,230
BUTCHER
   Anna 199,200
   Annie 199,200

CAMBERT
   G M 196
   G M, MD 196
CAMPBELL
   C M 11,12,13,119,120,121,129, 130,136,137,212,213,214,233,234, 239,240,267
   Chas M 266
   Edward H 120
   W C 20,21
CANTRELL, W T 240
CARLTON, W A 148,149
CARMICHAEL, J D 151
CARNEY, Susan 28
CARRELL
   I N 91,95
   I N, MD 91
CARTER
   Charles D 295
   Dorset 252,253
CHASTAIN
   J C 94
   J D 92,94,96
CHILDS
   J S 254
   Joseph S 254
CLARK
   M J 241
   Martha 242
CLAYTON & BRAINARD 126
CLEMENS, M S 258,259,260
CLEVELAND, Mrs J B 196
COCHRAN
   Carrie 244
   Corrie 244
   Mrs Carrie 244
   R M 134
   Vaughon 243,244
   W H 244
COFFMAN, Geo W 22
COLBERT
   C W 75,76,79
   Folsom Hume 231,232
   Francile 79
   H E 79
   Harley E 77,78,80
   Henrietta C 231,232

Index

Jewel 79
Mildred Francile 77,78
Mildred Francis 80
Mr Harley 79
Mr Harley E 78
Mrs Henrietta C 231
Mrs Pearl 78,79
Pearl 77,78,79
Pearl P 80
Peggy 29,30
Walter 231,232
COLLINS
   H A 94,96
   J P 10,11,197,198
CONNELLY
   Hannah 245,246,247
   John W 246
   John William 245
   John Wm 246,247
   Lesley 245
   Leslie 245,246,247
   Mrs Hannah 246,247
CONOVER, Jane 29
COOPER
   Demis M 171,174
   Demis Mattie 170,172
   Douglas 41
   Mrs Demis M 172
   Ruby Leah 170,171,173,174, 175,176
   Ruby Lean 172
   W W 175,176
   William W 170,171,172,173, 174,175
COTTOM, J D 209
COTTON, J D 208
COVINGTON, Effie 3
CROCKER, W B 214
CURTIS, Ollie 35
DABNEY
   J A 25,27
   J A, MD 25
DALE
   C D 193
   Charles D 195
   Chas D 194
   Chas D, MD 194
   Dr C D 193
DAVIDSON, Wm B 192,193,194
DEAN
   W N 248
   W N, MD 248
DEEN
   Dr J A 172
   J A 174
   J A, MD 172
DESHAN
   Albert 192,193,194,195
   Darcey 192,193,194,195
   Dorsey 192,193
   Iva A 193,194,195
   Iva Rilla 192
   Mrs Iva A 194
   Mrs Rilla 193
   Rilla 192
DOBSON, John H 202,203
DRAPER, T B 33
DRAUGHON
   Byrd Love 23,24
   H E 23,24
   Mrs H E 23
   Ruby Bel 23
   Ruby Belle 23,24
   Ruby Belle (Love) 23,24
DRENNAN, Bettie 1,2
DUCKWORTH
   Josephine 116,117
   Mattie Thomas 116,117
   Mrs Josephine 117
   Thomas 116,117
DUMAS
   Maggie L 267,268,269
   Miss Maggie L 266
DUNCAN
   Addie 58,59,60,61
   James 56,57,58,59,60,61
   John Otis 56,57
   Johnie Otis 57
   Johny Odus 56,58,59,60,61
   Mrs Addie 59
   Mrs Samantha 57
   Samantha 56,57
ELLIOTT, David G 323
ELLIS

Index

G H 48,49,51,52,54,56
G H, MD 48,50,51,52
ELMORE
   Claud Franklin 272,273
   George 272,273
   L F 273
   Lorena 272,273
   Mrs L F 273
ELTING, C H 112,113
EMBRY, Mary M 154
EZZARD, John T 321,322
FANNIN, E J 53,54,208,209,291,292
FITZPATRICK
   A Lena 136,141
   Miss A Lena 136
FOLSOM
   I W 231
   I W, MD 232
   Ii W 232
   Silas D 182,183
FORD, Miss Melvia 62
FOSTER
   Mr Siloman 222
   Siloman 222
   Solomon 223
   Thomas 223
FOWLER, O R 48,49,51,52,58,59, 60,319
FOX, O B 287,288
FRANCIS
   B L 204,205,206,207
   Kate A 204,206
   Katie 204,205,206,207
   Mrs Katie 205,206
   R Miller 204,205,206,207
FRANKLIN
   Joseph M 305
   Wirt 182,183
FROST, S W 131
GALE, Mary 18
GANARD, T M 185
GARDNER
   Annie 20
   B S 21
   Benjamin Shannon 20
   J G 30
   Mrs Susie 91

Robert 91,92,93,94,96,97
Robert M 94,95,97
Susie 92,93,94,95,96,97
Winona 91,92,93,94,95,96,97
Wynona 97
Zella 21
Zella Bernice 19,20,21
GARRISON, D W 121
GARSIDES
   Alex 283,284,296,300,301
   Ben 283,284,296,300,301
   Cecial Berthal 283
   Fannie 282,283,284,296,300,301
   Jim 283,284,296,300,301
   Joe, Jr 283,284,296,300,301
   Joseph 283,295,296,298,300,301
   Laura Etta 283
   Mattie 283,284,296,300,301
   Maude Lee 283
   Nellie 283,284,296,300,301
GAYLE, Mary 12,17
GILLHAM, C E 154
GIST, J W 304
GOLD, C B 253,254
GOLDEN, Mrs Deler 62
GOODENOUGH, A D 163,164,165, 166,167
GOODING
   Charles Lemuel 70
   Charles Lenuel 71
   Lem 71
   Mrs Willie 71
   Nellie May 70
   Sadie Bell 69,70,71
   Willie May 70,71
GOODWIN, G W 74,109
GRACE, Geo 53
GRADNER, Winona 96
GREEN
   G W 36,40
   G W, MD 36
   T F 214
GREENE
   G W 39,43
   G W, MD 39
GRINSLADE
   Henretta 80,82

Index

Henrietta 84
Henriyetta 80,81,82,83,84,85
Henry 80,81,82,83,84,85
Mrs Sallie 84
Sallie 80,81,82,83,85
GRIST, W W 287,288
HAMBLIN
   C M 213,214,215,223,225
   C N 223
   Charles M 220
   Charley M 216,217,218,219,221, 222,224
   Charlie M 225
   Lela Mildred Beatrice .. 212,217,218, 219,220,224,225
   Mary Ruth 212,215,216,217,221, 222,223,224,225
   Mrs Nina 215,217,218,219,221
   Nina 215,216,217,219,220,221, 222,223,224
HANNA, D H 38
HANNOND, E S 22
HARDWICK
   Alma Bell 1,2,3
   Alma Belle 3
   Brit 5,6
   Eastman 5,6
   Herman 1,2,3
   Joe B 1,2,3
   Waneta 1,2,3
HARDY, Summers 14,15,16
HARKIN, Thomas 222
HARPER
   J L 100,102
   Joseph E Johnston 99,100,101, 102,103
   Joseph Lea 101,102,103
   Mrs Viola 100,102
   Mrs Viola Harper 100
   Viola 101,103
HARRIS
   Cyrus L 188
   Nettie G 187
HARRISON
   Bettie Maud 22
   Betty Maud 21
   Geo W 22

George W 21
James Anderson 21
Jas Anderson 22
Mrs Bettie Maud 22
Mrs Bettie Maude 22
HARVEY, L F 46,47
HAWKINS
   Bertie 212
   Miss Bertie 208,209
HAWLEY
   Arthur E 198,199,200
   Daisy 198,200
   Lizzie 198,199,200
   Mrs Lizzie 200
   Nellie 198,199
HAYES
   Annie 198
   Charles 295
   Charley 282,283,296,298,300
   Daniel 282,283,296,298,300
   Edward 282,283,296,300
   Henry Charles Preston .. 296,297,298
   John Benjamin 197,198
   Maggie 282,283,296,300
   Minnie 282,283,296,300
   Mrs Annie 197
   Vivian 197,198
HAYWARD
   Edna May 106,107
   James L 107
   Mona E 107
   Mrs Mona E 107
HEANNA, D H 37
HEAYES
   Annie E 197
   John Benjamin 197
   Vivian 197
HENSLEY
   J W 158
   J W, MD 158
HIGHTOWER, N N 127,128
HOLDER, L L 100
HOLLINGSWORTH
   Luna 56
   Miss Luna 53
HOLT, B W 156
HOMER, Jacob 157

HOOVER, J T 62,63
HORTON, L J 202,203
HOWELL, John C 22
HUFF, Marietta 9,10
HULSEY, Wm J......................92,93,94
HULSEY & PATTERSON 95
   Winona 96
HUME, W R.. 6
HUNTER, J J...........................286,287
ILLEGIBLE
   J 20
   Jay, MD 20
   Norah E 201
   R D 274
INGE
   C M...101,102
   H R 101
INGLE, Erasmus A 187,188
JACK
   J T..168
   Mary 168,169
   Mrs Mary..168
   Rolan 169
   Roland 167,168,169
JACKMAN, F M................100,102,103
JAMES
   Ben 208,209,212
   Benjamin D....................................212
   Benjamin David....................210,211
   Birdie Stuard.........................210,211
   Jno G 265,266
   Mrs Birdie......................................210
   Mrs Birdie Stuard 210,211
   Rhoener 210,211
   Rubie Rhoener.......208,210,211,212
JEFFRESS
   J L..........................263,264,266,270
   J L, MD 264,266
JEFFRIES, J L...................................263
JENNINGS
   H L..230
   Henrietta L.....................................229
   Thenia.......225,226,227,228,229,230
JOHNS
   E A F 118,119
   S T....................................98,99,117,251
JOHNSON

Abel H 95
America 45,46,47
B S...250
D P... 7
Effie M 152,153,154,155
Elizabeth...............152,153,154,155
H B 152,153,155
Henry B 152
Henry Belton 153,154,155
Henry Bilton 155
J H 292,293
Mrs Effie 153
Mrs Effie M..................................154
JOHNSTON, D P 4,5,6,19
JONES
   E A 279,280,281
   E A, MD 279,280
   L T..116
JORDAN
   Edgar Ray.............162,163,164,165,
   166,167
   Edgar Roy....................................166
   Ethel 162,163,164,165,166,167
   Mrs Ethel......................163,164,165
   William Gaston............162,163,165,
   166,167
   Willis Gaston.......................164,166
KEARNEY, W M..............................22
KEFFER, Elvira 37,42
KELLER
   J R...109
   J R, MD 109
KEMP
   Joe 98,99
   Lorena E 98,99
   M E..99
   Marilons E................................98,99
   Mrs Anna..81
   Mrs Marilons E.............................98
   Mrs Susan A 32
   Otis..31,32
   Roberson....................................37,38
   Susan A 31,32
   W M...31,32
   Wellington M 32
   Wellington Martin 31,32
KENNEDY, D S.........................25,26

KENO
   Emily 157,158,160,161
   Josephine 157,158
   Josephine 156,159,160,161,162
   M 157,158,159,161,162
   Mrs Emily 158
KERBY, C A 32,317,318
KIEFFER, Elvira 35
KIMZEY, Alta 120,141,142
KING
   Annie 82,83
   Arthur 183,184
   Cornelia 180,182,183,184
   Mary 180,181,182,183,184
   Mrs Cornelia 181,182
   Philip 181
   Phillip 180,182,183,184
KIRBY
   C A 32,98,99,117,316,319
   Mrs C A 117,319
KLOSTERMANN
   Dr H W 82
   H W 84,85
   H W, MD 84
   H W, MR 81
KOOGLER, W G 185
KOOGLER & CO, W G 186
LANDMAN, A M 299
LANDRUM, Lula 321,322
LAUMANN
   T B 236,238
   T B, MD 236
LAWSON
   Nep 216,217,218,219,221,222
   Nina 213,214,225
LEFTWICH
   James 127,128
   Jewel Esther 126,127
   Minnie C 127
LEMON
   Maria C 72,73
   Mrs Maria C 73
   R B 72,73
   Robert Breckinridge 73
   Walter Harlin 72,73
LEMONS
   Maria 73

   Maria C 73,74
   Robert Breckinridge 73,74
   Walter Harlin 72,73,74
LEWALLEN, Alice A 99,117,319
LEWIS
   Anderson 92
   Dr E F 5,6
   E F 5,7,9,19
   E F, MD 5
LINDSAY
   Allie 3
   Ethel 271
   S S 1,2
   Sarah S. 3
   Saray S. 2
LINDSEY
   B H H 270,271
   Elizabeth J 271
   Ethel 270,271
   Girtha 270,271
LITTLE, J C 264,265,268,269
LIVELY
   C O 104,106
   C O, MD 105
LOOMIS, O H 216,218,219,221,222
LOVE, Ruby Belle 23
LOWRANCE
   Mrs Sophia A E 177
   Oscar Emmett 176,177,178
   Robert H 176,177,178
   Sophia A E 176,177,178
LUTTRELL
   C T 35,36,37,38,39
   Fannie 38
LYNCH
   Cherokee Rose 278,279,280,281
   Georgia V 279,280,281
   Georgia Vann 278,279
   J J 278,279,280
   Joseph 281
   Joseph J 279,280,281
MALCOLM, John 46,47
MANISS
   W J 115,116
   W J, MD 116
MANSFIELD, MCMURRAY &
   CORNISH 257

Index

MANSFIELD, MCMURRAY & CORNISH 308
   Ruby Leah 173
MAPLES, S W 30
MARSHALL
   Donald Speairs 249,250
   J Horace 249,250
   Lillie 249
   Mrs Lillie 250
   Wash 83,84
MARTIN
   A E 244
   A E, MD 244
MASSEY
   Enoch L 9,10,11
   Ernest Leon 9,10,11
   Marietta 9,10,11
MASSY, F B 6
MAUPIN, W H 36
MAXEY, Lanay 118
MCARTHUR, C L 145,146
MCBRIDE
   Aron Anita 319
   Hiram Young 319
   J B 138,139,140,141
   J B(illegible) 242,243
   J B, MD 138
   Lovica Colbert 319
MCCARLEY
   W H 71
   W H, MD 70,71,78,79,80
MCCLAIN, C M 216,217,218
MCCLURE, Alfred W 182,183
MCCOY, N H 11,119,212
MCDONALD, D J 13
MCGINNIS, J C 33
MCKINEY, Fannie 286
MCKINNEY
   Cecial Berthal 282,283,284, 296,300,301
   Cecil Berthal 298
   Emma Ma 296
   Emma May 296,297,298,299, 302,303,304,305,306,307,308,309, 310,311
   Fannie 284,286,287,288,289, 290,298

   Georgie 293,296,297
   Harris ...... 282,283,284,295,296,298, 300,301,302,303,304,305,306,307,309 ,311
   Laura Etta
   282,283,284,296,298,300,301
   Leona 282,284,285,286,287, 288,289,290,293,294,296,298
   Martha 282,283,300
   Mary Louise 296
   Mattie 296
   Maude Lee
   282,283,284,296,298,300,301
   Mollie 302,303,304,305,306
   Oid 291,292,293
   Oyd .... 282,283,284,285,286,287, 288,289,290,294,295,296,297,298,300 ,301
   Polly 283,285,295,296,297, 300,301,302
   William 296
   Williams 296,297,298
MCKINNIE
   Mollie 303
   Polly 283,295,300,301
MEAD
   E L 57,58,59,60,61
   F E 75,76
   G E 72,73
   L L 86,87,89
   Mrs F E 86,87,89
   S M 32,45,57,65,72,73,76,79,82, 83,86,87,88,89,90,91,246,317,318
   S M, Jr 72,73
MELTON
   A 138
   Ado 138
   J H 153
   W J 112,113
   W J, MD 112
MENTZER, J L 235,236,237
MEREDITH
   H D 238
   N C 235
MILLER
   Geo W 253,254
   Jno M 124,125

John M 126
Mrs Sophia 202,203
Mrs V P 125
Norma Elizabeth 203
Norma Elizibeth 201,202,203
Norman 201,202,203
Sophia 203,204
Sophia E 201,202
Tandy J 124,125,126
Virginia P 124,125,126
MILLS, S E 185
MOORE
   John C 248
   John Taylor 247,248
   Lemmuel Capel 108
   Lemmuel Caple 108,109
   Lemuel Capel 109
   Louisa J 62,63
   Lyda Amanda 62,63,64
   Lydia Amanda 63
   Mary Ellen 248
   Mrs Louisa J 63
   Mrs Mary Ellen 248
   Mrs Nora 109
   Nora 108,109
   Nora Vena 108,109
   T N 64
   Thomas N 63
   Thomas Nowel 63
   Thomaw Nowel 62
MORELAND
   C M 324
   Claud 321,322,323,324
   Claud Leonard 321,322,323,324
   Fannie 321,322,323,324
MORGAN
   Thomas M 63
   Thos M, MD 63
MORLAN, Fannie 323
MORLAND
   Claud 322,323
   Claud L 323
   Claud Linnad 322
   Fannie 322,323
MORRIS
   J D 266,267,268,269
   Joe 264,265,266,268,269,270

Joseph 262,263,269
Joseph D 262,263,265,266,268, 269,270
Joseph Daniel 264
Maggie 262,263,264,265,266,270
Maggie L 268
MURRAY
   Francis Albert 64,66,67,68
   Henton 65
   Mattie 65
   Maye 65,66,67,68,69
   Meigs Colbert 66,67,68,69
   Mrs Maye 66
MURRY
   Francis Albert 64,65
   May 64,65
   Meigs Colbert 64,65
   Mrs Mary 65
MUTZ
   Edna Crecia 4,5,6,7,8
   Edna Credia 9
   Geo 6
   George 4,5,7,8,9
   Ida 4,5,6,7,9
   Mrs 5
MYERS
   Alice Magnolia 178,179
   Mary J 179
   Mary Jane 179
   Mrs Alice Magnolia 179
   W S 180
   Winfield S 178,179
   Winnefred Clem 178,179
   Winnifred Clem 180
NASH
   H C 189,190,191
   Henry C ... 185,186,187,188,189,190
   Henry Clay 184,185,186,187,188, 189,190,191
   Lizzie 185,186,187,188,189,191
   Mrs Lizzie 185,187
NEEDLES, T B 284,285,302
NEIGHBORS
   Lillian Ethel 276,277
   Myrtle Jauneta 276,277
   William 276,277
NELSON

Emma 181,184	Blanch..142
J F 181,184	Blanche........... 119,121,122,123,124
NEWMAN, E A 26,27	Edward H.............. 120,121,122,123, 124,141
NOLETUBBY	Mrs Alta..122
John 24,27	PERKINS
John Anderson 25,27	Charlie 86,87,88
Johnnie 26	Fany...320
Johnson A 26	Laura B 86,88,89
Joohn 25	Laura Belle 87,90
Land 25,26,27	Mrs Laura B........................... 87,89
Mrs Land 25,26	Mrs Laura Bell............................. 88
NORMAN	Simon D....................................... 320
D S 317,318	W W 86,87,89
Daniel 316,317,318,319	W W, Sr....................................... 88
Danniel 317,318	Walter W, Jr 88
Sallie 316,317,318,319	Walter William 87,88,89,90
W G 317	Walter William, Jr 86,90
W J 318	PERRY
William J 316,317,318,319	Charles....................................... 242
O'BRYAN, J B 29,226,227,228, 229,230	Charles E 239,240,243
O'DONBY, W J............................... 246	Charley 240,241
O'DONLEY, W J..................... 110,111	Eli 106
OWENS	Lucy............................... 240,241,242
Douglas E 195	Mr C E....................................... 240
Douglas Elihu 196	Mrs Lucy 242
Duglas E 195	Raymon Edington....................... 240
Duglas Elihu 195,196	Raymond Edington 239,241,242
L F 196	PETER
Lafayette............................. 195,196	Harvey 27,28,29,30
Laffayett 195	Jane................................ 27,28,29,30
Minnie 195,196	Joseph............................ 27,28,29,30
PANTSKY	Mrs Jane................................. 28,29
M M..................................... 246	PETERS
Mary Mildon............................. 247	W L.. 134,135
PARKS	W L, MD 134
W H 325	PHELPS
W H, MR............................. 325	Andrew 33,34,35,36,37,38,39, 40,42,43,44
PARTAIN, W S................................. 169	Douglas.......... 33,35,36,38,39,40,41, 42,43,44
PATTERSON, W R........................... 95	
PAYTE	Emma ... 33,36,37,38,39,40,41,42,43
Arthur 289,290	Mrs Emma 34,35,36,37,39
J E................................286,288,289,290	Nicholas..40
J E, MD 286,288,289,290	Nickless 33,34,35,37,42,43
PENN, G H............................... 143,144	Nicolos 33,34,39
PERCIVAL	PILGRIM, James B 241
Alta....................... 121,122,123,124	

338

Index

PITCHLYN
   Edward E 114
   Peter..114
   Sudie..114
PITCHLYNN
   Edward E 111,112,113
   Mrs Sudie 112
   Peter P 111,112,113
   Sudie..111,113
POPE, L...319
POTTER, H C 271
POTTS
   Ittis..76
   Ittis Marie 74,75,76,77
   J B...75,76
   Joe B 74,76,77
   Mrs N V 76
   Nannie V 74,75,76,77
POWELL
   Cicel Perry............................250,251
   Ellen Jane 251
   Mrs Ellen J...................................251
   T P 251
   Thomas Porter 250,251
PRUITT
   Allice 110
   Hester 110,111
   Mrs Allice 110
   Willis 110
PUSLEY
   Easmon 114,115,116
   James 115,116
   James S 115
   Mary J.......................................115,116
   Mrs Mary J 115
PUTTY, Geo T 122
RAGON, S B.....................274,275,276
RALSTON
   Benh W 150
   Benj W 148
   Benj W, MD 143,144,145,147, 148,150
RATLIFF, Miss Lucy 239,240,243
REASOR, J M 104,105
REEVES, A 143,144
RENEAU, Walter I.........................158
REVES

G O 304
Geo O 305
REYNOLDS
   B F 129,132,133
   Ben F 131
   Bengaman F.................................131
   Bengeman F.................................130
   Benjamin F 132
   Ed 131
   Eddie Leroy 128,130,131,132,133
   Tennie L 131,132
   Tinnie L 130
   Wm H 291,292
REYNOLS, Mrs Tinnie..................131
RICE
   F E 143,144,145,146,147, 148,149,150
   T J 115
RIDER
   Gussie Agnes.......................312,313
   Mrs Nellie...........................313,314
   Nellie 312,321,322
   Thomas S............................312,313
RIGGS, L H.............................289,290
ROBINSON
   P F 1,2,3
   S B 267
ROLLER
   George Martin 44,46
   Geroge Martin 47
   Jack E 46,47
   Lucy Krouse 46,47
ROSSER, Malcolm E 276
ROWE
   Clyde 261,262
   Letitia 261,262
   Vera 261,262
ROWELL, W D..............................158
ROWLER
   George Martin 44,45
   J E 45
   Jack E 44,45
   Lucy..44,45
   Mrs J E 45
   Mrs Lucy 45
RUSHING
   Y M 250

SCOTT
  Y M, MD 250
  John G 312,313
  M E 304,305,306
SEALY
  Either 18,19
  Mrs Will 19
  Sussie 18,19
  Will 18,19
SEEARCE, W L 46,47
SEELEY
  George 35
  A H 202,203
  A H, MD 202,203
SEELY, Sussie 19
SEIFRIED
  Emma 258,259,260
  Henry D 258,259,260
  Jessie A 258,259,260
  Joe Maytubbie 252,254,255,257
  Joe Maytubby 252,253,254,256
  Joseph Maytubby 252,253,256
  Mary 253,256
  Mary F 253
  Mary Florence 253,254
  Wilfliam 255
  William 257
  William F 253,254,256
  Wm F 252,254
SELF
  Cecil Newton 296,297,298
  Fannie 298
  James 296
  Joseph W 296
  Sarah Arinda 296,298
SHAW
  E B 185
  Edward 189
  Edwin 189
  Edwin B 185
SHOCKEY, John 101
SHORT
  Cleo 57
  T W 57
SIMMONS
  J H 131,132
  J H, MD 131

SLATER, G B 91
SLOVER
  Dr Geo W 177
  G W 163,164,165,166,167,178
  G W, MD 163,164,166,177
SMITH
  B P 118
  C C 196
  E K 70,71,78,79
  Joseph P 215,216,315
  R W 234
  V 125
SPEAKE, J W 239
SPEARS, D A 205,206,287,288, 289,290
SPENCER
  Irene 324,326
  Margaret E 324,325,326
  Walter S 324,325,326
  Wesley 324,325
STAMP, E P 158
STINSON
  Jno E 119
  Jno E, MD 119
STRAIGHT, Mattie 220,221
STURDIVANT
  J F 262
  John F 262
TAXTON
  Lida 247
  Rosa 247
  W T 247
TAYLOR
  J N 251
  J N, MD 251
  John 115
TEMPLE, L E 246
TENY, L R 196
THAGARD
  W C 127
  W C, MD 127
THOMAS
  Alma 142,143,144,145,149,150
  Alpha 142,143,146,147,148,150
  C H 197,198
  Charles 142,143,144
  Charley 145,146,147,148,149,150

Index

Mrs Nancy 143,144,147,150
Nancy 142,144,145,146,148, 149,150
THOMES, C H 10
THOMPSON, Lee 203
TRAIL, Martha L 14,15
TRALLE
   Dr G M 217,218,219,222
   G M 215,220,221,223,224, 315,316
   G M, MD 217,218,219,222,315
TUCKER
   J W 125,126
   J W, MD 125
TURK, Idell.............................201,203
TURNER
   B F...272
   Daisy...............................314,315,316
   Hiram G........................314,315,316
   A J 117,171,172
   Roscoe Hampton 314,315,316
TYE, R P, MD........................151,152
UNDERWOOD, Ida..................233,239
VAN BUREN, President Martin 295
VAN ZANDT
   I L.................................153,154,155
   I L, MD..............................153,154
   K M 154
VANNOY
   W W 226,227,230
   W W, MD 226,227
VANTREES, Artie 31,32
WALKER
   C E..33,34
   Chas P..................................105,106
WALTER, James T 262
WALTER & FROST 132,133
WALTHALL
   Gracie 135,137,138,139,140,141
   Lena................ 137,138,139,140,141
   Mrs Lena 138,139
   Nicholas M 137,138,140
   Nicholas Mondavis.......139,140,141
   Nicklous 136
WARD, B 242,243
WATSON, Martha 26
WEBB
   Abrigale..........47,48,50,51,54,55,56
   George W ..48,49,50,51,52,54,55,56
   John Wesley ...47,49,50,51,52,54,56
   Luna................ 48,49,50,51,54,55,56
   Lune..56
   Mr G W 53
   Mrs Luna 48,51,52
WEBSTER, H B 277
WELCH
   Adelia 273,274,275,276
   Charles A.............................275,276
   Chas A 273,274,275
   Edgar Warren 273,274,275,276
   W A 275
WELLS
   A J 110
   A J, MD 111
WHISENHUNT, M E....................106
WHITE, Eugene E....................168,177
WIGAND, B C 81,83,84
WILBURN, J H 137
WILLIAMS
   J E............................28,240,243,280
   J Ernest 281
   A V..277
WILLIAMSON
   H...194
   J R...194
WILSON, H C 209
WIMBERLY, W H..................231,232
WOOTEN, J C.................................115
WRIGHT
   J G 299
   L W..130
YEISER
   C C 65,66,67,68,69,73,74,76, 77,87,88,89,90
   C C, MD 65,66,68,73,74,76,77, 87,88,89,90

www.ingramcontent.com/pod-product-compliance
Lightning Source LLC
Chambersburg PA
CBHW020242030426
42336CB00010B/583